PRAISE FOR

A Book of Lives Well Lived

"One of the main benefits of serving in our military is that we often get to know people in communities where we did not grow up. That was the case during our multiple tours in Tampa, where I got to know Mark Rosenthal and his wonderful wife, Deborah. They were the quintessential hosts for military leaders and their families, and their hospitality went beyond just opening their home. Mark's brainchild, the STAR Program, is a shining example of how communities support those who answer the nation's call by helping with their dreams. This book is a good read and more than a tribute to those who serve in uniform; it recognizes those on the home front who provide the intangible support that makes our military the greatest in the world."

—General Joseph L. Votel (Ret.), Four Star, Former Commander of US Special Operations Command (2014–2016) and US Central Command (2016–2019)

"The Rosenthals have put their own spin on using entertainment to boost morale and show support for our military. For many years they've channeled their patriotism into making our military members and coalition partners stationed in the Tampa area feel welcomed and appreciated. They have also played a very influential role in assisting in the critical transition of service members to the private sector. Using their perspectives as civilians entering a military world, this book offers a glimpse behind the scenes of these intriguing events that the general public rarely hears about."

—General Tony Thomas (Ret.), Four Star, Head of SOCOM (2016–2019)

"Mark Rosenthal and his wife, Deborah, have been pillars of support for the Tampa Bay military community for decades. Capturing and describing their many experiences in this great book provides a historical reference for future generations. Their generous spirit and selfless efforts have greatly benefited service members."

—General Richard D. Clarke, US Army (Ret.), Four Star, Commander of US Special Operations (2019–2022)

"I have known Mark Rosenthal for many years and saw his commitment to the people who decided to serve, defend their nation, and put their lives in danger—some sadly even giving their lives.

"Mark's professional attitude and his enormous willingness drove him to understand what these men and women are experiencing, and by doing so he was able to assist them. Mark is a unique person, a citizen who asks what he can do for his nation."

—Major General Mickey Edelstein (Ret.), Three Star, IDF Military Attaché in the United States

"I have known Mark and Deborah Rosenthal for years. They are truly national treasures and are passionate about—and are truly committed to—making our military members and coalition partners stationed in the Tampa area feel welcomed and appreciated. This wonderful book offers a fascinating look behind the scenes of all they've done and continue to do for our troops. Just as Bob Hope was famous to all of us because he recognized the importance of boosting morale through entertainment, the Rosenthals have become famous for all of us for how they've found their own unique ways to show their support."

> —General John Allen (Ret.), Four Star, Former Commander of United States Central Command (2010), Former Commander of the NATO International Security Assistance Force and US Forces – Afghanistan (USFOR-A), and Special Presidential Envoy for the Global Coalition to Counter ISIL (Islamic State of Iraq and the Levant)

"Mark has been, and remains, an incredible supporter of the US and allied military community in the greater Tampa Bay area. As an active-duty flag officer, and now retired in Tampa Bay, I've personally seen and participated with Mark in an extraordinary number of military-supporting events in which Mark was the driving force. His book is an exemplary look into the personal experience and fulfillment of one civilian making an real difference for our nation's fighting forces."

> —Vice Admiral Sean Pybus (Ret.), Three Star, Deputy Commander of US Special Operations (2014–2016)

"Mark Rosenthal and his wife, Deborah's, contribution to the Tampa Bay military community is nothing short of exceptional. Mark not only promoted the US military but also opened doors to the coalition and brought them into his home and the broader communities of Tampa Bay. His drive and energy to make a difference was demonstrated by his and his friends efforts in the STAR Program in assisting military to transition successfully after service. A true friend of Australia, we still remain in close contact twelve years after my posting into CENTCOM and USSOCOM. [Mark is] an international patriot and all around good guy who created a 'safe zone' for the military outside of MacDill AFB."

—Brigadier General Mark Smethurst (Ret.), Special Forces Australia

"This book is an outstanding, descriptive, behind-the-scenes look at the tremendous passion Mark and Deborah Rosenthal show for their US troops and coalition partners. Their hospitality and wonderful work welcoming and supporting troops to the Tampa area is so very much appreciated, and their tireless efforts will always be remembered."

—Major General Dean Milner (Ret.), CMM, MSC, CD Canadian Armed Forces

"Mark Rosenthal is a true patriot! His love for and dedication to the United States and the men and women of the armed forces who serve this great nation is unmatched. His life is truly well lived."

—Major Genereal Vincent K. Becklund (Ret.), Two Star, Special Operations Command

"How wonderful that you've chronicled the history of MacDill AFB and Tampa's unique culture as the crossroads of counterterrorism through arguably the most challenging times in recent history during our global war against violent extremism. Thank you for providing support and respite for senior leaders to take a . . . brief but needed break from the toil of unrelenting demands of leadership and command. You and Deborah most kindly and proficiently served those who served. God bless you and Deborah."

> —Frederick W. Humphries II, FBI Supervisory Special Agent (Ret.) for Counterterrorism in Tampa

"Mark and Deborah Rosenthal are true patriots who have devoted their lives to supporting the American military. A Book of Lives Well Lived tells the story of their experiences with a veritable Who's Who of senior American and Coalition military leaders for the past twenty years and is a must-read for anyone who has served in or supports the military. This book brought back many fond memories of my career in the Navy and of my friends Mark and Deborah."

> —CAPT Todd Schapler, USNR (Ret.)

A Book of Lives Well Lived:
The Military World through the Eyes of a Civilian
by Mark S. Rosenthal

© Copyright 2023 Mark S. Rosenthal

ISBN 979-8-88824-009-0

All rights reserved. No part of this publication may be reproduced, stored in a retrieval system, or transmitted in any form or by any means—electronic, mechanical, photocopy, recording, or any other—except for brief quotations in printed reviews, without the prior written permission of the author.

Published by

3705 Shore Drive
Virginia Beach, VA 23455
800-435-4811
www.koehlerbooks.com

A Book of Lives Well Lived

The Military World through the Eyes of a Civilian

Mark S. Rosenthal

VIRGINIA BEACH
CAPE CHARLES

I would like to dedicate this book to my brilliant and beautiful wife Deborah, my loving children, Jennifer and Jason, and their spouses, Connor and Shriya.

I believe I was put on this Earth to give to something greater than myself. I am so happy that my wife convinced me to tell my story and document these events. Sometimes civilians can find ways to support our military in ways that the government and the military can't, and I am honored that I've had the opportunity to show my appreciation to the dedicated men and women who serve our country.

Table of Contents

Introduction 1

Chapter 1: How It All Started: Our Introduction
to the Military 4

Chapter 2: Rosenthal "Games and Trains" Parties 6

Chapter 3: Coalition Parties Hosted by our
Civilian Communities 33

Chapter 4: Our First Invitation to MacDill Air Force Base 37

Chapter 5: Dinners and Receptions at
MacDill Air Force Base . . . We're Invited! 41

Chapter 6: Navy League of the United States:
Leadership and Events 51

Chapter 7: Middle East Briefings to Our
Civilian Community 64

Chapter 8: Army, Navy, Air Force, and Marine Balls
and Wounded Warrior Fundraisers 70

Chapter 9: Israeli IDF, AIPAC, Tampa Jewish Federation
and Temple Events and Speakers 92

Chapter 10: Military Demonstrations, Celebrations,
and Awards 119

Chapter 11: Sports, Antique Firearms, and Socializing
with our Military Leaders 148

Chapter 12: Department of Defense Warrior Games 155

Chapter 13: Visit Aboard USS *Dwight D. Eisenhower*
Aircraft Carrier 161

Chapter 14: Plunging Into the Sea Aboard the
USS Pittsburgh Nuclear Submarine 170

Chapter 15: Helicoptering onto the USS *Mesa Verde*
    Amphibius Assault Ship 174

Chapter 16: Aboard the Air Force Refueler KC-135
    Over New Orleans 179

Chapter 17: Special Visit to Fort Pierce and
    Military Maneuvers at Coronado, Little Creek, Fort Bragg,
    Quantico, and Fort Campbell 186

Chapter 18: US Air Force Special Operations Visit to
    Hurlburt Field, Duke Field, Eglin Air Force Base, and
    Tyndall Air Force Base 207

Chapter 19: National Naval Museum: America's First
    and Last on the Moon 217

Chapter 20: United States Army Military Academy
    at West Point 221

Chapter 21: The STAR Program: SOF Transition
    Assistance Resource 235

Chapter 22: Military Honors Treasured 248

Chapter 23: Military Retirement and Change of
    Command Ceremonies 261

In Conclusion . . . Gratitude 313

Military Reference List 314

Branch Creeds 319

Branch Songs 323

Branch Rankings and Positions 328

Military Management Positions: All Branches 332

Introduction

As an American citizen with no military experience, I have had the incredible opportunity to be introduced to the top military leaders in Tampa, Florida at Special Operations Command and Central Command. These amazing, brilliant American leaders could head any Fortune 500 company but decided to enter the military and dedicate their lives to protecting and defending our great country. These humble men and women work twenty-four hours a day, without concern of recognition or monetary rewards.

It is because of these men and women and my experiences with the military world that I, along with my friend Anthony Weiss, began to evolve the concept of STAR (SOF Transitions Assistance Resource), in 2015. The mission of STAR is to assist our special operations forces (SOF) in transitioning into the civilian sector.

The program has become very successful. I often get asked what inspired me to start STAR, and I think back to when I was first introduced to the military community in Tampa in 2008. This book describes a whole new world for my wife and me. Our relationship with the military was originally intended to make them feel at home while in Tampa. This included providing local information—our favorite restaurants, shops, hair salons, theaters, and social venues—for things they might enjoy while in our city. Little did we know at the time that we would become completely engaged in their world, and they in ours. We entertained them in our home, and they entertained us in theirs. I partnered with MacDill Air Force Base representatives in arranging events for staff from our International Coalition, United

States Central Command (CENTCOM) and United States Special Operations Command (SOCOM), as well as organizing briefings for the Tampa civilian community. I asked fellow Tampa business leaders to support a variety of military balls with proceeds going to the Wounded Warrior Project, and I attended a multitude of ceremonies like changes of command and retirements. These experiences ultimately led to deep relationship building between the civilians and the military members of our community. Now fourteen years after the start of this relationship, I want to share my story. As I reflect through the years, the people I have gotten to know, and the wealth of experiences I have had, I shake my head . . . how did all this really happen?

I suppose one thing just led to another! We introduced our civilian friends and family to the military community, which led to bringing our civilian business community to MacDill Air Force Base for briefings on the Middle East and the world at large. We assisted with the Army Ball for General Petraeus, the Marine Ball for General Allen, the Air Force Ball for General Schwartz, and the Navy Balls for Admiral Olson, Admiral Mulloy, and Admiral McRaven—which all helped finance wounded programs in each branch of the military. I later had the opportunity to be sent on practice missions to the aircraft carrier USS *Eisenhower*, the nuclear submarine USS *Pittsburgh*, a KC-135 mission to refuel six F-15 fighter jets, and to numerous military bases.

After becoming president of the Tampa Bay Area Navy League in 2012, I went to various local high schools and universities to promote the ROTC and the consideration of a military career. There are incredible opportunities available in the military for our young men and women. A career in the military offers the individual structure, education, pride, and confidence, as well as the possibility to travel the world, experience other cultures, and receive training in a multitude of jobs.

I have personally observed the vast knowledge and experience military officers and personnel have after serving. They have all the tools necessary to transition into the civilian sector and be confident and successful when they retire. Which leads me back to the STAR program.

This program is described in detail in a later chapter. I am extremely proud of the work we are doing. These men and women have selflessly served our country and we try to assist them with the next phase of their lives. Suffice to say, it is working, we are helping, and it is the least we can do for those who have done so much to help and protect us.

My goal for this book is to share some of the many experiences that I had the opportunity to enjoy with these great leaders so that all of you, both civilians and military, can appreciate this very special world of people. I am grateful for our men and women in uniform. Thank you for your service and all the sacrifices you make for all of us.

Special thanks to my wife, Deborah, who shared every minute of this unexpected life with me. It was at her insistence that I write down these experiences before too much time had passed. And thanks to her guidance, talent, and writing skills, the entire book was written and rewritten with great care, sensitivity, and as much precision as possible. I hope you enjoy reading this book—it is truly a book of lives well lived.

CHAPTER 1

How It All Started: Our Introduction to the Military

Our introduction to the military began on October 29, 2008. John and Leslie Osterweil opened their home and entertained a group of our civilian community in order to introduce us to the new heads of CENTCOM. That is, to meet and greet General David Petraeus, then head of CENTCOM, General John Allen, then deputy of CENTCOM and General Jay Hood, then chief of staff of CENTCOM.

John Osterweil had been a liaison between MacDill AFB and the community for many years prior. In 1988, General Norman Schwarzkopf came to Tampa to head CENTCOM. Soon after, his son was a classmate with John's son at Berkeley Preparatory School. And by 1989, the Schwarzkopf's invited the Osterweils over for dinner on the base and mentioned that it would be great to know more about the Tampa Community. John was delighted and began his journey as the civilian liaison for CENTCOM and SOCOM and as each leadership changed out every two years, he would host a meet and greet. These relationships, established early on, are why so many military leaders retire in the Tampa Bay Area. The generosity and goodwill of our community toward our finest was much appreciated and well received.

Deborah and I had been involved and volunteered in a multitude of nonprofit organizations over the years as well as having a strong presence in the business community and naturally, we were delighted to participate. We enjoyed the evening and participated in welcoming the generals and their wives and helping them feel at home and comfortable in their new community. Our experience at our first meet-and-greet party was wonderful. The generals were all down-to-earth and so humble. Each one was open and interested in our civilian fields and our great city of Tampa, which they expressed is well known as one of the best places to complete their service because of the public praise and support of our military.

Little did I know that Deborah had left that first gathering with the cell-phone numbers of the generals' wives—Holly Petraeus, Kathy Allen, and Lynne Hood. Since we'd had such an incredible time at the meet and greet, we decided to have one of our Rosenthal signature "Games and Trains" parties for friends and local military leadership. We'd been hosting these events for our family and friends for years and they were always well received. We thought they would offer a perfect opportunity for local military leadership to attend a unique function where they could relax and get to know some members of their new community.

CHAPTER 2

Rosenthal "Games and Trains" Parties

JANUARY 10, 2009: FIRST GAMES AND TRAINS PARTY WITH THE GENERALS

The Rosenthal Games and Trains parties occurred for years prior to meeting up with the military. It is our signature party mostly because we open our entire home to our guests, including a very special, unique feature: our train room. An avid train enthusiast, I had always dreamed of curating a working train collection. Our home's Train Room, as we call it, is a twenty-nine-foot by nineteen-foot room with three-dimensional decorations showing the scenery of Arizona's Red Rock State Park in the summer, the Colorado Rockies in the Spring, the Swiss Alps in the winter, and Zurmatt, Switzerland in the fall. This diorama depicts the challenging landscape in the US and Europe that train workers and engineers encountered when laying the first railroads there. The trains are Lehmann Gross Bahn (LGB) out of Nuremberg, Germany, and are of the G-scale, which is 1:22.5. So these are pretty big trains. There are fifteen different train lines comprised of ten to twenty cars on each line. All are run through a single laptop computer with technology designed especially for the Train Room. As an added effect, the train engines have smoke and sound recordings of the original real-life locomotives. According to the April 2018 *LGB Depesche* magazine for LGB enthusiasts, my Southern Railroad System won third place for indoor layouts in the world.

The first Rosenthal Games and Trains Party took place with twenty civilian couples and the Petraeuses, Allens, and Hoods in attendance. The invitation said *The Rosenthal Express . . . The generals are coming! The generals are coming!* I had heard that David Petraeus liked foosball, so I purchased a table and installed it in the center of the train room.

The night started with the security detail coming down our street at 5:00 p.m. to check everything out. When I received a call from security asking me how I wanted the general to arrive, I informed them that they could just come right in the front door. So, General Petraeus and Holly came up to the door at 7:30 p.m., and the Allens and Hoods promptly followed. General Petraeus was very cordial to all of our guests. I stood next to him and introduced him to each of the twenty couples and gave a background on each about their occupation, college, interests, etc.

When people arrive, Deborah is always in the foyer greeting them. She shows them the party layout detailing how the house is set up and ready for them to enjoy—dinner, dessert, bar, wine and beer stations, billiard table, ping pong table, foosball table, jigsaw puzzle, the giant adult-size pick-up sticks, and of course, the train room.

Sometime later, after everyone has a chance to eat, drink and socialize, Deborah rings her favorite, very loud, very old, brass school bell. She then asks everyone to gather in the train room for the presentation.

On this evening, I introduced the military guests and then presented General Petraeus with an honorary conductor's hat with all his medals on it. The train show was essentially the history of trains through time. It began with the first steam engine invented by George Stephenson in 1829; no invention in history has made more of a worldwide impact to civilians than the steam locomotive. Continents, countries, states, and cities were developed due to this incredible invention. I then proceeded to describe the development of our world over time through trains all the way to the most modern

Glacial Express Line in Switzerland in the 2000s.

After the presentations, General Petraeus immediately went for the foosball table. He was determined to take on each group who wanted to challenge him. People continued to mingle throughout the house and enjoy the company, assortment of desserts, and libations. General Petraeus went outside to get some fresh air and my friend, Richard Schwartz, asked him, "How do you come up with the names of each of the operations?" (Operation Desert Fox, Desert Shield, Enduring Freedom, Desert Storm). General Petraeus, or Dave, as he asked us to call him, told Richard that they sit around a table and come up with words that make an impact on the mission.

Later, Dave was back on the foosball table and was intent on taking all the guests out. The Allens and Hoods were enjoying watching the games and socializing with all the civilians. I had heard from his staff that General Petraeus would probably only stay for one hour. It was now 11:30 p.m. and General Petraeus was still there with his wife Holly. We were having a great time, so I jokingly asked him if he was going to spend the night. He smiled and expressed how much he had enjoyed the evening. He then mentioned that he had been with the vice president the day before and would be with the president the next day, but he would rather be here. The first Games and Trains party concluded just after midnight. What an incredibly memorable evening everyone had!

JUNE 14, 2009: FIRST GAMES AND TRAINS PARTY FOR THE INTERNATIONAL COALITION

On June 14, 2009, Deborah and I hosted our first coalition party for families from Albania, Australia, France, Greece, Italy, Jordan, New Zealand, Norway, Pakistan, Poland, Portugal, Sweden, and Ukraine, as part of the Coalition of CENTCOM. Also, in attendance were General Jay Hood, the chief of staff for CENTCOM, and his wife, Lynne.

As is the custom of my wife's propensity for detail, there was a table in the outside entry for name tags and a framed welcome sign; *welcome* was written in the native language of every attending guest. When they entered the house, they found their homeland flags printed on photo stock and lined along three sides of the upstairs portion of the foyer for all to see as further recognition of their countries.

After 9/11, President Bush wanted to have a representative from all countries that are working together to fight worldwide terrorism as part of CENTCOM. At this time, over fifty-nine countries are represented at CENTCOM. General John Allen, former head of CENTCOM communicated the following to me:

> It would be difficult for me to overstate how strategically important it is to host these foreign representatives. Each of these representatives was hand selected by their countries to be the quintessential representative of their state, and also, because they have the potential over the remainder of their career to leverage their exposure to the US. When these people leave CENTCOM and go back to their respective countries, because of the unadulterated military might of the US, they are left in awe. But many of these people have grown up in the shadow of an imposing military power before the Soviet Union, Russia, China, and North Korea. The difference for them about the US is that in the entire history of the world, there has never been a megapower like the US. At the very moment when the US military might be used to further our national self-interest, we use our national military for the good of the world, the cynics notwithstanding. So, for these folks, it is the idea of America that leaves them so indelibly changed, and that idea comes from being with you, Mark and Deborah. What you're doing has an immediate impact every day, but the real payoff will be in the years ahead as these officers, who eventually grow

up to be chiefs of defense and ministers of defense, will make national decisions on our behalf that could be of profound strategic importance to us. You should be proud of that truly strategic contribution to our national security.

The theme of our coalition party was to demonstrate American hospitality and generosity to our foreign guests. We served hotdogs, hamburgers, (all halal beef), waffle fries, and apple pie a la mode. What an icebreaker for all these representatives from disparate countries to interact with each other, as well as General Jay Hood, CENTCOM chief of staff, and his wife, Lynne, as well as Tampa Bay community friends and business leaders. It's interesting how games and trains, e.g. ping pong, billiards, and foosball, and experiencing the train room for the very first time, brought people together. The event was enjoyed by all, and Deborah and I felt like we connected people. We were thrilled that everyone had a very positive experience together at our home.

JULY 18, 2009: GAMES AND TRAINS PARTY—THE GENERALS ARE COMING AGAIN!

Our daughter Jennifer was taking a chemistry class at the University of Tampa as a prerequisite for Cornell University. What a coincidence that Anne Petraeus, General Petraeus's daughter, was attending the same class. The two started talking one day before class when Anne said to Jennifer, "My dad and your dad are great friends and I heard about your Games and Trains parties!" Immediately after class, Jennifer called me and said, "We need to have another party!"

Deborah began the planning and preparations. We coordinated the date and made all the arrangements for dinner, desserts, bar, wine and beer stations, etc. and of course, games and trains. Everything would be in place throughout the house, and all would be invited to make themselves at home. This party included General David and Holly Petraeus, General John and Kathy Allen, and General Jay and Lynne Hood, and of course, Anne Petraeus and Jennifer Rosenthal, as our star guests. We had thirty-nine attendees including our son, Jason, as well as friends and Tampa Bay business leaders. We also invited Jennifer and Jason's former civics teacher, Bob Bradshaw (a favorite of all students at Tampa Preparatory High School), as well as the principal, Kevin Plummer and his wife, Jennifer, to join us in meeting and mingling with our military friends.

You'll hear in a later chapter about my experience aboard the USS *Eisenhower* aircraft carrier; I used this party opportunity to invite my roommate on that excursion, Owen Roberts, and his wife, Susan. Another chapter on board the USS *Pittsburgh* will be forthcoming, and naturally I wanted to include my ship companion and University of Florida college roommate, Richard Schwartz and his wife, Sharon. And since it happened that Deborah's sister, Valorie, her husband, Ron Sanford, and their daughter, Jessica, were all in town, they too joined in the fun. Finally, our very dear, close friends, Ann and David Rosenbach, attended, as they have an open invitation for every Games and Trains party. And how perfect that both Daves—Petraeus and Rosenbach—had a lot in common, not the least of which was the fact that they both had attended Princeton. The party was a wonderful mix of amazing people.

Anne and Jennifer realized they were both members of the same sorority, Kappa Alpha Theta, and they proceeded to demonstrate a Theta cheer together. Afterward, the general challenged his daughter, Anne, to a competitive game of foosball.

The evening was another fabulous and memorable event. By the way, at the end of every party Deborah hands out party favors, usually a choice of dark or milk chocolate in the shape of the American flag, in a clear bag, tied at the top with red, white, and blue raffia.

MARCH 20, 2010: GAMES AND TRAINS PARTY—MORE VERY IMPORTANT PEOPLE

Since Dave and Holly Petraeus really enjoyed our Games and Trains parties, it was time to get together again! CENTCOM leader General Petraeus and his wife, Holly; Coalition head General Arnie Skjaerpe and his wife, Unni, from Norway; and Coalition deputy, General Gilles Lemoine and his wife, Laure, from France; Colonel Philippe Derathe and his wife, Lisa, from France; president of the Tampa Bay Rays, Dick Crippen and his wife, Penny; architect of the Dali Museum (who also worked with I. M. Pei on the pyramid at the Louvre in Paris), Yann Weymouth and his wife, Susana; owner of the Tradewinds Hotel in St. Petersburg, Florida, Mr. Tim Bogott and his wife Anje were the stars of the party.

It happened that a few of my University of Florida Tau Epsilon Phi (TEP) fraternity friends were in town, so Ralph and Margot Marcadis (Tampa natives), Michael and Jeanette Pincus (Dallas, Texas), Rocket and Robin Rosen (Sugarland, Texas), and Richard and Sharon Schwartz (Orlando, Florida) all came and partied with us, along with many others including our dear friends, Dave and Ann Rosenbach.

What is so amazing about General Petraeus is that he is genuinely interested in hearing about each and every occupation, career, and journey people have travelled to achieve their success. He was amazed at all the talent we had converged for the event.

To add a new dimension for Dave Petraeus, I recruited one of the nation's finest foosball champions, Tom Yore, to play the backcourt for him. I wanted to make sure that he was going to win every game that night. Tom and Dave took out Clif Curry (attorney-at-law) and Dr. Mark Frankle (orthopedic surgeon), who had both beaten Dave at an earlier party. The foosball table was intense as Dave and Tom took out the civilians throughout the night.

The evening was another fabulous and memorable event. We

had about thirty-four guests with wonderfully diverse and interesting backgrounds. By the way, at every party, we usually have our player piano playing and a continuous loop of photos showing on the big screen in the family room for all to enjoy.

The memory of that evening is even more precious to me today, as my fraternity brother Rocket Rosen passed away January 14, 2020, from amyotrophic lateral sclerosis (ALS), also known as Lou Gehrig's Disease. He was a brilliant attorney; a great teacher, coach, friend, and mentor to all of us at TEP, as well as a wonderful family man to his wife, Robin, and their four beautiful daughters, Jorden, Courtney, Portland, and Darby.

JULY 9, 2011: GAMES AND TRAINS PARTY—ADMIRALS, GENERALS—COME ONE AND ALL!

Deborah always prepares the house at least a week in advance of a gathering. Since she knows the menu, and she has already placed her order with Pane Rustica (her absolute favorite caterer for our parties), she knows exactly what platters, serving bowls, and utensils she will need. Everything is laid out with sticky notes indicating where each food and dessert item will be placed. She believes this is important because everything fits just right on the table and sideboard. Food is presented buffet style, and everyone serves themselves. Naturally, she saves the center of the table for a tall, beautiful flower arrangement, which she creates herself. Over the years, she switched out the black stones in the base of the vase to multi-colored golf balls and domino pieces. Under the arrangement, rather than a place mat, she uses the children's Monopoly board sprinkled with about twenty pair of dice, Monopoly hotels, houses, and playing pieces. The Games and Trains Party feel is everywhere.

In addition to the main buffet, bar, and beer and wine station, cheese and charcuterie platters (sometimes in lieu of the jigsaw puzzle), along with small bowls of nuts are sprinkled throughout the house. There is something for everyone.

As was customary, this party began with Deborah and me in the main foyer welcoming people into our home. Deborah showed our guests the layout for all the food, drink, games, and trains and asked everyone to please enjoy themselves. The layout of the house was printed on card stock and presented to our guests as she welcomed them. She always kept several on hand because people liked it so much, they asked if they could have one.

Naturally, the player piano was playing (sometimes we ask a pianist to play live throughout the evening), and the photos were on a continuous loop on the family room TV screen. I always try to include photos of those in attendance as an added treat.

This night would be our first time we would have the honor of hosting the entire Special Operations Command (SOCOM)—commander, Admiral Eric Olson and his wife, Marilyn; deputy commander, General David Fridovich and his wife, Kathy; and chief of staff, General Mark Clark and his wife, Lisa.

This night we hosted an astronaut too! The head of technology, astronaut Bill Shephard, also attended the event. Bill Shephard was the commander of the space shuttles *Atlantis*, *Discovery*, and *Columbia*, and was also the commander of the *Soyuz* TM-31, a Russian spacecraft. Bill explained a couple of the differences between NASA and the Soviet Space program. The American astronauts use a $100,000 writing device while the Soviets use a pencil; we use a $250,000 waste system, while they use a simple type of suction tube device; and finally, although the US does not allow alcoholic beverages, the Soviets have vodka in their drinking tubes for their cosmonauts—many of them insist on it. I can just imagine them squeezing the tubes while spinning without gravity throughout the spacecraft.

Our guest list counted forty-three confirmed attendees, including friends and business leaders—all there to interact and learn about each other's worlds.

The flow of the party continued—eat, drink, play billiards, ping-pong, and foosball, and socialize until the time comes for the train-room presentation. Deborah rang the school bell and invited people to gather in the train room, adding that desserts, coffee, and tea were waiting whenever guests were ready. After running the trains and explaining the history, I awarded each of the SOCOM leadership an official train conductor's hat, customized with pins representing their military services and distinguishing achievements, e.g. 1,2,3, or 4 stars, the branch of the military they served (Army, Navy, Air Force, Marine), their country (e.g. US, France, Israel, Australia, Canada), their specific field (infantry, artillery, aviation, intelligence). These conductor hats are special ordered through companies that supply the major railroads in the country.

After the train demonstration, everyone partied on and enjoyed the dynamics of the evening. At the end of the night, as Deborah disbursed chocolate party favors, we could sense that everyone had an amazing experience, taking home great memories. This was what it was all about for us—civilians and military members coming together and gaining greater knowledge and understanding of one another throughout the evening.

It's important to note a special history Deborah has with General David Fridovich. They were classmates at Nova High School in Davie, Florida. Deborah was a cheerleader and Dave was a football star on the team, both junior varsity and varsity. Until just before this gathering, they had not seen each other since 1970!

FEBRUARY 11, 2012: GAMES AND TRAINS PARTY—MORE INCREDIBLE HEROES AND STARS

This party was unique in that we invited the only two existing four-star Navy SEALs (Sea, Air, and Land team) at the time. They had both had the distinction of being the Navy's Bull Frog, or longest serving Navy SEAL still on duty. Admiral Eric Olson (Ret.), the former commander of SOCOM, had been involved in the Mogadishu rescue. And Admiral William McRaven, commander of the Joint Special Operations Command (JSOC), had spearheaded the capture of Saddam Hussein and the killing of Osama Bin Laden.

Also attending was Lieutenant General Marty Steele (Ret.), a three-star Marine, who had served in Vietnam and Operations Desert Shield and Desert Storm. He was the current president of the Intrepid Air and Space Museum in New York. Captain Devon Goldsmith, a Navy fighter squadron leader of numerous Iraqi bombings, had been my next-door neighbor and classmate at Jesuit High School in Tampa, Florida. Devin always sat in the front row in class, and I guess that served him well.

Marilyn Olson, Georgeann McRaven, Cindy Steele, and Vicki Goldsmith, all joined us with their husbands.

Speaking of Marty Steele, the first time I met him had been in 2010 when I was invited by General Petraeus to attend the nineteenth annual Salute to Freedom Dinner in Manhattan's West Side, aboard the *Intrepid*. The Intrepid Sea, Air and Space Museum pays tribute to our nation's heroes, and this event honored General Petraeus, then tenth commander of the US Central Command (CENTCOM). "The Intrepid Museum's mission is to honor the men and women who have served our nation. General Petraeus has led our troops overseas in that exact effort, and we are indebted to his leadership and love of country," said Susan Marenoff, executive director of the museum. "This annual event throws a spotlight on individuals who have gone above and beyond the call of duty for our nation." It was a fascinating evening.

Regarding Devon Goldsmith, it's interesting to note that I happened to read a 1990 *US News and World Report* article and there was a picture of the aircraft carrier *John F. Kennedy* briefing room. I noticed Devon sitting in the front row of the room. I hadn't seen Devon since 1975, so I was fascinated that he had gone into the military from college and then had become a Navy pilot. And yes, he was again sitting in the front row. I immediately contacted the magazine and asked how I could send a letter to Devon. I was given an address in Miami, Florida, and sent Devon a long letter telling him about our family and how I wished him all the best in the Navy. About six weeks later, I received a letter from Captain Devon Goldsmith with a map and pictures of all the targets he had bombed and the squadron he was charged to lead. I was proud of him for his service to this country and his many successes.

Another classmate of mine at Jesuit, Colonel Joe Miller, excelled in the military as director, strategy, plans, and policy, J5 for US SOCOM, and then the lead liaison between the US and Israel. He and his lovely wife, Carolyn, joined us for the evening.

Party guest and neighbor, Captain Jeff Cathey (Ret.) and his wife, Casey, joined us as well. Jeff was a top Navy pilot and had over 300 landings and one ejection on US aircraft carriers.

We were also honored to have Command Sergeant Major Gary Littrell, a Medal of Honor recipient for deeds performed in the Vietnam War. He was subject to intense enemy mortar attack and succeeded in defending a hill deep in Vietnam near Dak Seang for four days, not allowing the Vietcong an opportunity to capture or take over his position. He inspired confidence, directed artillery, and air support, and cared for the wounded.

Fred Humphries, special agent for the FBI in Tampa, Florida, also joined us that evening. He was a very humble and quiet guy who carried a big stick and another incredible military hero. On December 14, 1999, Fred had been involved in border control on the Canadian American border in Port Angeles, Washington, when a car with two men arrived on the ferry boat. Fred asked the two men their country of origin and one said with a French-Canadian accent, "Canada," and the other with an Algerian accent said "Canada." Fred knew that something was wrong since he'd had a platoon leader earlier in his career in the Army who spoke Algerian French. His suspicions were correct; upon inspecting the car, he found detonators, wire, firing caps, and explosives in the trunk. The car was heading to the Los Angeles International Airport to explode bombs and cause massive damage. This was the first Al Qaida plot that was foiled and unknown to all of us. Fred is truly a national hero.

Both Fred Humphries and Admiral McRaven were presented honorary conductor's hats for "Mark's Southern Railroad Systems." They were both very excited to receive the authentic hats with all of their medals and awards (or "lettuce," as some in the military call it) attached.

While recently attending a Special Operations banquet, I'd had the honor of meeting Sergeant Major Billy Waugh, and knew I'd want to invite him to a Games and Trains party someday. I had just read the book, *Hunting the Jackal*, which was all about Billy Waugh hunting, capturing and arresting Carlos the Jackal in Khartoum, Sudan. He had been to Sudan to perform surveillance and intelligence gathering on terrorist leaders, including Osama bin Laden. This was in 1990, when he'd had Osama Bin Laden in the site at close range and had requested permission to fire. The Clinton administration would not authorize the hit.

Billy Waugh was named one of the most highly decorated Special Forces and CIA operatives in the history of our country. He served over fifty years. Sergeant Major Waugh served in the US Army's elite Green Berets and received a Purple Heart and Silver Star in Vietnam. In the 1970s he retired from the military and went to the CIA to perform missions in Libya.

At the age of seventy-one, Waugh participated in Operation Enduring Freedom as a member of the CIA team in Afghanistan and parachuted into Tora Bora. According to Ambassador Coufer Black, US State Department coordinator for counter terrorism, "Billy Waugh is a man of exceptional character and courage who has served his country either in combat or in intelligence work since the middle of the last century. He has seen more, done more, and risked more in the interest of the United States than any man I know." He was an important honored guest at this Games and Trains Party.

What an incredible group of heroes and stars we had assembled for this gathering! Our civilian friends and business leaders were enthralled. We had a total of fifty-one guests for the evening who will never forget this extraordinary night. We had the man that foiled the first Al Qaida plot and the man that took out Osama Bin Laden, the head of Al Qaida.

AUGUST 10, 2013: GAMES AND TRAINS PARTY–REPEAT STARS AND MORE

Deborah prepared for another amazing party with all details fully covered. This gathering included a few repeats of stars that had attended before, such as Admiral Bill and Georgeann McRaven, Admiral Eric and Marilyn Olson, Lieutenant General Marty and Cindy Steele, Colonel Joe and Carolyn Miller, Captain Devon and Vicki Goldsmith, and Command Sergeant Major Billy and Lynn Waugh.

New stars included Rear Admiral Matts and Annette Fogelberg, Coalition of CENTCOM; Vice Admiral Joe and Kathy Maguire, director of the National Counterterrorism Center in Washington DC; Lieutenant General John and Miriam Mulholland, deputy commander of SOCOM, who they made the movie *12 Strong* about (the first counter to the 9/11 bombing in New York City); Brigadier General Mark and Monique Smethurst, an Australian and the first embedded foreigner in SOCOM leadership, he had also been assistant to General John Allen in Afghanistan and according to John was one of the bravest and most successful soldiers representing the ISAF Coalition; and Hal Walker, a retired medical doctor for SOCOM.

Many of our civilian friends are very supportive of the military. I think it's important to recognize Russ and Marti Kimball, owners of the Sheraton Sand Key in Clearwater Beach, Florida. I had met Russ a few years earlier at a function and introduced him to some of my military friends. Although he had never served, he expressed that he was very interested in assisting our nation's finest. Russ and Marti began their own tradition: they open their hotel beach area for CENTCOM Coalition families. They set up a huge tent with tables and chairs, food (lobster, shrimp, steak, chicken, the works), drink stations, and music. Probably going on ten years at the writing of this book, Marti and Russ are true American patriots for their generosity and hospitality toward our military families.

Our local community guests vary per party so that we maximize the interaction and involvement between "Tampans" and our military attendees. Everyone really enjoys and appreciates these unique parties. They moved throughout the house for food, cocktails, wine, beer (we had champagne whenever the French attended), games and trains, and socializing. When the time was right, Deborah rang the now-popular school bell and asked everyone to gather in the back room. I introduced all the military guests, including a little background on each, and then presented Billy Waugh and John Mulholland with their conductor hats customized with all their relevant "lettuce." By the way, little by little, over the years, every military participant in the Games and Trains parties received their own specialized conductor's hat.

After the train presentation, everyone continued to party in whatever area they were happiest. Some even moved to coffee and tea with their desserts. Others played foosball, ping pong, billiards or sat around the jigsaw puzzle talking as they placed their puzzle pieces on the 1,000-piece puzzle. At a minimum, Deborah always had the border put together prior to the party, hoping to encourage others to build off of it.

As we all enjoyed one another, I couldn't help but notice Bill McRaven at the billiard table. Quiet, humble, and under the radar, he proceeded to clear the table with shots hopping over balls with the acumen of a billiard shark. The party went on to the wee hours as he moved on to the ping pong table and partnered with Hal Walker against our friends, Carl and Lyda Lindell.

Later that evening, rather morning (around 12:30 a.m.), as we said our goodbyes and everyone expressed how much they enjoyed the party, Deborah handed out the chocolate American flag and added "God bless America."

The next day I emailed Dave Petraeus and wrote what an incredible billiard player Bill was; Dave responded, "Thanks for the intel." These incredible military leaders are competitive and yet so very humble. I shake my head in fascination, as I am so glad that they, and others like them are the leaders of our military. They want success, and they strive to win, and as they have always said, the most important win is through peace.

DECEMBER 14, 2016: GAMES AND TRAINS–SOCOM AND INTERNATIONAL COALITION

Admiral Bill McRaven, former head of SOCOM, first established the International Coalition in 2015 to allow nations across the world to work together as a joint force combatting global terrorism. There are twenty-nine countries in the coalition. This night included twelve of their representatives along with their spouses from Australia, Canada, Denmark, Finland, France, Great Britain, Lithuania, Netherlands, New Zealand, Norway, Romania, and Spain.

Military participants included General Tony Thomas, head of SOCOM and his wife, Barb; Admiral Sean Pybus, deputy of SOCOM and his wife, Patty; Major General Mark Hicks, chief of staff for

SOCOM and his wife, Lauren; Command Sergeant Major Patrick McCauley and his wife, Starla; General Dean Milner, deputy J-5 of CENTCOM (Planning) and his wife, Katrin; General Jay Hood, former chief of staff of CENTCOM and former commander of Guantanamo Detainee Center, and his wife, Lynne; Sergeant Major Billy Waugh, Green Beret and CIA officer (each for twenty-five years), and his wife, Lynn.

As always, the party "recipe" was a huge success. Civilians and military members mingling, eating, drinking, playing games, and experiencing the train room. Everyone had a great time and loved it all!

JULY 1, 2022: GAMES AND TRAINS WITH COMMANDERS OF CENTCOM AND SOCOM

Deborah and I had not hosted a Games and Trains Party for some time due to scheduling conflicts with CENTCOM and SOCOM as well as the COVID outbreak. Although they had us to their homes for dinners and other gatherings, there were times when military leaders were unable to attend our Games and Trains parties, such as General Joseph Votel, head of SOCOM (2014–2016); General James Mattis head of CENTCOM (2010–2013); General Lloyd Austin, head of CENTCOM (2013–2016); and again, General Joseph Votel, when he was head of CENTCOM (2016–2019); and General Ken McKenzie, head of CENTCOM (2019–2022).

In 2022 we wanted to welcome the new commanders—General Richard Clarke, head of SOCOM and General Michael Kurilla, head of CENTCOM—and their families to our community, Rosenthal style. It was time to do some serious catch up! Everyone, civilians and military members alike, needed a Games and Trains party! I contacted General Clarke's office and found a date that would work. He then suggested that I reach out to General Kurilla and check on his availability.

After receiving confirmations from both, we were on go! These are the two most important combatant commands in the world. And it would be the first time that both active heads of SOCOM and CENTCOM, and their wives, Suzanne Clarke and Mary Page Kurilla, would be attending a Rosenthal Games and Trains party. We were very excited.

After tending to all the preparations and house set up as usual, Deborah and I welcomed our guests at 7:00 p.m. Naturally, the military members were right on time as they exited their secure vehicles at the front of the house. We had forty-three attendees for the event with eleven either active duty or retired military members to honor.

The tone of the evening was different from previous parties; everyone had grown tired of the constraints of the pandemic and was hungry for a party. People were so engaged in conversation, eating and drinking, that introductions began later than usual, just after 8:30 p.m. when Deborah rang the bell and asked everyone to gather in the back room.

I began by introducing the military guests one at a time with a short bio and asking them to come over for their customized conductor's hats. That night we honored General Richard Clarke, commander of SOCOM; General Michael Kurilla, commander of CENTCOM; Admiral Collin Green, deputy commander of SOCOM; General Marcus Evans, chief of staff of SOCOM; General Charlie Holland (Ret.), commander of SOCOM, 2000–2002; General Tony Thomas (Ret.), commander SOCOM, 2016–2019; and General Vince Beckland, J3 head of operations for SOCOM.

I then recognized the other special guests present: Colonel Cary Harbaugh (Ret.) (SOCOM), Colonel Marty Jones (Ret.) (SOCOM), FBI Agent Fred Humphries (Ret.), and Major Or Karasin, first Israeli liaison officer (LNO) for CENTCOM.

After the introductions, I invited everyone into the train room and Deborah offered our guests desserts, coffee, and tea. I gave a briefing on the history of the trains and ran the twelve locomotives at the same time. Each of the attendees enjoyed the presentation and continued to socialize. And although the billiard, ping pong, and foosball tables were available for all to enjoy, this particular night people conversed and mingled with one another throughout the evening. There was great chemistry with all the guests. Deborah and I felt very gratified with the evening. It was a great success, and one of our best.

The event ended at about 11:30 p.m. with all guests departing with their chocolate American flag and Deborah's parting words of, "God bless America."

FEBRUARY 1, 2020: TRAIN ROOM VISIT AND LUNCHEON

I met Greg at a function in Tampa for SOCOM in 2018. He assumed the position of command chief master sergeant on July 11, 2019. As such, Gregory A. Smith is (as of this writing) the tenth command senior enlisted leader of US Special Operations Command at MacDill AFB.

He was so warm and welcoming and invited us to visit him in his position at the time, which was the command chief master sergeant, Air Force Special Operations Command at Hurlburt Field in Okaloosa County, Florida. I had taken a tour there before and witnessed the best of our Air Force special operators and enjoyed seeing an AC-130J Ghostrider, a powerful gunship. I learned from our conversation that Greg loved trains and knew all about the LGB trains that I had in my home.

Deborah and I invited Greg and his lovely wife, Tina, to our home to give a train presentation and have a nice lunch. Greg was in shock when he saw the Train Room and the setup of the fifteen train lines and the landscaping that was built. I gave Greg and Tina a briefing on the history of the trains and then ran them for the couple. Afterward, I presented him with one of my famous train conductor's hat with all of the medals Greg had achieved and presented Tina with her own hat. In addition, I had a replica made of the AC-130J Ghostrider airplane that we had seen at Hurlburt Field and had Greg autograph it since he was the commander at that time.

Afterward, we had a nice lunch and discussed their history in the military with all the different deployments and locations they had moved to over the years. Greg's current job at SOCOM as the highest-ranking noncommissioned officer allowed him to travel the globe as the assistant to General Richard Clarke, the head of Special Operations Command for the world. The day was very memorable, and I enjoyed introducing two great Americans to our home and welcoming them to our city.

DAYTIME TRAIN ROOM PRESENTATIONS: SINCE 2001

In the last section I described a Train Room visit and luncheon in 2020. This was one of many, probably hundreds, of daytime visits and Train Room presentations. I always look for opportunities to "show and tell" about the Train Room and I especially enjoy connecting the history of the world and the development of civilization through the perspective of trains.

People from all walks of life are welcome. And so, it has been for countless friends and family, new acquaintances, visitors to Tampa for special events (weddings, Bar and Bat Mitzvahs, birthdays, graduations), church parishioners, schools (sometimes bus loads), Temple members, railroad enthusiasts, Garden Railroad Convention participants, community business leaders, and of course, members of the military over the years. Most visitors brought their friends and families (spouses, children, grandchildren). We have become like a convenient local attraction for all to see. And naturally, prior visitors often tell others, and so, through word of mouth, our home was and is always open.

People see me around the community and say, "I heard about your Train Room! I'd love to show my family!" Our local NBC TV network interviewed and filmed it for the news, tying it to a holiday "feel good" piece. One time I got a call asking if I would show the Train Room to a group of people who were lobbying for high-speed rail throughout the state of Florida—it was great! They were delighted and very appreciative. That said, we still don't have high-speed rail in Florida.

The Rosenthal Train Room

Deborah, General David Petraeus, and me at our first Games & Trains Party

General Jay Hood, me, Captain Todd Schapler, Admiral Kid Donegan, and General Karl Horst

Me, Michael Pincus, General David Petraeus, and Rocket Rosen

Admiral Eric Olson, Astronaut Bill Shephard, me, General Mark Clark, and General Dave Fridovich

Sarah and Fred Humphries, Georgeann and Admiral Bill McRaven, Deborah and me

Sergeant Major Billy Waugh, me, and General John Mulholland

Admiral Bill McRaven, Colonel Hal Walker, MD, Colonel Philippe Derathe, Anthony Weiss, Brigadier General Mark Smethurst, and John McCoskrie

Command Sergeant Pat McCauley, General Tony Thomas, Me, Admiral Sean Pybus, and General Mark Hicks

General Tony Thomas, John McCoskrie, Patty Pybus and Admiral Sean Pybus playing Foosball

Command Sergeant Greg Smith, Tina, and Me in the Train Room

General Michael Kurilla, me, General Richard Clarke, General Marcus Evans, and Major Or Karasin In Train Room

CHAPTER 3

Coalition Parties Hosted by our Civilian Communities

As noted in the chapter about Games and Trains parties, we hosted the first International Coalition party. Guest families were from thirteen nations, but the list of coalition countries is much larger and so there would be more parties to be planned. The nations that were part of our coalition community at that time were: Afghanistan, Albania, Armenia, Australia, Belgium, Bulgaria, Canada, Croatia, Czech Republic, Denmark, Egypt, Estonia, Finland, France, Germany, Hungary, Italy, Japan, Jordan, Kazakhstan, Korea, Kuwait, Kyrgyzstan, Latvia, Lebanon, Lithuania, Mongolia, Morocco, Netherlands, New Zealand, Norway, Pakistan, Poland, Portugal, Qatar, Romania, Saudi Arabia, Singapore, Slovak Republic, Slovenia, Spain, Sweden, Turkey, Ukraine, Uzbekistan, United Arab Emirates, and United Kingdom (and for the first time in 2022, Israel).

I reached out to friends and leaders in our communities and asked them to host our coalition families. On June 14, 2009, Deborah and I hosted the first party. On October 23, 2010, Clif and Terry Curry hosted an outdoor barbecue at their home. Each nation's flag flew on a free-standing eight-foot flagpole arranged along the entire length of the property. A band kept the atmosphere lively with patriotic music. More than 260 guests attended, including one by air—we had a fly-over by an American pilot on an aircraft powered paraglider waving an American flag! We were also pleased to have in attendance Major General Michael Jones (chief of staff, CENTCOM) and Vice Admiral Michael Franken (head of J-5, CENTCOM). Russ and Marti Kimball of the Sheraton Sand Key Resort hosted a fun crab and beach fest on April 28, 2011, on the beach under a huge tent (it was such a hit that they repeated that same party theme there for the coalition countries on April 21, 2012, April 23, 2017, and May 1, 2022). On February 16, 2012, Chris and Alice Goslin hosted a party at their home where they lined the flag poles along both sides of the wide front entry walkway to the home. That night we were pleased to have in attendance Brigadier General Jens Praestegaard (Denmark Army); Rufus and Helen Marie Williams hosted a barbecue featuring hamburgers, hot dogs, coleslaw, baked beans, and apple pie on March 27, 2013. More than 150 guests attended, including Command Sergeant Major Frank Grippe (CENTCOM), Captain Jeff Cathey (Ret.) and his wife, Casey, and Sergeant Major Billy Waugh (Ret.) and his wife, Lynn. Tampa's infamous Bayshore Boulevard saw a party on June 27, 2014, hosted by and at the home of Harry and Carmen Barkett, as again each nation's flag flew proudly on individual flag poles lining the property. Finally another wonderful party hosted by and at the home of Rufus and Helen Marie Williams was enjoyed on May 4, 2018—flags and all.

There's one other important party worthy of mention—shortly after Admiral Bill McRaven made an important decision to make the Five Eyes (FVEY) countries (Australia, Canada, New Zealand, the United Kingdom, and the United States), part of the leadership of SOCOM, Rufus Williams III and his wife, Helen Marie, stepped up, being the patriots they are, and hosted the Five Eyes Party on September 12, 2014, at their beautiful Tampa home. Military officers and leaders from all of these countries attended, as well as many members of the civilian community. We were pleased to have in attendance Clay Pendergrass (SOCOM), General Jay Hood (Ret.) (CENTCOM), Command Surgeon Colonel Hal Walker (SOCOM),

Brigadier General Mark Smethurst (an Australian imbedded at SOCOM), Colonel Mark Blythern (Australia), Colonel Nathen Mutu (Australia), Colonel Dean Franklin (Australia), Lieutenant Colonel Scott Tatnell (Australia), and Colonel Paul Keddy (Canada).

These gatherings were wonderful opportunities for foreign nations to experience American hospitality. On all these occasions, civilians and the members of the military international coalition interacted and became better acquainted and appreciative of one another.

On each occasion I gave a short speech about how important each of our foreign dignitaries were and how we really are one big family working to keep peace in this world.

Our home's entrance with coalition country flags

Coalition party hosted by Rufus and Helen Marie Williams

Russ Kimball, General Richard Clarke, General James Linder and me at the Sheraton Sand Key

CHAPTER 4

Our First Invitation to MacDill Air Force Base

On September 19, 2009, Deborah and I were invited for dinner on the base by Colonel Lawrence Martin, MacDill AFB wing commander (also known as base commander or gate keeper), and his wife, Patricia. This was our first experience at a base dinner, and we looked forward to a new experience. We had a marvelous time at their Hawaiian-themed get together. Little did I know there was a very nice purpose to the gathering—they wanted to thank me for becoming an honorary Air Force commander of the 6th Mobility Wing.

The Honorary Air Force Commander Program in Tampa is very unique in that it bridges the gap between the military and civilians. The military community wanted to introduce the civilian community to the incredible base facility here in Tampa. Of course, as civilians, we want military members to feel at home while they are serving here in Tampa. Incidentally, the first mission I was privileged to go on as a part of this program was refueling five F-15s over Louisiana and then returning to MacDill AFB (I'll describe this more in a later chapter).

I think it's important and interesting to know a little history about the base. Established in 1939, the base was known as Southeast Air Base, Tampa. The US Army Air Force had been installed there just prior to World War II and was later renamed. In September 1947, it was named MacDill Air Force Base in honor of Colonel Leslie

MacDill (1889–1938), a World War I aviator in the US Army Air Corps (later US Army Air Forces) who had died on a training mission in an air crash of his North American BC-1.

During the 1950s, MacDill AFB was a Strategic Air Command (SAC) installation for B-47 Stratojet bombers. In the early 1960s, it transitioned to a Tactical Air Command (TAC) installation. This was set up as the first line of offense against the Cuban aggression during the Cuban Missile Crisis.

In 1983, the US Central Command (CENTCOM), taking over the previous responsibilities of the Rapid Deployment Joint Task Force, was established at MacDill AFB to monitor and advise the twenty countries of the Middle East and recently, in 2021, the addition of Israel. Although CENTCOM is one of the military's eleven Unified Combatant Commands (Africa Command, Central Command, European Command, Indo-Pacific Command, Northern Command, Southern Command, Space Command, Special Operations Command, Transportation Command, Strategic Command, and Cyber Command), it is arguably the busiest command, considering the military action throughout the Middle East.

In 1987, the US Special Operations Command (SOCOM) was created and established at MacDill AFB after the tragic mishap attempt to rescue the hostages in Iran. SOCOM is comprised of the best of the Army (Rangers and Green Beret), Navy (SEALs), Air Force (Combat Control, Pararescue, and Special Reconnaissance and Tactical Air Control Party), and Marines (Raiders). SOCOM is involved in a multitude of tasks throughout the world, such as clandestine activity (direct action, special reconnaissance, counter terrorism, foreign internal defense, unconventional warfare, psychological warfare, civil affairs, and counter narcotics operations).

It's important to recognize an extraordinary civic leader of our community and especially on behalf of MacDill Air Force Base. Al Austin, who passed away in 2014, worked tirelessly to stave off government cuts to MacDill AFB. Here are a few excerpts from a

1991 *Tampa Bay Times* newspaper article entitled "Task Force make pitch to preserve MacDill's runway:"

> With the military budget shrinking, supporters of MacDill AFB led by Al Austin told members of the Florida congressional delegation that he needs their assistance to find a new military tenant for the base. Across the country, groups like Austin's MacDill Response Team are working to persuade the Pentagon to reverse the planned closing of bases in their areas. MacDill was one of more than 35 bases a federal commission found to be obsolete and ordered fully or partly closed. Congress and President Bush have approved the closure list. The closure plan shuts down the MacDill runway and transfers its F-16 fighter wing to an Arizona base by 1994. Supporters fear that without the runway, the base will be a likely target for full closure later.
>
> Though no decisions were made, the ideas suggested to protect MacDill included: 1) Calling a meeting with Air Force Secretary Donald Rice to persuade him that the Defense Base Closure and Realignment commission erred in ordering MacDill partly closed. 2) The Senate Armed Services Committee has approved legislation by Senator Connie Mack, R-FL, that would order a reevaluation of the partial closure. 3) Keeping a specialized military unit, known as the Joint Communications Support Element, at MacDill. The unit, with nearly 500 employees, is set to move to Charleston, S.C. 4). Austin's group argues the move would cost taxpayers $15 million and leave the two military commands at MacDill without badly needed technical assistance. 5) Moving an Air National Guard unit, Air Reserve unit, or active Air Force wing to MacDill. 6) Representative C.S. Bill Young, R-FL suggested that the planned reorganization of the Air Force could bring MacDill new planes, such as tankers that refuel jets in the air.

As a result of the work and conviction of Al Austin, the base stayed, grew, and thrived. Today, MacDill AFB hosts over forty different governmental agencies and is the second largest employer in the city of Tampa with over $6 billion in revenue coming into the bay area. Over 25,000 people go on and off the base each day servicing the different entities. The Tampa Bay Area is proud of MacDill AFB and the important work they do through both CENTCOM and SOCOM.

CHAPTER 5

Dinners and Receptions at MacDill Air Force Base . . . We're Invited!

FEBRUARY 9, 2010: GENERAL JOHN R. ALLEN, DEPUTY COMMANDER OF CENTCOM

Deborah and I, along with John and Leslie Osterweil, were invited to have dinner with General John and Kathy Allen. They were living in the official home on MacDill Air Force Base for CENTCOM leadership. It is an older home but well maintained and well laid out. Its traditional detailing creates a very warm and comfortable atmosphere. Considered one of the best locations on the base, it has an open view of the Tampa Bay and downtown skyline. The home is adorned with many of their personal and generational family artifacts; both family ancestors had served in every battle and war since World War I. They even had a framed photo of American troops sitting on the side of a California hill before heading to Europe.

General Allen and Kathy were most hospitable and generous hosts, and dinner, wine, and desserts were delicious and delightful. We all enjoyed interesting conversation and a most comfortable evening. Later, I sent a thank-you card and the following day, John responded, "It was a great pleasure to host both the Rosenthals and Osterweils; it was as though we had family over." Deborah and I felt the same and have continued our close relationship to this day. The Allens are incredible Americans and have given much to this great country.

MARCH 7, 2010: GENERAL DAVID H. PETRAEUS, COMMANDER OF CENTCOM

Deborah and I were invited to have dinner with General Dave and Holly Petraeus. Like the Allens, they were living in an official home on MacDill Air Force Base for CENTCOM leadership. We were joined by Tim and Anje Bogott, owners of the TradeWinds Island Resort in St. Petersburg, Florida. We had first met them when we were all invited to join Dave and Holly in the president's box of a Tampa Bay Rays baseball game when Dave threw out the first pitch to start the game.

Also present at the dinner that evening were John and Leslie Osterweil, who were instrumental in introducing us to the military world. And finally, the guest of honor, Holocaust survivor and Nobel laureate, Elie Wiesel and his wife, Marion. Mr. Wiesel was a Jewish prisoner in both, Auschwitz and Buchenwald concentration camps and he lived to tell his story, having authored fifty-seven books including *Night*, which is often recommended reading in schools.

The evening began in the living room with cocktails and hors d'oeuvres. When we entered the dining room, Deborah and I were surprised and honored by the seating arrangement. Place cards seated me next to Marion and Deborah next to Elie. Notably, spouses were not seated together, which always makes the ride home ever so interesting as we share our mutual conversations. The dinner began with wine and a toast from Dave welcoming us to his home and expressing his delight that we were all there. Mr. Wiesel followed him with his own quite extraordinary toast. As he stood and held up his wine glass he began to speak in a low, wispy voice. Deborah later told me she felt a depth of sadness and pain within him. He began, "I would like to thank David and Holly for having my wife and me here for dinner with all of you. But most of all, I want to toast to the United States Military because if they had arrived one day later, I would not be standing here today." We were all deeply moved and rather teary-eyed by the weight of his words. He genuinely spoke from the bottom of his heart.

The meal began and was accompanied by multiple conversations around the table with periodical spurts of all of us joining together on various topics. Marion mentioned to me that she was also a Holocaust survivor and worked on many humanitarian projects. She was also instrumental on republishing her husband's famous book *Night* which was originally written in Yiddish and translated to French, English, and ultimately thirty languages. In 1986, Elie and Marion Wiesel cofounded the Elie Wiesel Foundation for Humanity, which is dedicated to combating indifference, intolerance, and injustice. He won the Nobel Peace Prize that same year.

Dave and Holly were gracious hosts, and every guest went home that night with a memory left indelibly in our hearts and minds.

MAY 22, 2010: GENERAL DAVID AND HOLLY PETRAEUS–OFFICERS' NEW QUARTERS

Deborah and I were honored to be invited to another interesting and educational evening with the Petraeuses. This time, they had moved into their new quarters in an entire new housing development for officers of CENTCOM and SOCOM that had recently been constructed. Dave and Holly welcomed us, John and Leslie Osterweil, Dr. Scott and Jill Kelley, and Natalie Khawam (Jill's twin sister), to their new home. We all sat around the dining room table and enjoyed the evening over dinner.

We had a nice time throughout the evening. We appreciated that we were part of the inner circle of Petraeus friends.

Who could have known that approximate three to four weeks

later General Petraeus would be sent to Afghanistan to relieve General Stanley McChrystal, who had resigned following a *Rolling Stone* magazine article quoting him criticizing the then leadership of the country, the Obama Administration.

AUGUST 12, 2010: GENERAL JAMES N. MATTIS, INCOMING COMMANDER OF CENTCOM

General John Allen was acting head of Central Command for forty-two days until General James N. Mattis was selected as the eleventh commander of CENTCOM (General Petraeus was now in Afghanistan). The day after General Mattis took charge, General John and Kathy Allen hosted a dinner party to welcome him to the command. We were honored to be invited among a small group of local civilians and to have the opportunity to meet the new leader.

General Mattis is a learned scholar, historian, and brilliant leader. He reminds me of a Patton or an Eisenhower. He is old-school and he knows that the only thing that dictators and communist leaders respect is force, which must be present and prepared to be used. He would feel that a weak leader would be an invitation to others that they can be aggressive and cause havoc in this world. General Mattis has a wealth of experience and is truly a great American.

The seating at the dining room table was consistent with our prior military dinners—husbands and wives were seated separately to maximize the couple's interactive experience with other guests.

By the end of the evening, Deborah and I reflected on the wonderful time we had visiting with John and Kathy and conversing throughout the night with General Mattis. We left feeling very good about our next leader of Central Command.

OCTOBER 20, 2010: PROGRESSIVE DINNER HOSTED BY CENTCOM OPERATORS

As a gracious gesture to thank Tampa Bay business leaders for their support of the upcoming October 22, 2010, Navy Ball, Rear Admiral Michael Franken and his CENTCOM team set up a progressive dinner at several homes on MacDill AFB. We had appetizers at one house, the main course at another, and then dessert at the third. Home hosts were Rear Admiral Michael "Mike" Franken (head of J-8 strategic plans and policy) and his wife, Jordan; Rear Admiral Kevin "Kid" Donegan (J-3 director of operations) and his wife, Debbie; and Rear Admiral Harold "Hal" Pittman and his wife, Rebecca.

This was such a treat for the civilian couples who participated. Many of them had never met military families, especially in their homes on the base with their children present. It was a "family" night for all, civilians and military alike. We were all very impressed with the confidence and resilience of the children of these military families. A normal part of their lives is moving from one school to another, starting over socially each time and making new friends, as their parents are stationed at base after base. Deborah and I continue to learn the great sacrifices these families make on behalf of our country.

MARCH 4, 2011: GENERAL JAMES MATTIS, COMMANDER OF CENTCOM

Deborah and I were honored to attend our first dinner reception at the home of General Mattis in the now new officers' quarters. He hosted over forty members of our Tampa Bay community—prominent business, entrepreneurial, and philanthropic leaders.

The dinner was laid out buffet style. People mingled, moving about the house, all while enjoying their meal and libations. Shortly into the evening, General Mattis gathered everyone for announcements, expressing how pleased he was that we were there, providing us with some insight about his position, and briefing us (unclassified information, of course) on what was happening in some of the twenty countries covered by Central Command. He is a delightful speaker and very organized and had pulled from his pocket a little piece of paper as a list of items he wanted to cover. He was brilliant and knowledgeable about the history of the entire Middle East. He explained that the major problem of aggression in the area come from Iran and that they undermine any attempts for peace in the Middle East.

Deborah sent General Mattis a nice thank-you note saying the following:

> *Dear Jim,*
>
> *Mark and I had the most wonderful time with you on Friday, March 4. Thank you for including us among such a fine ensemble of extraordinary people. We enjoyed every detail and considered the evening very special to us. We are honored to know you and look forward to our continued friendship.*

JULY 6, 2011: GENERAL JAMES MATTIS HONORS ADMIRAL ERIC OLSON

Deborah and I were invited to General Mattis' home again for a farewell dinner to honor the retirement of Admiral Eric Olson as commander of Special Operations Command. As a graduate of the United States Naval Academy, Admiral Olson was the first Navy SEAL ever to be appointed to three-star and four-star flag rank and was the first naval officer to be a US SOCOM combatant commander. Admiral Olson was also the Bull Frog at one point. Olson had participated in the Battle of Mogadishu and was later awarded the Silver Star for his actions which was cited as "... during combat actions in Mogadishu, Somalia, in October 1993, while under withering enemy fire during actions in support of UNOSOM II operations, Captain Olson demonstrated a complete disregard for his own personal safety in the accomplishment of his mission." This incident was made into the movie *Black Hawk Down*.

General Mattis was a gracious host and, as is his custom, he welcomed everyone, gave us a current explanation of Central Command and our position in the Middle East, and opened the floor to questions. He is an incredible, brilliant, and eloquent speaker as he explains the Middle East from a historic perspective and then brings us up to the present. Everyone was enthralled by his description of the issues, again depicting Iran as the aggressor in the region.

Throughout the evening we enjoyed food, libations, and conversation with our military and fellow civilians, and appreciated that many of our Tampa Bay business leaders were in attendance. We expressed our best wishes to Admiral Olson and his wife, Marilyn, and their children, Dan and Alyssa.

OCTOBER 4, 2011: GENERAL JAMES MATTIS WELCOMES NEW LEADERSHIP

Deborah and I were very excited to join General Mattis, military personnel, and fellow Tampa civilians to welcome incoming SOCOM commander, Admiral William McRaven and his wife, Georgeann, as well as CENTCOM deputy commander, Admiral Robert Harward and wife, Jane. Both admirals are Navy SEALs, and I would later play golf with them whenever they had time off from their duties in the Middle East.

As was customary, we thoroughly enjoyed the evening.

NOVEMBER 6, 2011: ADMIRAL BILL MCRAVEN HONORS LIEUTENANT GENERAL DAVID FRIDOVICH

Admiral William McRaven, commander of SOCOM, and his wife, Georgeann, hosted a dinner party in honor of Lieutenant General David Fridovich's retirement as deputy commander of SOCOM. General Fridovich was a Green Beret in the Army had an incredible thirty-seven-year military career. We wished him and his wife, Nancy, a wonderful retirement. As you may recall, Deborah and Dave were classmates at Nova High School in Davie, Florida, so she would be saying goodbye to an old friend who was, also a great football player.

Admiral McRaven became commander of SOCOM in August, 2011 after an illustrious military career including being the commander of the Joint Special Operations Command (2008–2011), a Navy Seal, Bull Frog, and while in Tampa, he would ultimately engineer the plan with SEAL Team Six to take down Osama Bin Laden.

We thoroughly enjoyed the evening. Bill and Georgeann were gracious hosts in every way and made everyone feel at home.

MARCH AND OCTOBER 2012: GENERAL JAMES MATTIS, COMMANDER OF CENTCOM

Tried as we did, we were never able to set a date for General Mattis to attend a Games and Trains Party, so regrettably, he missed out on playing billiards and foosball. Still, he loved entertaining at his home on the base and we were always delighted to attend with our fellow civilians, as we all became better acquainted with the many military officers and personnel who were his guests as well.

We also looked forward to his briefings as well, which generally came after appetizers, libations, and socializing. He gave us an update on the Middle East, the US strategy, and our performance. He enlightened us on the many complexities of the region and invited us to ask questions. After the briefings, we were directed to enjoy the beautiful buffet that had been set up by the military chefs. The food was always delicious, and we never failed to continue to mingling and enjoying the company of everyone there.

As always, Deborah and I left each gathering with such a positive sense of comfort knowing we had—and have—such a great military.

MAY 29, 2013: GENERAL LLOYD J. AUSTIN, NEW COMMANDER OF CENTCOM

Deborah and I were invited to meet the new head of Central Command, General Lloyd Austin, and his wife, Charlene, at their home on MacDill AFB. Have you noticed a pattern? The command positions each have a particular house on the base. As the commanders come and go, they move in and out of the official house for their particular command position. It is quite extraordinary, the relocations our military members constantly undergo. They say they are accustomed to it and that it is their normal, but my hat goes off to them for the sacrifices they, their spouses, and their children make throughout their careers, often moving ten to twenty times within their military careers.

Upon arriving, we met up with about twenty-five Tampa civilians, military officers, and personnel, as well as General Austin's staff. We had the pleasure of enjoying those present, the food, and libations, and we were delighted that General Austin had prepared some remarks. He gave a rousing speech about his history in the military as well as his goals as the leader of CENTCOM. General Austin was very down-to-earth and answered questions eloquently. Prior to this command, General Austin was the Army's vice chief of staff and following his CENTCOM post he was sworn in on January 22, 2021 as the twenty-eighth secretary of defense.

It was another great, feel-good evening with our military friends.

DECEMBER 13, 2018: GENERAL JOSEPH L. VOTEL, COMMANDER OF CENTCOM

The invitation read: "The Commander, United States Central Command and Mrs. Michele Votel request the pleasure of your company at dinner on Friday, the Thirteenth of December at six-thirty in the evening at MacDill Air Force Base, Florida."

Deborah and I were honored to be invited to the Votel home on the base for our final dinner with this great patriotic family. We were joined by several civilian couples and enjoyed one another's company throughout the evening.

The meal was deliciously cooked by the CENTCOM chefs. General Votel mentioned that they planned to head back to Minneapolis, live in a housing community, and take up golf. He had dedicated over thirty-nine years in the military, commencing at West Point. He commanded SOCOM, followed by CENTCOM in Tampa, which was a first, as it is unusual for someone to be the head of both commands. As a result, Joe and Michele were able to spend a good deal of time in Tampa.

As is the case with every military spouse we have had the privilege of knowing, Michele was a big supporter of his career. She also made a difference in the lives of wounded service members.

They have both made such an incredible impact on our nation. Deborah and I are honored that they came into our lives. The evening was a nice farewell, and we hope to keep in touch. I look forward to playing golf with Joe when he's ready for another challenge.

CHAPTER 6

Navy League of the United States: Leadership and Events

DECEMBER 16, 2009: THE NAVY LEAGUE—A HOLIDAY DINNER

As new members of the Navy League, Deborah and I went to the holiday dinner to support the organization. The Navy League of the United States was founded in 1902 with the encouragement of President Theodore Roosevelt. The Navy League is unique among military-oriented associations in that it is a civilian organization dedicated to the education of our citizens—including our elected officials—and the support of the men and women of the sea services and their families. You do not need to have served in the military to be a member of the Navy League.

The event was very nice and included the presentation of the colors by the high school Naval Sea Cadets and a great speech by former Florida governor Leroy Collins and his first lady Mary Collins. Their son, Admiral Leroy Collins (Ret.), a two-star Navy admiral, was also present. We had a good turnout of over sixty attendees for the holiday dinner.

MAY 3, 2010: TRIP ABOARD THE COAST GUARD CUTTER *CROCODILE*

As vice president of the Navy League Tampa Bay Council, I had many interesting opportunities. One of these was an invitation to travel around Tampa Bay aboard the United States Coast Guard Cutter (USCGC) *Crocodile*.

Based at the St. Pete Coast Guard Station, the *Crocodile* is one of the Coast Guard's seventy-four Marine Protector Class patrol boats. At eighty-seven feet long, the diesel-powered boat carries a crew of ten and patrols the Gulf of Mexico, protecting Gulf coast harbors.

The cutter handles drug interdiction, illegal human transportation, and search and rescue. She is also responsible for monitoring depth buoys. For two hours, we sailed Tampa Bay to check buoys and ensure they were at their anchored positions. I left the pier in St. Petersburg with a great understanding of our fine Coast Guard team!

OCTOBER 19, 2010: CAPE CANAVERAL AND CAPTAIN OF THE FIRST SPACE SHUTTLE MISSION

As president of the United States Navy League Tampa Council, I was invited to Cape Canaveral to witness the last space shuttle on the launch pad. Chris Paddock, the regional president of the Navy League was invited as well. Chris served twenty-four years as a Naval officer.

We arrived at the Cape at 9:30 a.m. and were greeted by astronauts John W. Young and Robert L. Crippen. Both men had been on STS-1, the maiden test flight of the space shuttle program in 1981. STS-1 was the first American manned space flight since the Apollo-Soyuz Test Project in 1975. It was preceded by atmospheric testing of the orbiter and ground testing of the space shuttle system. The astronauts escorted us inside the Vehicle Assembly Building. We saw the cranes, the backup shuttle (in case of rescue), and the block wall that all previous pilots had signed before their missions.

Then we boarded the bus and headed to the launch pad. We viewed STS-135, the 135th and final mission of the American space shuttle program. STS-135 used the orbiter *Atlantis* and hardware originally intended for contingency mission STS-335. Shuttle missions that start with a "3" are rescuers or launch on need (LON) missions. No STS mission of that type was ever needed to be flown, thank goodness.

We were taken up to the shuttle and had pictures with Robert Crippen, the first shuttle pilot, with the final space shuttle in the background. STS-135 launched on July 8, 2011 and landed on July 21, 2011. It was an incredible experience.

JANUARY 25, 2011: THE NAVY LEAGUE TAMPA COUNCIL– ELECTION AND INSTALLATION

That dinner in 2009 was my first introduction to the Navy League. I enjoyed the camaraderie and friends that I met in the organization. I started out assisting with the Navy Ball. I then went on to be the secretary, vice president, and then president of the Tampa Council from 2013 and 2014.

The event on this January 2011 evening was the installation dinner for the new leadership of the Navy League. Jose Gutierrez, attorney-at-law in Tampa, was installed as the new president. John Lehman, an executive with Boeing, became the vice president, and Cheryl Brown was the secretary for part of the year, with me taking care of the end of the year. Tina Bollenback was installed as treasurer, and Gail Ryan became the Navy League chaplain.

The dinner commenced with the presentation of the colors, which was done by the Navy Sea Cadets. We then said the Pledge of Allegiance, followed by an invocation by Gail Ryan. The dinner was very nice at the Wyndham Hotel on Westshore Boulevard in Tampa. Our guest speaker was Dean Mosher, a nationally known artist and historian. His paintings are in museums and national parks throughout the United States. Dean has succeeded in creating paintings with incredibly accurate and comprehensive historical depictions. Of particular interest to Navy Leaguers are Dean's series of paintings depicting "Great Moments in the United States Naval History where character and circumstance met to produce victory." Dean Mosher gave a wonderful briefing to the organization. We then closed the evening with having the colors retired by the Tampa Division 6 of the Naval Sea Cadets. It made me swell with pride as we concluded the evening of another year of the Navy League.

MARCH 3, 2011: ANNUAL SEA SERVICES AWARDS DINNER

John Lehman, a Navy veteran who is an executive with Boeing was the master of ceremonies for the event. The presentation of the colors was conducted by the Navy League Junior ROTC. The Pledge of Allegiance followed and then the invocation by Gail Ryan. I was impressed with the formalities that made everything so authentic and official.

Admiral Eric Olson, commander of the US Special Operations Command was the guest speaker. He was the eighth commander of the USSOCOM located at MacDill AFB in Tampa, Florida. Admiral Olson is a native of Tacoma, Washington, and graduated from the United States Naval Academy. He was the first four-star Navy SEAL in our military. Olson has participated in several conflicts in contingency operations, including Mogadishu. He has also served as a United Nations military observer in Israel and Egypt, and as an assistant deputy of the chief of Naval Operations for plans, policy, and operations.

Admiral Olson gave an excellent briefing to our Navy organization about the status of Special Operations Command. All in all, it was a very memorable evening. One thing that stayed with me was my conversation with Admiral Olson. I said to him, "I bet Osama Bin Laden is dead." He said to me, "Don't be too sure of it; he could still be alive." Of course, Bin Laden was still alive at the time, but within two months, that would change.

JULY 25–27, 2011: US NAVY LEAGUE HOSTS THE JAPANESE NAVY

As the then vice president of the Tampa Bay Council of the Navy League, I helped welcome our friends in the Japanese Navy. The Japanese commander of the Japan Training Squadron, RADM Umio Otsuka, hosted our city of Tampa government leaders, business leaders, and the Navy League on their training ship *Kashima* (TV 3508).

The invitation read:

> The commander of the Japan Training Squadron and the Consul General of Japan in Miami Request the honored company of Mr. Mark Rosenthal and guests at a reception on board the Training Ship *Kashima* (TV 3508)
> Date: Monday, July 25, 2011
> Time: 6:30 p.m.
> Place: Port of Tampa, Cruise Terminal 3
> Dress: Class B for Military
> Business Casual for Civilians

The event was held promptly at 6:30 p.m. at the Tampa's Cruise Terminal. Over 500 Japanese sailors, along with the leaders of the Japanese Command, arrived in all whites for the ceremony prior to boarding the ship. Mayor Bob Buckhorn was present for the event, along with approximately 100 guests. The ceremony was very nice with a thank you to the Navy League for hosting the Japanese sailors. We boarded the ship and walked around the entire bow and stern and were enamored at how immaculately clean and shiny everything was. The ship looked like it had just been given a fresh coat of battleship-gray paint.

The commander and his staff were very gracious in welcoming us and many other civilians aboard the ship. After the viewing of the ship, we went to the stern where we were amazed at the spread of food and beverage. The largest seafood and sushi towers I have ever seen were presented. The food and libations were delicious, as the Japanese are fine hosts.

That evening Deborah and I hosted two Japanese sailors at our home for the night. They were so happy to be invited. We cooked them a nice filet mignon along with the accouterments for a meal they would never forget. Everyone enjoyed the evening playing ping-pong and billiards and communicating via a translation app on an iPad. Our son, Jason, had a blast meeting and telling them about life in America and they in turn showed us on the map where they lived in Japan. We had such an enjoyable evening sharing our lives. I reminded them that they could stay in the shower for more than a minute if they wanted, knowing that showers on their ship can only be for thirty seconds or less. The next morning, they were off to board the ship. On the way, they wanted a Big Mac from McDonald's, so we stopped and made sure they had a goody bag to take back to their compatriots. It was sad to see them go after a memorable twenty-four hours with them. We said our goodbyes—Sayonara!

DECEMBER 8, 2011: TRIP TO WASHINGTON DC FOR THE ARMY-NAVY GAME

I was invited to attend the Army-Navy Game, typically played in Philadelphia, but on this occasion held in Washington DC. Deborah and I and a group of Tampa Bay business leaders, Blake Casper, Steve and Sandra Gardner, John and Leslie Osterweil, and Ray and

Jan Sandelli, flew to DC and checked in to our hotel. We chose the historical Willard InterContinental Hotel.

Prior to the American Civil War in 1861, the Willard hosted a peace convention, considered to be a last-ditch effort to avert the outbreak of the war. Around the same time, Abraham Lincoln had to be smuggled into the hotel in order to avoid several assassination plots. There he would spend the ten days leading up to his presidential inauguration. Nearly a century later, Dr. Martin Luther King, Jr. wrote his iconic *I Have a Dream* speech at that same hotel. Across the decades former US presidents either visited or stayed there, leading to its nickname: "the residence of the presidents." It was the habit of Ulysses S. Grant to drink whiskey and smoke a cigar while relaxing in the lobby, where he was often approached by favor seekers, from which originated the term "lobbying."

Once everyone settled into the hotel, we attended a party that evening where we were introduced to the vice chief of operations for the Navy, Admiral Jonathan Greenert. It was a lot of fun and included all the energy of a rivalry football game that had been going on for 112 years.

The following day we enjoyed visiting the many monuments and museums throughout the city, then returned to our hotel to change for our evening. The then director of the CIA, David Petraeus, and his lovely wife, Holly, had invited all of us to join them for dinner. It was wonderful to see them again and spend time together catching up. Dave and Holly were warm and gracious hosts, and we thoroughly enjoyed the evening.

The next day we woke up early and headed for FedEx Field in Landover, Maryland for the big Army-Navy game. We had been invited by the president of the National Navy League, Daniel Branch, to join him in the skybox overlooking the 40-yard line and witness the 112th game between the Army and the Navy. The patriotic traditions and marching bands prior to the game and during the halftime ceremonies were very moving and we all felt great pride in our men and women in uniform and of course, for our country. The Navy won that year, 27–12.

As we returned to Tampa the following day, we appreciated our quite extraordinary weekend.

MAY 14, 2013: AWARD PRESENTATION FOR WHARTON HIGH SCHOOL NJROTC

As vice president of the United States Navy League Tampa Bay Council, I was invited to go to Wharton High School and present the outstanding Navy Junior ROTC Award to the outstanding male and female student. This award is presented to the NJROTC student who exemplifies honor, courage, and commitment to the Navy core values. Over 10 percent of the high school students participate in the Junior ROTC programs in the Tampa Bay Area. The top JROTC students are given scholarships to one of the military academies (Army, Navy, Air Force, and Coast Guard). Over 200 people were on hand for the presentation.

JANUARY 9, 2014: THE NAVY LEAGUE TAMPA COUNCIL– ELECTION AND INSTALLATION

For the last three years, I had been a member of the Navy League, serving as the recording secretary, an advisor, a vice president, and assisting and supporting the Navy Ball each year, rotating between SOCOM and CENTCOM.

John Sarao, a former Navy captain and associate director of the Joint Military Leadership Center at the University of South Florida, was the master of ceremonies for this installation dinner. He was in charge of the ROTC program and very active in the Tampa Navy League as the academy sponsor.

The program started with the presentation of the colors by the Junior ROTC from the Tampa Bay Area. The invocation was given by Gail Ryan, the team leader of the Junior ROTC program in Tampa. In my opinion, she operated one of the finest programs in the country. The number of these Junior ROTC members that ended up at military academies was above average because of her incredible leadership.

As part of the program the following people were installed:

Mark Rosenthal—President
Jennifer McCoskrie—Vice President
Bob Easterday—Treasurer
Roger Mitchell—Secretary
Gail Ryan—Chaplin
Skip Witunski—Florida Region President
Chris Paddock—Central Florida Area President

I was honored to take the baton and lead our Tampa Navy League of 300 members for the next two years.

We had Dean Mosher, who is a historical architect, serve as our guest speaker. He gave a presentation called "The Battle of Lake Erie, September 10, 1813." It was interesting to learn so many details about the event. I gave a report on all the events we are planning for the upcoming year and promised to exceed the number of events and increase the membership in the Navy League. The program ended with the retiring of the colors.

JUNE 19, 2014: PRESENTATION OF US FLAG TO WWII VETERAN

As president of the Navy League, I had the honor of presenting the American flag to Dickie Lee James, a WWII Navy veteran.

Jeff Patterson of the NBC affiliate contacted me in early in June about a WWII Navy veteran who had recently died. Her son, Todd

James, wanted to honor her with a proper military flag ceremony. Todd had contacted numerous governmental agencies but had gotten the runaround. He then contacted Jeff Patterson of WFLA News Channel 8 "On Your Side" and Jeff in turn, contacted me. I immediately stepped up to the plate as the president of the Navy League and said I would make it happen.

Dickie Lee James was a parachute rigger as the Second World War commenced and was a very integral part of our success.

On June 19, I had the Navy League junior cadets assist me in the presentation. They were the flag bearers and marched in with a perfect cadence to the Salvation Army in Lakeland for the service. Dickie Lee had been a long-time volunteer there and it was a perfect venue for the ceremony. As Jeff Patterson stated on the TV clip later that night, the event went off without a hitch and Todd was happy about this special tribute to his mother.

In front of the US Coast Guard Cutter *Eagle*

Deborah welcoming the Japanese sailors to our home

With Coast Guard Rear Admiral William Baumgartner

With Astronaut Bob Crippen at the launching pad for the final space shuttle mission at Cape Canaveral

(From top left to right) Me, Steve Gardner, Holly Petraeus, Blake Casper, Jan Sandelli, John Osterweil, and Ray Sandelli. (From bottom left to right) Sandra Gardner, Deborah, David Petraeus, and Leslie Osterweil

Me as president of the Navy League presenting the ceremonial sword to an ROTC Naval cadet at the University of South Florida

CHAPTER 7

Middle East Briefings to Our Civilian Community

MARCH 24, 2010: BRIEFING BY GENERAL PETRAEUS AT CENTCOM

The first formal briefing on the base was presented by General David Petraeus, at his headquarters (CENTCOM) at MacDill Air Force Base. John Osterweil and I were present. I was in awe at the incredible state-of-the-art facility—the offices, conference rooms, auditoriums, and secure rooms (not open to the public) were very impressive.

The general briefed us on CENTCOM's area of responsibility. This covers twenty countries including Iraq, Iran, Pakistan, and Afghanistan. It also covers the countries of the Arabian Peninsula, the northern Red Sea, and the five republics of Central Asia. CENTCOM military operations include the Persian Gulf War (1991), the Iraq War (2003–2011), and the Afghanistan War (2001–2021).

As of this writing, CENTCOM operations and exercises include Operation Inherent Resolve and the US Military Training Mission (USMTM). Operation Inherent Resolve is a Middle East operation against terrorist threats from groups such as ISIS. USMTM is a "train, advise, and assist" operation based in Riyadh, Saudi Arabia.

There are six American regional unified combatant commands.

CENTCOM is one of three headquartered outside its operational area. MacDill AFB in Tampa, Florida hosts CENTCOM's main headquarters. A forward headquarters was established in 2009 at Al Udeid Air Base in Qatar.

General Petraeus led us on a tour of the CENTCOM facility and proudly introduced us to his staff. He explained that even with the technology available, the most important things were the personnel. I was impressed with the dedication and professionalism of each person I met. It was comforting to know that we have freedom and security thanks to these great Americans. When I got home, I told my wife and children about my experience and the incredible facility we have just down the street.

OCTOBER 12, 2012: BRIEFING BY GENERAL KARL HORST AT CENTCOM

As the president of the United States Navy League, I was able to set up a briefing by General Karl Horst, chief of staff of Central Command under commander General James Mattis. General Horst was an amazing briefer. He gave all the eighty attendees a realistic view of what CENTCOM does and the state of affairs in the world.

During the briefing, Karl stopped and called me up to the stage along with the head of the Coalition, Rear Admiral Matts Folgelberg from Sweden. He presented me as an honorary ambassador to the Coalition of sixty countries that are a part of CENTCOM. The US Central Command Coalition at MacDill Air Force Base is one of the largest military coalitions in US history. Following the 9/11 terrorist attacks in 2001, the coalition began to form with a common purpose—to fight terrorism.

The following is a description of CENTCOM by Army General Tommy Franks, CENTCOM commander in 2001:

Beginning on September 12, we worked our way to a plan, which we executed or started to execute on October 7. By the time we reached the end of September, we had a coalition here in Tampa of senior national representatives of some fifteen or so nations. By June 2002, the coalition had grown to thirty-four national flags.

[They] placed their forces into Operation Enduring Freedom, placed their forces—naval forces, air forces, special operations forces, ground forces—under our operational control. They remain that way today [June 2002], very, very effective, and managed through some of the best coordination that I've seen between our own State Department, between this command, between the office of the Secretary of Defense, and the joint staff involved in Washington.

The strength and importance of the CENTCOM Coalition have continued for more than a decade. Having coalition members in Tampa has proved invaluable and helped ensure focused coordination and synchronization. Coalition forces have made important contributions to fighting terrorism across the spectrum of operations. Particular contributions include, but are not limited to, providing vital intelligence, personnel, equipment, and assets for use on the ground, air, and sea. Coalition members also have provided liaison teams, participated in planning, provided bases, and granted overflight permissions, as well as sizable contributions of humanitarian assistance.

The CENTCOM Coalition nations are working to promote peace and stability in CENTCOM's area of responsibility and beyond. Their contributions are an example of how the international community is working together to enhance capabilities, share information, and address destabilizing issues in the region. I was honored to receive this title of honorary ambassador, and I remain committed to see that each year I have a Tampa Bay community leader host an American barbecue for these foreign leaders and their families. I like to expose them to our diet as well as the American generosity and hospitality for all. I want them to understand that we are working for peace in the world.

DECEMBER 19, 2018: BRIEFING BY RETIRED SERGEANT MAJOR BILLY WAUGH

On December 18, 2019, I went to Colonel Cary Harbough's Christmas party to meet the CARE Coalition team. The coalition is set up for wounded SOCOM members. Major General James Linder and Barb Thomas (wife of General Tony Thomas) were also in attendance. General Linder wanted to know how to get a signed copy of *Bern's Rare and Well Done* from the owner of Bern's Steak House. Coincidentally, I was taking Deborah to Bern's for my birthday, so I told the general I would make this happen.

Upon arriving at Bern's, I found that the front entrance featured a table set up to sell the book. I bought the book and asked the maître d', Frank, to have David Laxer sign it. David is the son of Bern (1923–2002) and Gert Laxer (1926–2020) and current president and owner of Bern's Steak House. After a delicious dinner, Frank brought the signed book to our table.

On December 19, 2018, I contacted General Linder and asked how to deliver the book to his office. I told him that I was attending the Billy Waugh speaking event and I could meet him afterward. He was interested in the event and mentioned he would like to attend.

At 3:00 p.m. General Linder arrived at the Davidoff of Geneva (cigar and liquor boutique venue) and met with all the attendees. Everyone was impressed that the chief of staff of SOCOM came to listen to Sergeant Major Billy Waugh (Ret.). Billy did not disappoint the group. He gave an amazing PowerPoint demonstration depicting the beginning of Special Forces after World War II, then its involvement in the Korean War, Vietnam War, and then on to Afghanistan.

Billy Waugh experienced over twenty-five years as a Special Forces officer and twenty-five years as a CIA operator. No one in the history of our country has dedicated more to our military than Billy Waugh, according to Cofer Black, ambassador at large in charge of counterterrorism. He operated in almost every country in the world. He parachuted behind enemy lines in North Vietnam for intelligence and military actions. Billy also saved the lives of pilots that had parachuted behind enemy lines.

After Vietnam, Billy Waugh moved on to the CIA where he performed intelligence on Osama bin Laden and captured Carlos the Jackal. At the age of seventy-two, while still with the CIA, he parachuted into Tora Borra looking for Osama Bin Laden. At eighty-seven years old he went to Vietnam to relive the downing of numerous American pilots in a bombing mission to Hanoi.

Billy Waugh tells the story of his life as a Green Beret and his special operations experiences as a CIA operative in the way that only one who has been there and experienced it can. Billy gave out his book, *Hunting the Jackal*, and autographed it for each of us. Meeting this real American hero was an incredible experience.

Rufus Williams, me, Sergeant Major Billy Waugh, and General James Linder at the *Hunting the Jackal* briefing

CHAPTER 8

Army, Navy, Air Force, and Marine Balls and Wounded Warrior Fundraisers

OCTOBER 2, 2009: US NAVY BIRTHDAY BALL, PEPIN HOSPITALITY CENTRE

In 1902, President Theodore Roosevelt supported the formation of the Navy League of the United States: Citizens in Support of Sea Services. This is a nonprofit civilian, educational, and advocacy organization that supports America's sea services: the Navy, Marine Corps, Coast Guard, and Merchant Marines.

The Navy League's mission is to: enhance the morale of sea service personnel and their families through national and council level programs; provide a powerful voice to educate the public and Congress of the importance of our nation's defense, well-being, and economic prosperity; and support youth through programs that expose young people to the value of our sea services.

Locally, when ships enter Port Tampa such as the USS *Lassen*, USS *William Flores*, USS *Independence*, USS *Mahan*, USS *Florida*, and USCGS *Tampa*, the Tampa Bay council supports these visits by offering the opportunity to Navy League members to board and tour the ships.

The council also provides support to the Wounded Warrior Foundation and other nonprofit missions aligning with the Navy

League. These include sponsorship of the US Naval Sea Cadet Corps and the Navy League Foundation Scholarship Program. There are five Sea Cadet units in the Tampa Bay area: Tampa Bay Division, American Victory Division, Manatee Division, Suncoast Squadron, and Marvin Shields Seabee Battalion. The University of Florida and the University of South Florida both have Navy ROTC programs. There are also Junior ROTC programs in twenty-two bay area high schools.

Once I learned about the Navy League I promptly got involved, I became a member, and ultimately became the president of my local council. Over the years, my involvement prompted me to support and participate in the US Navy Balls.

In October 2009, Deborah and I attended our first Navy Ball, and it came complete with pomp and circumstance, beginning of course, with our national anthem. Traditional formalities throughout the evening were customary to Navy officers, enlisted sailors, and wounded warriors present, but to us, it was all very moving and struck our patriotic heart strings. We both loved the entire experience.

We arrived at the Pepin Hospitality Centre, in the northeast part of Tampa, at 6:00 p.m. We were greeted by Admiral Eric Olson. As you may recall, the admiral was the United States SOCOM commander (the first Naval officer to hold that position); the first Navy SEAL ever to be appointed to three-star and four-star flag rank; the first four-star admiral to be the Bull Frog; was well known for his heroics in the Battle of Mogadishu in Somalia (as depicted in *Black Hawk Down*) and as a result, was awarded the Silver Star. Admiral Olson later took command of the Navy's counterterrorism unit, SEAL Team Six, and afterward, led the SEALs as commander of Naval Special Warfare Command. What this man has accomplished can't be overstated.

The night kicked off with a cocktail hour where service members and guests mingled. A bagpiper provided the call to dinner. The University of South Florida Navy ROTC presented the colors. Then, a sailor sang "The Star-Spangled Banner." The dinner of filet mignon with all the accouterments was delicious.

Admiral Olson introduced the guest speaker, Brigman Owens. Owens was the vice president of Bennet Group, a public relations firm based in Hawaii, but he was most known to the general public as a thirteen-year veteran of professional football. He had played for the Dallas Cowboys and the Washington Redskins (now known as the Commanders). After his stint as a player, Owens served as assistant director and associate counsel to the NFL Players Association. He helped develop the collective bargaining agreement for the NFL.

In 1983, Brig founded Super Leaders, a nonprofit program to provide high-school students with positive leadership skills. More than 22,000 students had completed the program and achieved a 98 percent high-school graduation rate. Owens was an incredible speaker with a great message about success in life. He was one of the best motivational speakers I have ever heard.

The evening ended with a cake cutting, but not just cutting a cake as we know it. The Navy tradition is to call up the oldest and the youngest sailor and together, they join hands on a ceremonial sword and cut the very large sheet cake to celebrate the birthday of the Navy. That night was the Navy's 234th birthday.

JUNE 18, 2010: US ARMY BIRTHDAY BALL, A LA CARTE PAVILION

General David Petraeus, the commander of Central Command (CENTCOM) hosted the 235th Army Birthday Ball. I was interested in assisting and gathering civilian support, so I contacted friends from high school, college, and the business world to help sponsor the event. The proceeds would go to the Wounded Warrior Project, so I wanted to make this event as successful as possible, all while giving the civilian population the opportunity to experience this military tradition.

The event began with the VIP reception—a receiving line and social hour for civilian sponsors to meet and be photographed with military dignitaries. General Petraeus graciously met and took photographs with my group of sponsors. Thereafter, we all entered the ballroom and once seated, the ceremonies began. The posting of the colors was carried out by a group of enlisted soldiers who carried the US flag, the CENTCOM flag, and the Army flag. A rifleman oversaw the detail as they marched to the front of the pavilion. An enlisted soldier sang the national anthem.

After the invocation, there were toasts from the heads of CENTCOM and various civilian business leaders. I was honored to have been asked to make a toast for the state of Florida. The guest speaker for the evening was General Ann Dunwoody, commanding general of the Army Material Command. She was the first woman in the US Military and uniform service history to achieve a rank of four-star general.

Deborah and I were delighted and honored to sit at the table of General David and Holly Petraeus. As we approached the table, I jokingly brought Dave a bottle of Gatorade, since the week before, the general had become light-headed during a congressional testimony. He was amused and even brought it to the podium when introducing General Dunwoody.

There were over 400 attendees for this memorable event. My civilian friends were in awe of the event and of the dedication and professionalism of our military, as were Deborah and I. Participating in this incredible military event made me very emotional.

OCTOBER 22, 2010: US NAVY BIRTHDAY BALL, PEPIN HOSPITALITY CENTRE

A resolution on October 13, 1775, of the Continental Congress established what is now the United States Navy with "a swift sailing vessel, to carry ten carriage guns, and a proportionable number of swivels, with eighty men, be fitted, with all possible dispatch, for a cruise of three months. . ." After the American War of Independence, the US Constitution empowered the new Congress "to provide and maintain a navy." Acting on this authority, Congress established the Department of the Navy on April 30, 1798.

In 1972, chief of naval operations, Admiral Elmo R. Zumwalt, authorized official recognition of October 13 as the birthday of the US Navy. Since then, each CNO has encouraged a Navy-wide celebration of this occasion "to enhance a greater appreciation of our Navy heritage and to provide a positive influence toward pride and professionalism in the naval service."

I was invited to assist in the preparation, scheduling, and production of my first Navy Ball along with SOCOM. This was a very rewarding experience as I introduced many civilian business leaders to many of our military members there. The event was first class, with all the leadership of SOCOM and the chief of naval operations, Admiral Jonathan Greenert, as the guest speaker. Admiral Olson of SOCOM was the host for the event at the 235th birthday celebration for the Navy. Both Olson and Greenert were gentlemen and took pictures with all the guests as a keepsake. Deborah's sister, Valerie, and her husband, Ron, happened to be in town, so we invited them to join us and experience this great military event. We all left the event with such a strong feeling about supporting our men and women in service.

Rear Admiral Michael Franken even sent me a personal note on November 9, 2010:

> *Mr. and Mrs. Rosenthal,*
> *On behalf of the Tampa area Navy community, I extend my sincere appreciation to you for helping to make the 2010 Navy Birthday Ball a resounding success. Your contributions helped make this worthy event possible and will provide a lasting impact to select organizations and charities long after the ball's conclusion.*
> *Because of your generosity, the Navy's 235th Birthday will*

be remembered as a radiant affair.
Best wishes,
Michael T. Franken
Rear Admiral, US Navy

Mark, as you know "The event" wouldn't be as grand without you. Thank You. V/R MF

NOVEMBER 6, 2010: US MARINE CORPS BIRTHDAY BALL, DOWNTOWN HYATT HOTEL

Deborah and I were honored to be the guests of General John Allen and his lovely wife, Kathy. We had such great chemistry with both of them and we felt very fortunate to experience our first Marine Ball in Tampa. There were over 200 attendees present for the gala, which included many Marines in their exquisite and sharp formal uniforms. The host of the event was Lieutenant General Thomas D. Waldhauser, the commander of Marine Corps Forces Central Command (MARCENT), a decorated Marine and former commander of the US Africa Command.

MARCENT is the Marine Corps service component of the US Central Command, located at MacDill AFB in Tampa since 1990. The area of responsibility (AOR), is the twenty countries of the Middle East and over 500 million people, featuring mountain ranges with elevations of more than 24,000 feet, desert areas below sea level, and temperatures ranging from below freezing to 130 degrees Fahrenheit. The Arabian Sea, Red Sea, Arabian Gulf, and part of the Indian Ocean are also included in the region.

Three of the world's major religions—Christianity, Judaism, and Isla—have their roots there. The region contains major maritime trade routes that link the Middle East, Europe, Asia, and the Western Hemisphere. Petroleum products that fuel the economies of Europe and its Asian allies pass through three maritime choke points in the region: the Strait of Hormuz, the Suez Canal, and the Bab El Mandab.

Major General John Archer Lejeune (1867–1942) described the Marine Corps in the following message on the anniversary of the founding of the Corps:

> On November 10, 1775, a Corps of Marines was created by a resolution of Continental Congress. Since that date many thousands of men have borne the name "Marine." In memory of them it is fitting that we who are Marines should commemorate the birthday of our corps by calling to mind the glories of its long and illustrious history.
>
> The record of our corps is one which will bear comparison with that of the most famous military organizations in the world's history. During 90 of the 146 years of its existence the Marine Corps has been in action against the nation's foes. From the Battle of Trenton to the Argonne, Marines have won foremost honors in war, and in the long eras of tranquility at home, generation after generation of Marines have grown gray in war in both hemispheres and in every corner of the seven seas, that our country and its citizens might enjoy peace and security.
>
> In every battle and skirmish since the birth of our corps, Marines have acquitted themselves with the greatest distinction, winning new honors on each occasion until the term "Marine" has come to signify all that is highest in military efficiency and soldierly virtue.
>
> This high name of distinction and soldierly repute we who are Marines today have received from those who preceded us in the corps. With it, we have also received from them the eternal spirit which has animated our corps from generation to generation and has been the distinguishing mark of the Marines in every age. So long as that spirit continues to flourish Marines will be found equal to every

emergency in the future as they have been in the past, and the men of our nation will regard us as worthy successors to the long line of illustrious men who have served as "Soldiers of the Sea" since the founding of the Corps.

Maj Gen John A. Lejeune
13th Commandant of the Marine Corps

The Marine Corps Ball began with the "First Call," which is a call for all to take their seats. Next came a beautiful invocation and then the adjutant's call to "Present the colors," followed by the singing of the national anthem, at the end of which guests were seated. After we were all settled, General Waldhauser, as master of ceremony (MC) introduced General Allen as the deputy commander of US Central Command.

General Allen graduated with military honors from the Naval Academy with the class of 1976, receiving a Bachelor of Science Degree in Operations Analysis. He holds a Master of Arts Degree in Government from Georgetown University, Master of Science degree in Strategic Intelligence from the Defense Intelligence College, and a Master of Science Degree in National Security Strategy from the National War College. Following the commissioning, he attended the basic school and was assigned to Second Battalion, 8th Marines, where he served as a platoon and rifle company commander.

General Allen served as a Marine Corps fellow to the Center for Strategic and International Studies and then taught political science at the Naval Academy, while serving as a jump officer and jump master of the Academy. He was then selected as the commandant of the Naval Academy in 2002 and was the first Marine Corps officer to serve in this position at the Naval Academy.

General Allen's first tour as a general officer was as the principal director, Asian and Pacific Affairs in the Office of the Secretary of Defense for three years. From 2006 to 2008, Lieutenant General Allen served as the deputy commanding general, II Marine Expeditionary

Force and commanding general for the 2nd Marine Expeditionary Brigade, deploying to Iraq as well as serving as deputy commanding general of the Multinational Force in Al Anbar Province, Iraq. On July 15, 2008, Lieutenant General Allen became deputy commander of CENTCOM.

Deborah and I enjoyed being with the Allens throughout the evening of our first Marine Ball. As we drove home, we both shared how moved we were about our incredible Marines.

SEPTEMBER 17, 2011: AIR FORCE BIRTHDAY BALL, TAMPA CONVENTION CENTER

As a new civilian volunteer at MacDill AFB, I dedicated many hours to the success of the Air Force Ball. I contacted several friends in the business community who wanted to support the military and asked them to donate to the 64th birthday celebration of the United States Air Force. I recruited more than twenty-five couples to sponsor and participate in the event of over 250 attendees. This was our first exposure to the traditions and formalities of the US Air Force and particularly, the Airlift/Tanker Association Tony Jannus Chapter.

The evening began with a cocktail reception for sponsors, supporters, and military leadership with an opportunity to have a photo with the evening's guest speaker, Dan Clark, a motivational speaker and *New York Times* best-selling author of more than twenty books. The reception hour was followed with bells as a call to the banquet.

We began to understand that the customs and traditional ceremonies at the balls are similar in all the military branches—posting the colors, singing of the national anthem (this time sung by an Air Force enlisted airman), the invocation, the toasts, and cake cutting (the oldest and youngest service members together).

At each ball, the toasts are specific, as are the responses from the guests (there is a program at each place setting that guides guests in the appropriate response). On this occasion, they were as follows:

- To the flag of the United States of America: "To the colors."
- To the United States Air Force on its 64th birthday: "Hear, Hear."
- To the president of the United States: "To the president."
- To the chief of staff of the United States Air Force: "To the chief of staff."
- To the chief of naval operations: "To the chief of naval operations."
- To the commandant of the United States Marine Corps: "To the commandant."
- To the secretary of commerce of the United States: "To the secretary."
- To our guest speaker, Mr. Dan Clark: "Hear, Hear."
- To our honored heroes: "Hear, Hear."
- To the airmen and fellow service members who are serving away from home, their families, and those who have served in the past keeping the bell of freedom ringing loud and clear: "Hear, Hear"

After the presentation of the POW/MIA table came another toast:

- To our comrades: "Hear, Hear."

To say this was all very moving and emotional is an understatement.

The dinner, dessert, and conversation were wonderful. Dan Clark gave us a very emotional motivational speech and shared many of his life experiences as a CEO and businessman, author, and adventurer (flying fighter jets, sky diving, racing automobiles and dog sleds, and carrying the Olympic torch in the 2002 Olympic Games). The speaker and the entire evening had quite an impact on Deborah and me, as did the traditional cake cutting ceremony. Our military branches have so many meaningful traditions.

OCTOBER 14, 2011: US NAVY BIRTHDAY BALL, A LA CARTE PAVILION

As the incoming president of the United States Navy League, Tampa Bay Council, I was honored to serve on the Navy Ball Committee with Admiral William McRaven, commander of SOCOM, the host for this incredible ball. That year's theme was "236 Years of Service to the Nation." When we met about two months prior to the event, Admiral McRaven provided details about what he wanted the evening to include, namely a grog, and a silent drill team. As president of the Navy League, I had invited the Coast Guard drill team to perform at a previous event, so on behalf of Admiral McRaven, I lined them up for the Navy Ball.

Once again, I went to work recruiting community business leaders, friends, and family for this formal event. We confirmed 600 attendees, which was the largest crowd to date for the Navy Ball in Tampa. We set up a cocktail hour before the dinner with a photographer so each of the donors could have a picture with Admiral McRaven. He and his wife, Georgeann, were delightful throughout the evening.

One of this year's honored guests was Michael Edwin Thornton, born March 23, 1949. Michael was a retired United States Navy SEAL and recipient of the US military's highest decoration, the Medal of Honor, for his actions in the Vietnam War. He was awarded the medal for saving the life of his senior officer, Lieutenant Thomas R. Norris, who also earned the Medal of Honor in an unrelated incident. Lieutenant Thornton was also taking pictures with the civilian business leaders along with Major General Mark A. Clark, chief of staff, SOCOM.

Following the reception, chimes rang to signal everyone to enter the ballroom and take their seats. The order of events began with the national anthem followed by an invocation for our military and our country.

As is traditional at the balls for all branches of the military, a POW/MIA memorial table is featured. The table was described in that evening's program:

> As you entered the banquet hall this evening, you may have noticed a small table in a place of honor. It is set for one. This table is our way of symbolizing the fact that members of our profession of arms are missing from our midst. They are commonly called POWs or MIAs, we call them "Brothers and Sisters." They are unable to be with us this evening and so we remember them.
>
> This table set for one is small—symbolizing the frailty of one prisoner alone against their oppressors.
>
> The tablecloth is white—symbolizing the purity of their intentions to respond to their country's call to arms.
>
> The single red rose displayed in a vase reminds us of the families and loved ones of our comrades-in-arms who keep the faith awaiting their return.
>
> The yellow ribbon tied so prominently on the vase is reminiscent of the yellow ribbon worn upon the lapel and breasts of thousands who bear witness to their unyielding determination to demand a proper accounting of our missing.
>
> The candle is lit—symbolizing the upward reach of their unconquerable spirit.
>
> A slice of lemon is on the bread plate to remind us of their bitter fate.

There is salt upon the bread plate—symbolic of their families' tears as they wait.

The glass is inverted—they cannot toast with us this night.

The chair is empty. They are not here.

All of you who served with them and called them comrades, who depended upon their might and aid, and relied upon them, for surely, they have not forsaken you, remember! Remember! Until the day they come home, remember!

After the dinner, Admiral McRaven gave an incredibly articulate speech about our current US Navy and a patriotic tribute to our great country. Then the Coast Guard silent drill team went through their presentation exercise of throwing their rifles backward and forward. Overall, they were great, with one mishap—a weapon dropped, and the bayonet stuck into the wood floor rather close to Admiral McRaven's table. They clearly felt some pressure of all eyes of a large crowd upon them.

Once all the traditional military ceremonies and demonstrations were completed it was time for Admiral McRaven's personally favorite tradition, presenting the grog. He asked a Navy officer to describe the grog bowl for the attendees.

The Navy lays claim to the grog, which originally referred to a drink of water, honey, citrus juices, and copious amounts of rum. It was introduced to a naval squadron commanded by British Vice Admiral Edward Vernon in 1740. Today, the grog takes on many forms and is used in many ways by all the services. While not required at formal events, the grog ceremony is often embraced by those attending. The components of the drink are left to the imagination of those planning the event, and usually have loose ties to the military unit's history. The alcohol and other items that are poured into the grog have significance to that particular unit. Sometimes it is alcohol from a foreign country, where the unit served in World War II, or Kentucky bourbon from when the unit was stationed at Fort Campbell. Sometimes even inedible (and unappealing) objects are thrown in as a joke, like an old boot sock, but as just about everyone ends up drinking from it, most units keep that stuff to a minimum. Some units even mix it up and serve it from toilet bowls—sterilized, I'm sure.

Once the grog was mixed, all the guests followed Admiral McRaven's lead as he dipped his mug in the grog and took a swig. Throughout the night the guests dipped and swigged. The mix was powerful, and many people took mere sips, but not all . . . the grog bowl was emptied in no time.

The evening ended with the cake cutting followed by music and dancing. As people left for home, we all had memories we would never forget. I was pleased that the event was so successful. What an incredible night!

Following the event, I received a letter from Admiral McRaven:

> *Dear Mr. and Mrs. Rosenthal:*
>
> *Thank you for your substantial contribution in making this year's Navy Birthday ball a resounding success! Throughout the evening, I heard nothing but glowing comments, and I know they did not come without your assistance and strong desire to make it truly great.*
>
> *The food was excellent, the entertainment was inspiring, the GROG did not last beyond first contact! All told, the event was well planned, coordinated, and with over 600 people in attendance, fantastic representation by Tampa's military and civilian communities.*
>
> *Events like this do not come together easily, and this one was exceptional! Your outstanding efforts were obvious from the quality of the result. Please accept my personal thanks, and BRAVO ZULU to you for your help in making the 2011 Navy Birthday Ball an unforgettable memory for all who attended.*
>
> *Sincerely,*

William H. McRaven
Admiral, US Navy
Commander

SEPTEMBER 11, 2012: US NAVY BALL, A LA CARTE PAVILION

As president of the Navy League, I was honored to be involved with the Navy Ball. This year it was hosted by Central Command (CENTCOM) with Commander James Malloy, who was in charge of operations, coordinating the event. In advance of the ball early that day, we set up a briefing at CENTCOM, which we often did when scheduling allowed, for all the Navy Ball sponsors and community business leaders.

The briefing was incredible, which was expected since it was given by representatives of both General James Mattis of CENTCOM and Admiral Bill McRaven of SOCOM, providing their mission statements and state of affairs in the Middle East and other hot spots around the world. There were eighty attendees at MacDill Air Force Base for the briefing. Everyone was hit with some hard truths combined with being comforted that we were in such capable hands. We all went on to the gun range on the base where each civilian had the opportunity to shoot some of the latest Special Ops weapons. At the end of the day, everyone returned to their homes and hotels (out of town civilians also participated) and got ready for the Navy Ball.

Admiral McRaven made sure that the silent drill team was more seasoned, so he flew in the Annapolis Navy Silent Drill Team. I had entertained them the day before with a dear friend of blessed memory, Richard Weiss. We took them to lunch at the Oyster Catchers Restaurant and then went on to MacDill Air Force Base to view the CENTCOM Operations Center.

The Navy Ball went off without a hitch with over 500 attendees.

After guest speaker Rear Admiral Michelle Howard gave a rousing speech about the current state of our incredible Navy, Admiral McRaven gave the toast to start the grog. Everyone lined up to dip and swig. It was very fun—the grog did not last long, as the guests all wanted to participate and taste the concoction.

It was another memorable evening. We were all appreciative more than ever of the many incredible Navy leaders serving our great country.

A few days later I received a letter from V.G Mercado, the vice director of strategy, US Central Command.

> *November 9, 2012*
> *Dear Mr. Rosenthal,*
>
> *Please accept my gratitude and thanks for your outstanding support for this year's Navy Ball. We could not have pulled off such a memorable event without your exceptional support.*
>
> *In all the years that I have attended the Navy Balls, none was better or more enjoyable than this one.*
>
> *On behalf of the Navy Team at US Central Command, we are eternally grateful and look forward to next year's ball.*
>
> *Sincerely,*
>
> *V. G. Mercado*
> *Vice Director, Strategy, Plans and Policy*
> *United States Central Command*
>
> We would not have had such a great ball without your outstanding leadership and support!

SEPTEMBER 29, 2012: US AIR FORCE BALL, TAMPA CONVENTION CENTER

As a member of the MacDill AFB Air Force Advisory Board, I was asked to assist in the production and sponsorship of the 65th Annual Air Force Ball with the theme of *Generations*. I contacted numerous Tampa-area business leaders and retired Air Force veterans, and we promoted the ball as a fundraiser for Monroe Middle School. The school serves students from MacDill AFB and the funds would serve to assist in academics and safety.

Over 200 people gathered to hear guest speaker General Norton A. Schwartz. He served as the twenty-second chief of staff of the US Air Force. As chief, he was the senior uniformed Air Force officer responsible for the organization, training, and equipping, of 680,000 active duty, national guard, reserve, and civilian forces serving in the United States and overseas.

General Schwartz was an excellent speaker and was applauded for his description and accolades about the professionalism and dedication of our Air Force. The Airlift/Tanker Association Tony Jannus Chapter did a fantastic job presenting the Air Force Ball to our civilian community. I was proud to be able to assist with and sponsor the event. I had a nice discussion with General Schwartz during the event and gave him high praise for his position in keeping our Air Force the best in the world.

OCTOBER 10, 2014: US NAVY BALL, A LA CARTE PAVILION

As the president of the Navy League, I was honored to work with Admiral Mark Fox, the deputy commander of CENTCOM, and Rear Admiral James Mulloy, commander in chief operations briefer, a J3, at CENTCOM, on the 239th Navy Birthday Ball. Admiral Fox is credited with scoring the first Navy MIG kill of Operation Desert Storm in 1991 and leading the opening "Shock and Awe" strike of Operation Iraqi Freedom on March 21, 2003. Admiral Mulloy would later become deputy commander of CENTCOM in 2020.

Before the ball, I introduced over eighty civilians to Central Command Operation at MacDill AFB for a briefing by Rear Admiral Mulloy, followed by time at the gun range where we were allowed to shoot some of our special operations weapons. The civilians were impressed by the professionalism of our military and the importance of the Navy Ball that many of those who had not planned to attend or sponsor the ball became major sponsors.

The Navy League of the United States is comprised of civilians with several missions, including public education designed to inform civilians and political leaders of the vital importance the US Navy is to our country as well as the significance of maintaining comprehensive and fully prepared sea services. Additionally, the Navy League, through its councils, provides support for active duty and wounded personnel and their families, both financially and educationally. The Navy League sponsors the US Naval Sea Cadet Corps (twelve to eighteen-year-old boys and girls), and the Navy League Scholarship Program to assist with the Naval Academies.

The guest speaker was Admiral Michelle J. Howard. In 1999, after taking command of the USS *Rushmore*, she became the first African American woman to command a ship in the US Navy. Admiral Howard assumed command of Expeditionary Strike Group 2 and Combined Task Force 151 (CTF 151) aboard the amphibious assault ship, USS *Boxer*, in April 2009. *Boxer* was the flagship for CTF 151, a multinational task force established to conduct counterpiracy operations in the Indian Ocean. She played a key role in the rescue of Captain Richard Phillips, of the *Maersk Alabama* cargo ship, whose kidnapping by Somali pirates became a major motion picture film, *Captain Phillips*, with Tom Hanks. As vice chief of naval operations, which she began that same day, she was the first African American and the first woman to hold that post.

On July 1, 2014, Admiral Howard became the first woman to become a US Navy four-star admiral to command operational forces, when she assumed command of US Naval Forces Europe and US

Naval Forces Africa. Admiral Howard retired on December 1, 2017 after nearly thirty-six years of service in the United States Navy.

We were thrilled to have Admiral Howard for the ball. It was exciting to have the person responsible for saving the *Maersk Alabama* crew. I thought it would be fun to have the *Maersk Alabama*'s lifeboat, which is housed by the National Navy-UTC Museum in Fort Pierce, Florida, temporarily moved to the Navy Ball event for all to see. Cool idea, but ultimately cost prohibitive.

The sponsors and donors were excited to meet and take pictures with Admiral Mark Fox, Rear Admiral James Mulloy, and our guest speaker, Admiral Michelle Howard. The format for the evening was the same as previous balls from the presentation of the colors to the cake cutting. It was a successful event with over 400 attendees. Once again, I was excited to share the experience and to expose our civilians to our incredible military, giving them lifetime memories of our nation's finest.

With General Norton Schwartz at the Air Force Ball

With the Navy Silent Drill Team in the Train Room prior to the Navy Ball

Me, our daughter Jennifer, Kathy Allen, Deborah, our son Jason, and General John Allen

Navy Ball with Admiral Greenert, the commander of the US Fleet Forces Command

Me, Jason, Jennifer, Deborah, Katie Hood, and Lynne Hood at the Army Ball

Me and Deborah with Admiral Bill McRaven

CHAPTER 9

Israeli IDF, AIPAC, Tampa Jewish Federation and Temple Events and Speakers

JANUARY 2007: FEDERATION'S 4TH ANNUAL PRESIDENT'S DINNER—KEYNOTE SPEAKER, GENERAL COLIN L. POWELL (RET.)

My wife, Deborah, has been active in the Jewish Community for over thirty years, serving in leadership roles and chairing events at our Temple, Congregation Schaarai Zedek, and for the Tampa JCCs and Federation organization.

The Tampa Jewish Federation's Annual President's Dinner is one of the most acclaimed events in the Tampa community, having hosted an extraordinary number of speakers. Since inception in 2004 and chronologically thereafter, keynote speakers have been Thomas Friedman, Rudolph W. Giuliani, the Honorable Madeleine Albright, General Colin L. Powell (Ret.), a panel of Senator Bill Bradley and Dr. Charles Krauthammer moderated by Judy Woodruff, Doris Stearns Goodwin, David Brooks, Dr. Charles Krauthammer, Admiral Eric T. Olson, Cokie Roberts, the Honorable Ehud Barak, Ambassador Dennis B. Ross, Jeffrey Goldberg, Ambassador Ron Prosor, Frank Luntz, Alan M. Dershowitz, Deborah E. Lipstadt, Ambassador Michael Oren, and Dr. Daniel Gordis.

Deborah served on the committee for all those years and chaired the event on five occasions. It happens that the year General Colin Powell spoke she was chair and accordingly, it is customary that the chairs and their spouses are seated at the speaker's table. So it was that I was asked to sit next to General Powell. Since my wife asked me to become familiar with his background, I studied all I could for our interaction and also read General Powell's book, *My American Journey*.

That evening, at A La Carte Pavilion with over 950 attendees, I was honored to sit at the main table with perhaps one of the most distinguished leaders in the entire world. Deborah, on the stage at the podium silenced the crowd and asked everyone to be seated. I must say, she was quite effective. Her strong presence and assertiveness—all with a beautiful smile—settled the entire room in no time. You could have heard a pin drop. And so, the program began. After the US and Israeli national anthems were sung, as well as Hamotzi (blessing over the bread), the program continued. Deborah was effectively master of ceremonies (MC), and she was excellent.

During our dinner conversation, I asked General Powell what it was like working with all the presidents. He said he enjoyed working for Ronald Reagan, who was always very courteous and warm to Powell's family. He said George H.W. Bush, really made Powell and his family feel included and treated them like members of the Bush Family. General Powell and his wife, Alma, were often invited to Kennebunkport, Maine, and had the nicest time with the Bush family during the entire presidency. As far as Bill Clinton, he said that the Powell family was treated warmly, but added that Bill was easily forty-five minutes late to every meeting, and then usually left thirty minutes early, telling his cabinet as he left to "work it out." As to George W. Bush, the Powell family was treated with warmth and always welcomed. When I asked him jokingly if he ever went shooting for ducks with Vice President Cheney, he laughed and said "No!"

Since Secretary Powell was also a four-star general, I asked him if the State Department was as bureaucratic as the military's Department of Defense; he said they were both tied to one big bureaucracy. He said it was a miracle that we were able to get men and materials to the Middle East in the first Iraq War because there had been such a backup in logistics in both departments.

The program included remarks from Laura Kreitzer, Federation president; a presentation of the Tikkun Olam (repair the world) award by Federation CEO, Gary Gould, to a community member (that year the recipient was Jack Roth); and a pitch asking for donations to the organization (that year the ask was given by Mark Wilf, vice chair of United Jewish Communities). Once this happens, the speaker refers everyone to the envelopes at the center of each table. Each envelope has the name of everyone present at the event.

I picked up the envelopes and handed them around the table, including one with General Powell's name. When he was a bit surprised there was one for him, I jokingly responded that in general, at Jewish events, there is usually a request for donations. I then said kiddingly, "They're probably trying to get some of the speaker fee back." He laughed and put the envelope in his pocket.

General Powell was an incredible speaker and shared charming tidbits of his upbringing, including a story about the time his family took a trip to the South in the 1960s before the days of the extraordinary Dr. Martin Luther King and how unwelcomed he had felt. He reminded us that in those days, Blacks were restricted to certain restaurants and hotels. Relating further to the crowd, he expressed that both Blacks and Jews have had to deal with many similar challenges. He also shared his rather unique experiences with the Jewish community growing up. As a child, he worked at an Orthodox Jewish children's store. He was there so much that he learned to understand Yiddish and added a funny story about the occasions when the customers would speak to each other in Yiddish in front of him, thinking he didn't know what they were saying, and then he would tell the store owner what they said—usually about pricing, bargaining, etc. He would effectively provide intel on what amounts the customer would be willing to spend for a stroller, toys, etc. Other duties included turning the lights on and off during the Sabbath. He was also a *shabbos goy* at a synagogue, performing certain activities that Orthodox Jewish religious law prohibits on the Sabbath. In addition to turning lights on and off, he pushed the button on the elevator for congregants.

I was very honored to meet and interact with such a distinguished man in this very special setting. It is a tragedy that in 2021, he passed away a result of complications from COVID-19.

FEBRUARY 18, 2011: HOLOCAUST PRESENTATION BY SIDNEY SHACHNOW, HOLOCAUST SURVIVOR

After an illustrious career in the military, Major General Steven Hashem's final assignment in the Army was as director of coalition coordination for US Central Command. There, he was responsible for coordinating international support to coalition operations in Iraq and Afghanistan as well as serving as the primary interface between CENTCOM and senior national representatives from sixty nations.

It was through General Hashem that I first learned about the International Coalition based in Tampa. Steve and his lovely wife, Martha, were very involved in the civilian world. Deborah and I would frequently see them at military social gatherings as well as one of the coalition parties I had arranged. I also played many rounds of golf with Steve when he found time away from serving this great country.

One day Steve said, "You should read this book about a great American that was in the Holocaust and then came to the United States and became a two-star general, Sidney Shachnow. The book is entitled *Hope and Honor* and it tells the story of his extraordinary life."

The story begins with young Sid, a Lithuanian Jew born Schaja

Shachnowski, as he watched the Nazis march into his town of Kaunas. Sid, his family, and the entire Jewish population were confined to a ghetto which was designated Concentration Camp #4, Kovno. They struggled to survive using their wits, bribery, help from the Jewish camp police, and the occasional assistance of local Lithuanians. After almost three years in the camp, he and his family were smuggled out to live with a local farming family. Of the original 40,000 Jews confined at Kovno, only about 2,000 survived.

Shortly after the end of the war, Sid and his family escaped Lithuania to Nuremberg, Germany. Then thirteen years old, Sid worked on the black market, befriended an American Army sergeant, and later in 1950, the family immigrated to the United States. Settling in Salem, Massachusetts, he learned English while working to help support his parents and attended school regularly for the first time. In 1955 he enlisted in the Army. This began a forty-year military career. He started as an infantry private, rose to captain in the Special Forces, or Green Berets, and fought in Vietnam, twice receiving the Silver Star for valor. In 1970 he was transferred to West Berlin to command an elite Special Forces unit. After other postings, including director of the US Special Operations Command in Washington DC, he returned to West Berlin as the Army's commanding officer. His long career ultimately resulted in his becoming a highly decorated major general.

Sid's life certainly demonstrates remarkable qualities, as well as high professional integrity and a ferocious will to survive. The telling of it is not always graceful, but his story comes through clearly and with conviction. I was so impressed with the book that I mentioned to Steven that I would like to invite Sid to Tampa to speak with the coalition countries to educate and describe what the Jews went through during the Holocaust. I set up briefings at CENTCOM for all sixty Coalition country representatives and at our Temple, Congregation Schaarai Zedek. I decided to fly Sid and his charming wife, Arlene, whom he called his angel, to Tampa. This would be an opportunity for Sid to tell his story to so many people needing to hear it.

For the Coalition countries, Sid had a PowerPoint show about the Holocaust in Europe that was honest, gruesome, and revealing. There was no denying the Holocaust with such vivid pictures being displayed. To say that each representative of the foreign countries was taken aback by the images of the ruthlessness and inhumanity by the Schutzstaffel (SS), especially the four German representatives present, is an understatement. It was an eye-opener for all; they were in shock. After the presentation, Sid commented that persecution and torture are still present in communist and dictatorships around the world. He ended with, "We must stop this."

I mentioned to Sid that I thought giving the same PowerPoint presentation to the Jews at Schaarai Zedek would be a mistake—although real, it would be too hard for them to view. Sid toned down the presentation. Still, it was important that they see it firsthand from a Holocaust survivor.

While transporting Sid and Arlene to MacDill AFB and the Temple, we talked informally in the car. He shared with me that as a US general living in Berlin, Germany, his headquarters had been that of the powerful Nazi official Hermann Goring, who's residence had once belonged to Fritz Reinhardt, a finance minister under Hitler. He added that in 1989, every couple of weeks the East Germans, Russians, Americans, British, and the French would meet at the Berlin Wall and discuss visitation. One day Sid asked the East German representative when the visitation would begin? The East German representative, without being given permission by the higher-ups, agreed to allow the visitation immediately. Sid felt that this action influenced the removal of the Berlin Wall. There began to be an onslaught of East Germans crossing the wall. The momentum of the masses accumulating at the wall was too much for the Russians and the East Berlin military to stop. Thus, Major General Sid Shachnow was indirectly responsible for the reunification of Germany.

This day will always be remembered as the day sixty Coalition countries were more enlightened than ever before about the horrors of the Holocaust. Hopefully, would never happen again. I was so glad to have met two great American patriots who had made such a difference in the world.

It would happen that twelve years later, on February 8, 2023, I set up a dinner at Bern's Steak House with the new commander of SOCOM, General Bryan Fenton, along with Command Sergeant Major Shane Shorter. The head military attaché of Israel, Major General Hidai Zilberman, and Israeli Major General Eyal Zamir also attended.

The conversation at the table began with the key heads of US and Israel, General Fenton and Major General Zilberman, becoming better acquainted as they shared their backgrounds and experiences.

General Fenton mentioned that he had worked under General Shachnow, a Holocaust survivor, as his aide-de-camp in Germany from 1990–1991. He proceeded to describe one of their meetings with the Russian garrison commander in East Berlin—after the fall of the wall—in which the Russian commander mentioned that their rations were scarce. General Fenton said that General Shachnow wanted to provide the Russians with groceries and deliver them across the border to the Russian representative as a gesture of good will.

General Fenton was surprised, as this was very unusual, but indicative of the great man Shachnow was. General Fenton got the groceries and the two men crossed the border and went to the Russian base. General Shachnow asked General Fenton to go inside and pass off the food supplies. They then headed back into West Berlin. Shortly thereafter, General Fenton received a call from the Pentagon asking to speak to General Shachnow. During the telephone conversation, General Fenton wondered what was in store. Sure enough, when he asked General Shachnow what had transpired, his response was, "They heard about your escapade Fenton and they fired me." General Shachnow then said he was just kidding. "They wouldn't have the guts to fire a Special Forces officer." General Fenton shared with us that working under General Shachnow was the greatest experience of his life. It made a great impression on him and it was then that he decided to become a member of the Special Forces.

Clearly, dinner at Bern's was delightful and insightful. I was honored to host these great leaders and enjoy such a memorable evening.

JANUARY 26, 2014: FEDERATION'S 11TH ANNUAL PRESIDENT'S DINNER—KEYNOTE SPEAKER, PRIME MINISTER EHUD BARAK

As mentioned previously, including the list of speakers, the Federation's Annual President's Dinner is one of the most acclaimed events in the Tampa community. This dinner has a tradition of bringing world leaders and nationally recognized speakers to address our community, celebrating the growth and successes of the Tampa JCCs and Federation.

In 2004, Ann Rosenbach created the model and was the first event chair along with Rande Weissman. It is fair to say that Ann is the Founder of the event with complete support of fellow community member, Maureen Cohn, honorary chair in perpetuity. The event continues to this day with speakers being secured annually by Ann. And so it was that in 2014, Ann was able to secure a very special speaker.

That year, Ann was also event chair along with Harry Cohen and they had the distinguished honor of featuring keynote speaker Prime Minister Ehud Barak, the tenth prime minister of Israel from 1999 through 2001. Speaking with the former prime minister directly about logistics, and knowing he would have some free time, she asked if there was anything special he wanted to do while in Tampa. He promptly replied that he would like to go to Special Operations Command to see how they had progressed.

Ehud Barak is perhaps best known as the father of Special Operations for Israel. He was one of the architects of the Entebbe

Raid, and he dressed up as a woman in Lebanon and killed one of the killers of the Israel Olympic team in Munich. He later dressed up as a flight mechanic in the Sabina French Airliner hijacking and was successful in taking over the plane. Barak was a student in the United States in the 1950s and took classes at Stanford, where he met with William J. Donovan, who is considered the father of our CIA and Special Operations.

Ann asked me if I could help with this request, so I sent an email to Admiral Bill McRaven, who was the head of SOCOM at that time. He did not respond immediately, so a few days later I contacted him again. The second email received an immediate response with numerous military associates copied. I contacted Ann and informed her that Admiral McRaven would like to host the prime minister and his wife, Nili. He requested that Deborah and I be present and informed me that Bill and his wife, Georgeann, would be present as well. Bill asked that Deborah and I come early to SOCOM so we would all greet them at the front entrance to the facility. This would all take place on the day after the annual dinner, Monday, January 27.

Prior to his arrival in Tampa, I contacted General Petraeus and General Allen and told them that I was going to be meeting with Prime Minister Ehud Barak and asked if there was anything they wanted me to tell him on their behalf. General Petraeus asked me to tell him that he was very proud of his achievements, and he considered him a good friend. General Allen mentioned that he was working on a Middle East Peace Plan with John Kerry and the talks had stalled because the Arab countries were not entirely in favor of the treaty.

On Sunday, January 26, prior to the start of the annual dinner, I had the opportunity to meet and brief Ehud Barak. I gave him the remarks from both Generals Petraeus and Allen and presented him with a couple of boxes of fine cigars, one from Thompson Cigar (the largest cigar mail-order house), and one from J.C. Newman Cigars, which is the last of 150 automated cigar factories in Tampa. Prime Minister Ehud Barak was excited to see the fine cigars that he told me he couldn't wait to get back to Israel and smoke them with "Bibi" (Prime Minister Benjamin Netanyahu). I also gave him a train conductor's hat with four stars and made him an honorary conductor of Mark's Southern Railroad Systems. I had the Prime Minister autograph a small version of Israel's Cobra helicopter for the train room, where it hangs to this day.

The evening of the annual dinner Prime Minister Barak spoke eloquently about the past and the current state of Israel and received a standing ovation from the crowd.

On Monday, January 27, Prime Minister Ehud Barak and his lovely wife, Nili, arrived at MacDill AFB around 9:00 a.m. escorted by Tampa's finest—our police. They drove right up to the front entrance of SOCOM where Admiral McRaven and Georgeann, along with Deborah and I greeted them. After Admiral McRaven gave us a tour of the front entrance mini museum, we were escorted to a small room in the facility for a breakfast meeting. Admiral McRaven sat in his chair with four stars on the back and started the conversation with how good the relationship is between the US and Israel. Then Ehud Barack continued by telling us about his military background and how he led Special Ops teams in Israel.

Admiral McRaven then briefed him on how we have come since the failed rescue attempt in Iran in 1980, Operation Eagle Claw. We then walked to the Joint Operations Center (JOC Room) and met with some of the staff and then on to the new room called the War Games Room that Admiral McRaven had designed. The floor looked like an iPad on steroids. It was about twenty-four feet by thirty-two feet that can project holograms and elevated images so they can strategize on war situations. Ehud Barak was so impressed with the facility that he said, "You guys have come a long way since the Iranian hostage attempt." He seemed really pleased and I felt like a mensch for putting the two together. During the three-hour visit, there wasn't even a fifteen-second break in conversations.

McRaven and Barak were the best special operators of our

time. They had a lot in common, and they really appreciated the opportunity to be together. I was so excited to have made this happen. I later found out that since a civilian had brought them together there was no need to go through the red tape of the State Department. They could now pick up the phone and call each other anytime.

Besides my wedding day and having two beautiful children, this was the most important day of my life.

MAY 11, 2015: AIPAC AND SENATOR LINDSAY O. GRAHAM

Deborah and I went to an AIPAC Convention (American Israel Public Affairs Committee) in Washington DC from March 1–3, 2015. AIPAC is a lobbying group that advocates pro-Israel policies to Congress and the Executive Branch of the United States. Last count, AIPAC had over one hundred thousand members, seventeen regional offices, and a vast pool of donors. It is considered one of the most powerful lobbying groups in the United States. One of the missions of the organization is to strengthen, protect, and promote the relationship between the United States and Israel.

I met Senator Lindsay Graham briefly at the convention and then later, Deborah and I met him at the Capitol Hill Club in DC. We offered to host a social event to support his potential run for president of the United States whenever he planned a trip to Florida. Even though his constituency is South Carolina, not Florida, I wanted to support this great Air Force military JAG (Judge Advocate General) and senator.

It happened that he was planning a trip to Orlando to visit his sister and her family, and he could easily drive over to Tampa. He asked us if May 11 would be a good date. We agreed and Deborah was on go, preparing the invite list, ordering from our favorite caterer, Pane Rustica, and setting up the house. Essentially, it would be one of our Games and Trains Parties.

We had over forty-five attendees including General Jay Hood (Ret.) and General Karl Horst (Ret.). When Senator Graham arrived, I showed him around the house and of course, the Train Room. He was taken back when he saw the train layout. I presented him with a conductor's hat pinned with the JAG logo and all the Air Force medals he had received. He was so excited that he immediately had his assistant take the conductor's hat to his car for safekeeping.

Senator Graham gave a very informative and positive briefing to a supportive crowd. He was kind enough to take pictures with the entire group of attendees. He conversed with General Hood, who had briefed him years prior, when Jay was commanding general of Joint Task Force Guantanamo Bay, Cuba. He was briefed by General Horst when Karl was chief of staff for General Jim Mattis, then commander of CENTCOM.

He is a gentleman with a good and kind spirit who seems to genuinely care about our country. Our family was in awe that such an accomplished man had joined us and our friends in our home. Senator Graham left with a positive support group in Tampa.

JANUARY 29, 2017: FEDERATION'S 14TH ANNUAL PRESIDENT'S DINNER—KEYNOTE SPEAKER, AMBASSADOR RON PROSER

The Tampa Federation's Annual President's Dinner featured keynote speaker Ambassador Ron Proser. Ambassador Proser was the former Israeli Ambassador to the United Kingdom, former vice president of the United Nation's 67th General Assembly, former director general of the Israeli Ministry of Foreign Affairs. This was another occasion when the speaker asked for a visit to MacDill Air Force Base. I promptly made the arrangements for a tour of SOCOM with the chief of staff, Major General Marcus Hicks. His Air Force background included commanding the 374th Airlift Wing at Yokota

Air Base, Japan, and the Combined Joint Special Operations Air Component at Joint Base Balad, Iraq.

I picked up Ambassador Proser on that morning and drove him to the base. We were greeted by General Hicks, who briefed us on Special Operations in Tampa and explained that it is a unified combatant command composed of the finest of the Army, Navy, Marine Corps, and Air Force. He said the Tampa operation is where planning and logistics take place. General Hicks also mentioned that as a pilot, he'd had the opportunity to fly with Israeli IDF pilots. Ambassador Prosor was very impressed with the knowledge, professionalism, and dedication of General Hicks.

We then went to the Bryan Glazer Family Jewish Community Center where I introduced the ambassador to Saru Seshadri, COO of Florida-Israel Business Accelerator (FIBA). He was particularly curious about the work being done within this organization because his son was working on a special drone invention. FIBA is involved in Israeli start-up companies interested in coming to the United States. They assist with marketing, networking, legal, distribution, angel money, and other facets of the businesses.

Ambassador Proser's remarks that evening were very insightful. Among other things, we learned that to be an Israeli ambassador to a foreign country, you need to have extensive education in a particular country, speak the language, and have overall knowledge of foreign affairs through Israel's specialized training schools. On the other hand, US ambassadors are generally a politically based selection. He also spoke about his United Nations experiences as well as Israel's position being surrounded by friendly as well as unfriendly neighbors. He added that American Jews who are truly pro-Israel should be Republican, and not value social issues over the well-being, protection, and survival of Israel.

It was yet another successful Annual President's Dinner.

MARCH 3, 2017: ISRAELI IDF DINNER AT BERN'S STEAK HOUSE

At 9:00 a.m. I received a telephone call from the Israeli Embassy in Washington DC. I was issued a protocol informing me that Colonel Eyal Beinart, head of Israeli IDF to the US/Canada assistant defense attaché, would be available for dinner in Tampa, along with two of his colleagues, Brigadier General Dror Shalom, head of the Research and Analysis Division and the Israeli Cyber Intelligence Unit, and Major Danny Citrinowicz, assistant attaché. I looked forward to having dinner together.

Deborah and I included our friends, Anthony and Nancy Weiss, and we all enjoyed a delicious meal at Tampa's renowned Bern's Steak House. During dinner, Dror said that because of ISIS there are millions of displaced people in the Middle East. Their average age is twenty-five years or less, most are uneducated, without skills, without jobs, and need necessities. As a result, they are susceptible to ISIS influence. These issues will be problematic for an entire generation, perhaps longer.

Additionally, Dror told us that a large number of refugees entering Lebanon and Jordan cannot be accommodated. This is a long-term problem for the whole Middle East. Eyal said that he was concerned about the US abandoning the Middle East, as each presidency has not been consistent to convey solidarity. He said the allowance of Iranian aggression via Hezbollah and Hamas, in addition to Syria, all affect the balance of the Arab nations.

After dinner, we toured the Bern's wine cellar, dessert room, and afterward, the Rosenthal Train Room. At the end of the evening, I dashed off to get them to the airport to catch their flights to Washington DC. It was an enjoyable and eye-opening experience.

MARCH 16, 2017: CONGREGATION SCHAARAI ZEDEK—GUEST SPEAKER, ARI SACHER

Upon hearing Ari Sacher speak at AIPAC, I got his phone number and asked if he would have an interest in speaking at our synagogue. The temple brotherhood agreed it would be a great idea and so, arrangements were made to bring him to Tampa.

Ari Sacher is an engineer for Rafael Advanced Defense Systems, Israel's largest government owned defense contractor. His specialized field is as a rocket scientist, and he is best known as the inventor of the Iron Dome, which is a short-range missile defense system strategically placed in twelve locations within the state of Israel. In addition to covering the technology aspects of his field, his remarks included a multitude of topics as they relate to Israel—politics, surrounding neighbors, cultures and communities within, and Jewish humor.

After the event, my close friend, David Rosenbach, and I, hosted Ari for dinner at Bern's Steak House. Ari ordered Chilean sea bass and an assortment of vegetables. Since he is kosher, he asked for the meal to be double wrapped in aluminum foil, baked, and served (still in foil) on the plate. He joked that an Iron Dome protected his meal.

Ari and his wife have eight children. He noted that in recent days, Israelis are having more children and they are less concerned about Arab citizens populating the country in greater numbers than the Israelis. It was an insightful conversation.

SEPTEMBER 3, 2019: ISRAEL IDF CHANGE OF COMMAND— MAJOR GENERAL MICHAEL EDELSTEIN

I was honored to be invited by the Israeli ambassador to the United States, Ron Dermer, to witness the defense attaché change of command ceremony and farewell reception in honor of Major

General Michael Edelstein, head Israeli military attaché to the US, at the Israeli Embassy in Washington DC.

After enjoying the US Open tennis match in New York, I made a point to travel to Philadelphia to visit some old friends, brothers Danny and Gary Zlotnick. I had been very upset that Danny, at just sixty years old, had a stroke and was no longer able to use or feel the left side of his body. From Philadelphia, I took Amtrak to Washington DC and arrived around noon. I took a cab to my favorite hotel in DC, the Capitol Hilton, and checked in. From there, I prepared myself for the retirement ceremony. I arrived at the Israeli Embassy at approximately 4:30 p.m. and a small crowd was queued up at the entrance.

At 5:00 p.m. sharp IDF (Israel Defense Forces) security let us in the gate to the front conference room of the building. Inside the approximately 3,000 square-foot room was a nice spread of Middle Eastern food, including salads and lamb. Over 150 attendees entered the room and socialized until the 6:30 p.m. ceremony, which was hosted by Ambassador Dermer. Most of the attendees were Israeli officials along with military attachés from many Israeli allied countries that are present in Washington DC.

From the Jewish Institute for National Security of America (JINSA) I met Leo Nayfeld, managing director, Harris Vedeman, director of programs and outreach, and Jeffrey Nadaner, senior vice president of defense and military affairs. This organization brings current American military leaders to Israel and gives them a tour of the country while briefing them on the military leaders of the IDF. I also met the commander of the police and public security ministry attaché to North America, Mr. Yitzhak Almog. He was very personable and mentioned that he may be coming to Tampa in the near future.

I was honored to meet Major General Yehuda Fox, who would be the replacement for General Edelstein. I met his wife and family and wished them much success in the new position. I also met Brigadier General Amir Keren, the Air Force attaché and deputy defense attaché for Israel. He is the assistant to Air Force commander

Major General Amikam Norkin, who was supposed to speak the week before in Tampa but unfortunately, had to go back to Israel due to a military incident. Another interesting person at the event was Major General Meir Klifi-Amir (Ret.), national director and CEO of Friends of the Israeli Defense Forces. I had such a nice time meeting all of these Israeli patriots.

Ambassador Dermer led the ceremony with an introduction of General Edelstein. He told the audience that in the three years that General Edelstein had held the position of the military attaché, the relationship between the US and Israel was the best that it had ever been. Mickey had made an everlasting impression on the leadership of Israel and the US.

I was honored to have been mentioned by Mickey during his speech in which he thanked all the military and civilians that had made his stay in DC so special. Later when I spoke to Mickey, he mentioned that his family had already left for Israel. I wished Hadar and the children all the best. Mickey gave me a hug and was so happy that I had attended the event. I felt good about being there to celebrate his success and knowing that we would continue our friendship going forward.

That night at 12:02 p.m., I received an email from Mickey.

> *Dear Mark,*
> *I want to thank you for attending the farewell event tonight. I feel so grateful. It was very moving to see you there; you're not another guest but a real friend.*
> *Thank you for your friendship and I look forward to hosting you in Israel. Big hugs from Hadar and me to Deborah and many greetings for the coming wedding—Mazal Tov.*

I went to sleep feeling great about the trip and the impact that patriots like these make around the world.

SEPTEMBER 13, 2021: ISRAELI IDF OFFICER, MAJOR OR KARASIN

Major Or Karasin is the first Israeli officer in history to be embedded at Central Command as a representative of Israel. The Trump Administration on their final move to engage the Israel and Arab nations, convinced the twenty countries of Central Command to incorporate Israel. This was an incredible act, moving Israel from European Command to Central Command, so the Israelis could communicate one on one with their Arab counterparts. Therefore, over time, relationships could be built, and issues could be resolved in Tampa, Florida rather than within the political wave of Washington DC or the United Nations.

Since my involvement with the US military, I have come to know many Israeli IDF officers. On many occasions when they came to Tampa, I would get a telephone call requesting that I set up a dinner at Bern's Steak House. And so it was that my friend, Anthony Weiss, his wife, Nancy, me, and Deborah, were all honored to host a reception dinner for the new Central Command now-embedded Israeli officer Major Or Karasin and his wife, Roni. Also present at the dinner were Major Eyal Rechnitz, aide-de-camp to the defense attaché embassy of Israel, his wife, Michelle, and Peter Belk, deputy director of J-5 plans and strategy, and director of weapons of mass destruction.

The conversation throughout the evening was engaging and most enjoyable. Deborah and I were pleased to welcome our new friends, Or and Roni, into our community. We felt like we were part of a new chapter in history. Certainly, Or will play an important role getting better acquainted with their Middle East neighbors at MacDill Air Force Base. I explained to Or that the Arab representatives are some of the most brilliant young military leaders of their respective countries with the potential of one day leading their military. And I felt like Or, with his warm and cheerful personality, will have a great impact building relationships with the representatives of the other twenty countries—Afghanistan, Bahrain, Djibouti, Egypt, Eritrea, Ethiopia, Jordan, Iran, Iraq, Kenya, Kuwait, Oman, Pakistan, Qatar, Saudi Arabia, Seychelles, Somalia, Sudan, United Arab Emirates, and the Republic of Yemen. Now, with the inclusion of Israel, they number twenty-one.

Hopefully, this is a huge step toward lessening tensions in the region and building peace among neighbors.

JUNE 23, 2022: ISRAELI FIRST RESPONDERS TO THE SURFSIDE, FLORIDA CONDO COLLAPSE

Israeli officer Major Or Karasin called me and asked if I would entertain a group of Israeli officers visiting Tampa. Naturally, I was happy to be of service. At 12:00 p.m. Or arrived at my house with Lieutenant Colonel Moti Dayan, the HFC liaison officer to NGB, Major General Ori Gordin, home front command commanding general, Colonel Sagi Baruch, south district commanding general, and Lieutenant Colonel Vered Chen Zagron, director of international affairs. We all boarded my SUV for lunch and a tour of Tampa. We drove down Bayshore Boulevard, which in the 1970s was considered the longest continuous sidewalk in the world, then we drove through Ybor City along 7th Avenue and arrived at the Columbia Restaurant for lunch. The 1903 corner saloon transformed into the Columbia Restaurant in 1905 and grew from there. Now, 117 years later, they are still operating and serving some of the best Spanish food in America.

General Gordin sat next to me at the table and generated most of the conversation. He mentioned that his small group of representatives was stopping in Tampa for a visit to CENTCOM and then going to Miami to give a speech about the Surfside condominium collapse. He explained that a year before, while he and his wife were on vacation in Martha's Vineyard, Massachusetts, he had received a phone call from his superior officer informing him of the collapse of the Champlain Towers South, a twelve-story beachfront condominium in the Miami suburb of Surfside, Florida. He was asked if he would put together a team and assist in the recovery. General Gordin immediately contacted his group of seventeen specialists for this type of recovery and flew back to Israel. Thereafter, Florida Governor Ron DeSantis was contacted by the Israeli government and the diplomatic interaction began between the two nations. Within twenty-four hours the specialized Israeli search and recovery team flew directly to Miami to assist over 3,000 American first responders at the collapse site. At first the Americans wondered why seventeen Israelis had come to assist. According to General Gordin, the Israelis have a unique way of searching for the remains of bodies in an incident such as this. They contacted the next of kin and had them document the existing building plans and the location of their family members' condominiums. The Israelis directed the US first responders and low and behold, the first body was recovered. Then the second and so on until over a dozen bodies were recovered with the help of Israeli leadership. After that, the American first responders became the workforce for the seventeen Israeli experts with tremendous respect.

Ninety-eight people died in the tragedy. Four people were rescued from the rubble, but one died of injuries shortly after arriving at the hospital. Eleven others were injured. Approximately thirty-five were rescued the same day from the portion of the building that had not collapsed, which was demolished several days later.

General Ori Gordin and his team were heading to Miami Beach the day after our lunch, to mark the anniversary of the Surfside tragedy, the third-deadliest building collapse in US history, to give a speech and receive recognition from our dignitaries for a job well done. I was in shock and got teary-eyed as he told me his story.

After lunch, we went to the Newman Cigar Factory for a tour

of one of the last remaining cigar factories in Tampa. At one time Tampa was known as the cigar capital of the world because it was home to 150 cigar factories. The tour of the factory was fabulous and the owners, Eric and Bobby Newman, came out and presented all the guests with cigars and took group pictures with us. I told the Newmans about the significance of this team, and they were very impressed. They said to them, "God bless your team."

Next, we traveled on to the University of Tampa and went to the museum. The main building at the University of Tampa was the original 1891 Tampa Bay Hotel built by Henry Plant. Henry Plant built the railroad to entice northerners to come to Florida to fish, hunt, and enjoy the weather in the winter. Besides being a railroad tycoon, Henry Plant was in the steamship business and had a line going from Florida to Cuba. Everyone enjoyed the museum.

We then headed back to my house for a train show. I gave the team a brief history of the evolution of the trains and ran the fifteen lines. I then presented General Gordin with a conductor's hat with three stars for his great accomplishments, not only here in America, but now he was being promoted to head of the Northern Command, which is the most active post. He in turn presented me with a large Mezuzah and a beret worn by the special Israeli team. It was a special day spent with incredible patriots who risked their lives for American citizens.

JULY 20, 2022: UNITED ARAB EMIRATES (UAE), ISRAEL, AND ME

Major Or Karasin, now settled in at his post as the new Israeli Liaison officer (LNO) for Central Command, called to tell me that Special Operations in America was hosting Israel, UAE, Bahrain, and England as well as the Israel Defense Forces (IDF) representatives, and they would like to come to my house and say hello. Most of these IDF special operators had visited me before and I had developed a nice relationship with these true patriots, such as Israeli Major General Itai Veruv. In addition, Or mentioned that he had a great relationship with the representatives of the UAE and asked if I could set up a dinner for seven of their team members at Bern's Steak House for Wednesday night. The representatives had previously been told that it could take as long as six months to get a reservation for seven people. I immediately called my contacts at Bern's and explained how important it was to show our American and local Tampa hospitality to our new friends from the Middle East. When I heard back from Bern's I was told that the only time available was 10:00 p.m. I contacted Or and he confirmed from the UAE contingent that the time would work.

So, on Wednesday at 4:30 p.m., the Israeli contingent of seven officers came over for a social hour and to see the Train Room. I was honored to have them over and wished them the best of success. The Israeli leadership thanked me for making the reservation for their new friends in the UAE and mentioned that it would be very important for me to join them for dinner, even at the late hour.

I was honored. After our conversation I called Bern's owner, David Laxer, and mentioned the importance of the dinner tonight. I asked him to sign a copy of Bern's recipe book to give to the UAE team as a remembrance of the evening. I then called Bobby Newman, owner with his brother, Eric Newman, of the J.C. Newman Cigar Company. I thought it would be a great gesture to present a nice box of the latest American cigars.

I arrived at Bern's at 9:15 p.m. and discussed the group's arrival with the maître d', Frank Russo. We would not have any alcohol or mention pork for the dinner to our guests. At around 9:30 p.m., I was sitting in the lounge, and a couple of gentlemen dressed in American garb came in and sat by me. I heard an Australian accent from one of the gentlemen and felt like he must be the leader of the UAE I had been briefed about. I walked over to them and asked if they were from the UAE and sure enough, they introduced themselves as

General Mike Hindmarsh, the presidential guard commander and leader of the UAE military, from Australia, and UAE Colonel Faisal Almahmod, the director of the J-3 in PG. We talked briefly until the remainder of the UAE team arrived. Then UAE staff colonel Dr. Rashed Almoudi, the SNR of the UAE in CENTCOM, UAE Major Essa Almonsori, the CSAG officer in Central Command, and UAE Captain Ali Ahmed, LO in Central Command arrived. Our maître d', Frank, escorted us to the senior waiter, Drew's, room. Incidentally, when Bern's first opened at this location, it started with one bay of a retail shopping center. That bay was Drew's room. Over time, Bern's occupied the entire building and eventually the entire block. Bern's has provided excellence in food to our community since 1956.

We all sat around the table for dinner, and I sensed that they wondered how I was involved. At first, they thought I was in the military and not just a caring civilian who was so proud that the UAE had joined Israel through the Abraham Accord. I started by explaining to Mike that I was in Australia playing tennis in 1979 and then went to Perth for the America's Cup in 1987. Mike was delighted and our conversation became even more engaging. He explained that although unusual as an Australian, he was the top military officer in UAE reporting directly to the monarch, UAE leader, Mohammed bin Zayed Al Nahyan. I further clarified my involvement as a citizen of the United States, and fourth generation living in Tampa. We went around the table to say a little bit about our families and how many children we all had. The numbers went from eight to six to five to three, and of course, my two. I realized our Arab partners have very large families compared to America. We also discussed the access that UAE has to our television networks, and I realized they watched our news, sports, and television shows. They were fully immersed in our American ways.

Mike then gave me an introduction about the UAE and its main cities of Dubai and Abu Dhabi. Mohammed bin Zayed has built the main cities from the sea by dredging and developing incredible residential subdivisions and commercial sites. The downtown office buildings are some of the most modern and tallest buildings in the world. The leader realized that even though the country of UAE has the sixth largest reserve of oil in the world, once the oil is dry, the country would need other ways of supporting itself financially. He decided to create a tourist destination, along with a high-tech mecca for business in the future. His goal was to achieve a sustainable empire that would last for generations and benefit his country and its people.

Mike added that it was Mohammed bin Zayed's idea to have his diplomatic representative meet with the Trump Administration to negotiate a peace treaty in the Middle East. The Trump administration immediately recognized the importance and made it happen. The monarch realized it was a great idea that would allow UAE and their partner Bahrain security in the Middle East by having Israel and the US protect them from Iranian aggression. I asked him why Saudi Arabia did not join the peace treaty and he mentioned that UAE had upstaged Saudi Arabia by unilaterally meeting with the Trump Administration without conferring with them. As Mike mentioned, the Arab nations have a common enemy in Iran but unfortunately, they do not see eye to eye on other issues, so they are not all united.

I was told that Mohammed bin Zayed is like a father figure to Emirates and is loved by all. Even though the country is not considered a democracy, Mohammed has provided them wealth, safety, and security for a long-standing future with Western values. I mentioned Lee Kuan Yew of Singapore and Mike said that Mohammed is loved by the Emirates like Lee Kuan Yew is loved by the Singaporeans, even though Singapore is a democracy and UAE is a monarchy.

I was so impressed with each of the UAE representatives and their passionate love of their country. They also told me that within the last four years Mohammed bin Zayed had required all Emirates to serve at least one year in the military. This would help bind them to their country and give them a stronger feeling of allegiance.

After dinner, I presented the team with the Bern's book, *Bern's*

Rare and Well Done, autographed by owner, David Laxer, and the American Newman cigars. Next, we were treated to a tour of the wine cellar and then on to the upstairs Dessert Room. Everyone enjoyed the famous banana cream pie and macadamia nut ice cream. We all took pictures throughout the night to remember this memorable evening. I closed out the dinner by saying that we, as Americans, are so proud of the UAE for helping bring peace to the Middle East and for their relationship with Israel and America. What an incredible day with the IDF and our new friends from the UAE!

With Israeli Major General Michael Edelstein

Prime Minister Ehud Barack and his wife Nelly, Deborah, me, Georgeann McRaven, and Admiral Bill McRaven

Senator Lindsay Graham with the Rosenthal family

Senator Lindsay Graham in the Train Room.

With Major General Ori Gordin, who led the Israeli team at the Surfside Collapse, presenting me with an Israeli mezuzah and beret

CHAPTER 10

Military Demonstrations, Celebrations, and Awards

NOVEMBER 9, 2009: THE WOODROW WILSON AWARDS DINNER

Deborah and I were honored to be the guests of General David and Holly Petraeus for the Woodrow Wilson Awards Dinner in the beautiful ballroom of the Vinoy Hotel in downtown St. Petersburg, Florida. Woodrow Wilson Awards are given out each year in multiple countries by the Woodrow Wilson International Center for Scholars of the Smithsonian Institution. Recipients of the award are individuals from both the public and business spheres who have shown an outstanding commitment to former president of the United States, Woodrow Wilson's dream of integrating politics, scholarship, and policy for the common good. Created in 1999 as a local award for leadership in Washington, DC, the awards were expanded in 2001 to recognize great leaders and thinkers throughout the world. Funding from the awards supports additional research, scholars, and programs in Washington and in the home community of the recipients.

The Woodrow Wilson Award for Public Service is given to individuals who have served with distinction in public life and have shown a special commitment to seeking out informed opinions and thoughtful views. Recipients of this award share Woodrow Wilson's steadfast belief in public discourse, scholarship, and the extension of the benefits of knowledge in the United States and around the world. These leaders devote themselves to examining the historical background and long-term implications of important public policy issues while encouraging the free and open exchange of ideas that is the bedrock of our nation's foundation.

The Woodrow Wilson Award for Corporate Citizenship is given to executives who demonstrate a commitment to the common good—beyond the bottom line. They are the people who demonstrate that private firms should be good citizens in their neighborhoods, as well as in the world. The award is given to those who have done tremendous work to improve their local communities and the world at large.

General Petraeus was honored to receive this prestigious award as the recipient for public service and Tom James received the award for corporate citizenship. Interestingly, I have known Tom for a long time—since my junior years as a tennis player. We have played doubles numerous times in the past. He is an incredible athlete and brilliant businessman who took his father's business from a local brokerage house to an international firm, Raymond James Financial, Inc., with offices in over ten countries and with 7900 financial advisors throughout the United States.

Some of the award recipients for public service include Vice President Cheney, Hon. William Cohen, Betty Ford, Senator John Glenn, Dr. Henry Kissinger, Andrew Lloyd Webber, General Colin Powell, and the Honorable Andrew Young. Deborah and I had such a great time meeting all the dignitaries at the event and we felt honored to be the guests of one of the greatest military leaders of all time.

The next day Deborah sent a thank you note to General Petraeus.

> *Dear David,*
>
> *Thank you for inviting me and Mark to be your guests Monday night at the Woodrow Wilson Awards dinner. It was truly a delight to join you and share in your well-deserved*

honor. We are blessed to call you and Holly friends.
With appreciation always,
Deborah

MAY 27, 2010: THE INTREPID FREEDOM AWARD

The Intrepid Sea, Air, and Space Museum is a military and maritime history museum in New York City. The museum pays tribute to our nation's heroes and on this occasion, its 19th Annual Salute to Freedom Gala, honored General David H. Petraeus.

Museum president Susan Marenoff Zausner stated, "The museum's mission is to honor the men and women who have served our nation. General Petraeus has led our troops overseas in that exact effort, and we are indebted to his leadership and love of country. This annual event throws a spotlight on individuals who have gone above and beyond the call of duty for our nation."

General Petraeus invited Deborah and me to this black-tie event in NYC, and since Deborah could not attend, I represented the family. The gala dinner was held aboard the decommissioned aircraft carrier USS *Intrepid* and over 250 attended. Invited dignitaries included Nobel Laureate Elie Wiesel and Secretary of State Henry Kissinger. Also in attendance was Colonel Gregory Gadson. A former garrison commander, Colonel Gadson is a motivational speaker and actor. He may be best remembered for his role in the 2012 science fiction film, *Battleship*, directed by Peter Berg, who also made *Lone Survivor*.

I was seated at the table of our dear friend, General John Allen. He would later succeed General Petraeus as commander of the International Security Assistance Force in Afghanistan.

Past recipients of the Intrepid Freedom Award include:

✦ Presidents George W. Bush, George H.W. Bush, Ronald Reagan, and William Jefferson Clinton

- Senators Hillary Rodham Clinton and John McCain
- Congressmen Newt Gingrich and Bill Young
- His Excellencies Yitzhak Rabin, Silvio Berlusconi, and Boris Yeltsin
- The Right Honorable Baroness Margaret Thatcher
- Defense Secretaries Robert Gates, Donald Rumsfeld, William Cohen, and Dick Cheney
- Chairman of the Joint Chiefs General Richard B. Myers, USAF
- General Henry Shelton, USA, General Colin Powell, USA, and General Tommy R. Franks, USA
- His Eminence John Cardinal O'Connor
- The Honorable Michael R. Bloomberg and New York City Police Commissioner Ray Kelly

After the gala, we gathered at a beautiful apartment overlooking the east side of Central Park. There we met many of the international dignitaries who were present for the event. What a great time meeting the movers and shakers of the world.

SPECIAL OPERATIONS COMMAND (SOCOM) AWARDS DINNER–2011, 2013, 2017, 2018, AND 2019

Deborah and I were honored to attend several Special Operations Command (SOSOM) awards dinners. These events give out prestigious awards, most notably the Colonel Arthur D. "Bull" Simons Award, the Dr. Christian J. Lambertsen Award, the United States Special Operations Command Patriot Award, and the Commando Hall of Honor Award,

The Bull Simons Award is a lifetime Special Operations Forces (SOF) achievement Award presented annually by the commander of SOCOM during SOF Week. The Bull Simons award recognizes demonstrated leadership excellence and selfless support in improving the quality of life for SOF soldiers, sailors, airmen, and marines; significant contributions leading to advancements in SOF operational capabilities; the highest ethical and moral standards; and personal embodiment of the spirit, values, skills, and professionalism of our SOF warriors. In 1979, Bull Simons was contracted by Ross Perot of Electronic Data Systems to rescue his workers in Iran. He was able to rescue and return them all to safety back to the United States.

The Dr. Christian J. Lambertsen Award for Operational Innovation recognizes those individuals whose audacity, insight, and ingenuity embody innovation as an enduring operational skill and hallmark of the Special Operations Forces mindset and culture. While deployed in Afghanistan, Dr. Lambertsen recognized a critical problem with mine-resistant armored personnel (MRAP) vehicles if they were hit by a mine and turned over in a river.

The United States Special Operations Command Patriot Award was established in 1994 to recognize individuals for outstanding contributions to and in support of special operations and who greatly support wounded warriors, their families, or surviving families through significant and enduring contributions. Michael G. Vickers, undersecretary of the defense for intelligence and assistant secretary of defense played a central role in shaping US strategy for the war with Al-Qaeda and the war in Afghanistan. During the 1980s, Secretary Vickers was the principal strategist for the paramilitary operation that drove the Soviet Army out of Afghanistan.

The Commando Hall of Honor Award recognizes individuals who have served with distinction within the Special Operations Forces community. The recipients include Major General Frank D. Merrill (Ret.), who distinguished himself by commanding the 5307th Composite Unit, part of the US Army's 75th Ranger Regiment in WWII, which was later called "Merrill's Marauders." Major General Robert Frederick (Ret.) distinguished himself by receiving eight purple hearts for organizing, training, and commanding the Joint

Canadian American First Special Service Force in World War II. Brigadier General Russell W. Volckman (Ret.) distinguished himself by evading capture from the Japanese in the WWII and establishing a guerrilla force to counter the Japanese in the Philippine Mountains. After the war, he served as the chief of plans, Special Operations Division, Office of Psychological Warfare during the critical period when Special Forces were established at Fort Bragg, North Carolina. Colonel Jeffrey B. Jones (Ret.) distinguished himself during a lifetime of service to the US Special Operations Forces as chief, special operations division, and assistant deputy director for operations of the Joint Staff from 1995 to 1998. Colonel Christopher P. Costa (Ret.) distinguished himself during a twenty-five-year career as both a commissioned intelligence officer and civil servant. He was instrumental in the successful evolution of significant national capabilities, including the Joint Unconventional Warfare Task Force, Naval Special Warfare Task Force, and Naval Special Warfare Tactical Development and Evaluation Squadron One. Chief Master Sergeant Wayne G. Norrad (Ret.) distinguished himself by injecting special tactics capabilities into the formation of the nation's premier Joint Special Operations Team while developing high-altitude, high-opening parachute tactics and integrating air and ground assets. He participated in the planning and execution of some of our nation's most sensitive operations in Cambodia, Just Cause, Desert Shield, and Desert Storm. Chief Master Sergeant Gordon Scott (Ret.) distinguished himself as a Special Operations loadmaster in the MC 130E/Talon aircraft. He directed, organized, trained, and equipped the Air Force Special Operations Command loadmasters and implemented a joint operations guide for all Air Force special operators. He also made key contributions to the development of the *Mother of All Bombs*, known as a MOAB. Master Sergeant Scott C. Fales (Ret.) distinguished himself by dedicating thirty-three years of service to the Department of Defense and continues to serve as the director of personnel recovery operations at the 724th Special

Tactics Group. He was personally responsible for the program tasked with tracking and locating American hostages around the world. His lifetime commitment to the Special Operations community has greatly impacted the future of personnel recovery for the Special Operations mission and left a tremendous mark on the Department of Defense.

On May 18, 2011, Deborah and I were excited to be invited to our first US Special Operations Awards Dinner by Admiral Eric and Marilyn Olson, the head of SOCOM. The black-tie event was held at the Marriott Waterside in downtown Tampa and included a great many leaders, past and present.

That year's recipient of the Dr. Christian J. Lambertsen Award was Staff Sergeant Craig S. Cooper USMC. Staff Sergeant Cooper distinguished himself while serving as the motor transportation chief, Special Operations Task Force 82. The factory-supplied egress wrench was inaccessible in the design and Staff Sergeant Cooper designed, fabricated, and placed the tool so if the MRAP did flip over in a river, all four operators could free themselves and escape.

That year's Bull Simon Award recipient was Major General John K. Singlaub (Ret.) who distinguished himself throughout a lifetime of service to our nation's military and its Special Operations Forces. As a SOF warrior of over thirty-five years, in 1943 he was an Army officer who parachuted as part of the Allied invasion of mainland Europe into France. He led an Office of Strategic Services (OSS) Jedburgh team and aided the French Resistance in preparations for the Allied breakout from Normandy. He then deployed to China to train and lead Chinese guerillas in the fight against the Japanese. In the waning days of World War II, he parachuted onto Hainan Island in the South China Sea with an OSS team, liberating more than 400 Allied captives from a Japanese prisoner of war camp. From 1968 to 1969 he was instrumental in the establishment of the US Army Ranger Training Center at Fort Benning, where he also served as an instructor. General Singlaub's unwavering loyalty, dedication, and devotion to duty reflect distinct credit on him, Special Operation

Forces worldwide, and the US Special Operations Command.

Deborah and I arrived dressed in our formal attire at 6:30 p.m. and were first greeted by General Joe Votel, the chief of staff of SOCOM, and his wife, Michele. We took a beautiful picture together. Then we met up with Lieutenant General David Fridovich, deputy to SOCOM, and his wife, Kathy. As I mentioned earlier, Dave and Deborah had been classmates at Nova High School in Davie, Florida over forty years earlier.

Prior to the event, my dentist Dr. Charles Martin had given me a book to read. It was about an amazing military hero, Sergeant Major Billy Waugh, called *Hunting the Jackal*. When they introduced Major General John Singlaub, they mentioned that one of his assistants in many of his incredible military assignments was Sergeant Major Billy Waugh. After I heard this, I made sure I met Billy Waugh before the event ended so I could introduce myself. I wanted to tell him that I had read his book. Realizing I needed to invite Sergeant Major Waugh to a social event, I immediately asked him for his business card. I thought it would be fun to invite him and his wife to come to a Games and Trains party (they ended up coming to several). Some of the other attendees that we had pictures with were Ross Perot, General James Mattis, along with the award recipients, Under Secretary Michael Vickers, and Major General John Singlaub.

On May 15, 2013, Deborah and I, along with our friends John and Jennifer McCoskrie, were invited by the commander of Special Operations Command, Admiral Bill McRaven, to attend the Special Operations Awards Dinner held at the Marriott Waterside in downtown Tampa. Heads of Special Operations Command were all present along with many of their personnel. Prior award recipients attended as well. Since very few civilians are invited, we were truly honored and appreciative. Over 400 attendees enjoyed the event as several awards were presented.

That year's USSOCOM Patriot Award was presented to Kathy Maguire. Kathy has served as a mother figure for young wives, organized holiday parties for the children of deployed service members, comforted families of the fallen, cooked food for hospitalized warriors, and impacted policies to better the lives of SOF families past, present, and future. What an incredible gift she is to SOCOM! I met Kathy and her husband, General Joseph Maguire, a few years prior. Joe was the director of the National Counterterrorism Center. They are two of the most patriotic people I have ever known.

That year, the recipient for both the Commando Hall of Honor Award and the Bull Simons Award was Chief Warrant Officer Fred Arooji (Ret.). As a Special Operations aviator, he was an unconventional warfare professional who pioneered numerous tactics, techniques, and procedures that are still in use on the battlefield. The doctrine he devised, tested, and authored for night vision goggle operations and intelligence, surveillance, and reconnaissance aircraft is the basis upon which all modern Special Operation aviators operate.

I was in awe of how each of these incredibly brilliant warriors had made a difference to our Special Operations Command.

The event was memorable and filled with incredible military leaders and heroes. We took pictures with many of the award recipients. I also had the pleasure of again meeting and speaking with Sergeant Major Billy Waugh. The entire evening was truly an honor.

On April 16, 2017, General Tony Thomas, commander of SOCOM invited me, Deborah, Anthony, and Nancy Weiss, to join him and his wife, Barb at the 30th Anniversary Dinner of SOCOM. We were invited, as well, to the VIP room, where we enjoyed conversations with Tony, Barb, General Joe Dunford, head of the Joint Chiefs of Staff, General Doug Brown, former head of SOCOM, and Major General Marcus Hicks, chief of staff of SOCOM, among others.

General Dunford spoke highly of General Jim Mattis, secretary of defense, as well as Rex Tillerson, secretary of state and former CEO of ExxonMobil. These incredible leaders build excellent teams to defend and protect our country.

The evening was most enjoyable, and it was quite exciting to speak with so many influential people.

On April 18, 2018, Deborah and I and Anthony and Nancy Weiss were again honored to be invited to join this esteemed group of national heroes for the USSOCOM Awards Dinner. We entered the Tampa Convention Center and were promptly directed to the VIP room. Inside were the who's who of incredible past SOCOM leaders such as retired Admiral Eric Olson (Ret.) and General Doug Brown (Ret.), and the current head of SOCOM, General Tony Thomas. In addition, I was honored to meet the head of the Joint Chiefs of Staff once again, General Joseph Dunford. General Dunford was approachable and graciously introduced us to his support staff. I handed him one of my STAR coins and thanked him for his dedication to this country.

The event started with my friend, Dick Crippen, former sports director of our local ABC and NBC networks, and currently a senior advisor with the Tampa Bay Rays baseball team, as the master of ceremonies. The SOCOM Joint Color Guard presented the colors followed by the national anthem and the flag folding ceremony.

General Thomas gave a warm welcome and introduced the keynote speaker for the evening, General Doug Brown (Ret.). The room was filled with over 500 attendees. The dinner was delicious, and the speakers were excellent.

That year's recipient of the most prestigious Bull Simons Award was US Army Sergeant Major Dennis Wolfe (Ret.). His remarkable five-decade career—in and out of uniform—pioneering explosive ordinance and disposal tactics for Special Operations was the basis for the award. His expertise established a world class program to counter weapons of mass destruction becoming the standard for the United States government and our international partners. As mentioned earlier, this lifetime achievement award recognizes recipients who embody the true spirit, values, and skills of a Special

Operations warrior.

Deborah and I had the most memorable time and were honored to be invited to such a prestigious event. What a great evening!

The 32nd SOCOM Awards Dinner was held on April 18, 2019 at the Florida Aquarium in Tampa. Prior to the event, a letter arrived at my home:

> *The Commander, United States Special Operations Command, cordially invites you and a guest to attend the 32nd Anniversary Awards Ceremony on 18 April 2019 at the Florida Aquarium.*
>
> *The Commander will recognize a number of recipients for the following awards:*
>
> *Bull Simons recognizes recipients who embody the true spirit, values, and skills of a Special Operations warrior.*
>
> *Lambertsen is awarded for recipients whose audacity, insight, and ingenuity embody innovation as an enduring operational skill and hallmark of the SOF mindset and culture.*
>
> *Excalibur is awarded for leadership, courage, integrity, and gallantry during military operations or training.*
>
> *SOCOM Colors is awarded for extraordinary leadership and sacrifice of SOF.*
>
> *Service Member of the Year is awarded to an enlisted member of USSOCOM who has demonstrated exceptional performance and superior leadership in his/her primary duty.*

At the event, there were approximately 200 attendees, mostly from SOCOM around the world, and a dozen or so civilians. I brought my friend, Nick Zambito, as my guest. He had served for four years during WWII. The event started at 6:00 p.m. with a light social cocktail hour, following by the program and dinner.

At 8:30 p.m., General Richard Clarke, head of SOCOM, introduced the award recipients and, I was delighted to hear, recognized our STAR program, naming the founders, Anthony Weiss and myself. We were quite honored. The event officially concluded at 10:00 p.m., but still accommodated people who wished to socialize with one another.

I spoke to General Mark Hicks, who was the former chief of staff for SOCOM and had since moved to AFRICOM Special Operations. He said his family was doing well and mentioned that he kept the conductor's hat I had given him in a special place in his home in Stuttgart, Germany. I appreciated hearing how much he treasured it and enjoyed catching up with him.

This was the night that Anthony and I were introduced to Lieutenant General Bryan Fenton, the deputy commanding general of the US Indo-Pacific Command (INDOPACOM). Coincidentally, a year prior, Jay Wilton and Ed Kobel, two of our STAR civilians, had gone to Honolulu, Hawaii on vacation. They wanted to bring our program to the special operators in the Indo-Pacific Command and so, they had met with General Fenton. They set up a dinner and described and carried out our STAR model at the Four Seasons Hotel in Hawaii for twelve of the operators. Anthony and I were astounded that General Fenton was now here in Tampa and that our STAR program had made it all the way to the Pacific. What a connection! Our STAR program was now in two states! Clearly our civilian members were so moved that they carried our mission in their hearts and acted upon it. General Fenton had discovered Tampa's STAR program in Hawaii.

MAY 23, 2012: SPECIAL OPERATIONS FORCES INDUSTRY CONFERENCE (SOFIC)

Each year a symposium called the Special Operations Forces Industry Conference (SOFIC) is held in Tampa followed by an awards dinner sponsored by SOCOM. During this event, the Tampa Convention

Center is turned into a defense contractors' exhibition hall, displaying all the latest armaments, technology, and communications equipment from all over the world. This is like a James Bond gadget show.

The conference was an eye-opener for me because I realized that America not only has the most brilliant military in the world but also leads in military technology. Each year during the symposium there are break-out sessions along with demonstrations of the new technology. The conference is followed by a gala dinner. Every two years all the special operators from our Allied Coalition come and participate in the event.

This year Deborah and I were invited by Admiral Bill McRaven to be his guests for the star-studded Special Operations Awards Dinner. We were honored to take pictures with special operators from South America, Europe, Asia, and Australia. Attending the Gala were Brigadier General Arnie Skjaerpe (head of the Coalition in 2009), and his lovely wife, Unni; the entire leadership of the Israeli Special Operations; head of the Coalition for Central Command, Rear Admiral Mats Fogelmark of Sweden. By the way, this Coalition for Central Command was formed by President George W. Bush after 9/11 to coordinate a concerted effort to prevent terrorism around the world. Over sixty countries have representatives in Tampa. I was introduced to the Coalition in 2009 by General John Allen and have been supporting the cause ever since.

During the dinner, Colonel Joseph Miller, a close friend and Jesuit High School classmate, introduced me to the Israeli contingent. Joe works at SOCOM and has a special relationship with the Israelis. He was kind enough to make the formal introductions. The Israeli contingent included Colonel Eyal Rozen, Brigadier General Etay Virob, Brigadier General Boaz Hershkovitz, Major General Shai Avital, and Major General Mickey Edelstein.

The evening was held at the Marriott Waterside in downtown Tampa and included more than 500 attendees. Admiral Bill McRaven was the emcee for the evening and gave a tremendous speech about how important it is to have the Special Operations Coalition partners. Incidentally, shortly after the event, SOCOM began embedding allied countries into their staff in Tampa.

The guest speaker was Secretary of State Hillary Clinton. She gave a rousing speech about how important Special Operations is to the stability of the world. She also said that we lead the world in technology and that she wanted to make sure we have the funding to keep it that way.

After the event, Deborah and I were invited to take pictures with the recipient of the Special Operations Medal and the Bull Simons Award. I mentioned to Deborah that we should invite the Israeli Special Operations Contingent over for breakfast the next morning. That night she put me in charge of hunting down lox and cream cheese, fresh fruit, and orange juice at an all-night grocery store while she laid out platters, plates, and silverware. The next morning, I would be doing a run for fresh bagels.

They arrived at our home at 8:00 a.m. and we made sure to invite our Congregation Schaarai Zedek Rabbi Richard Birnholtz as well as General Joe Miller. We all sat around the table like one big family, breaking bread, and sharing stories of our children, our relations with Israel, and international perspectives. After breakfast, we all took pictures in the Train Room.

Deborah and I were pleased to have been able to host the Israeli leadership and make them feel at home. Since then, we have stayed in touch with these very special Israeli officers, and we continue to be supportive of Israel in every way we can.

APRIL 26, 2016: SPECIAL OPERATIONS FORCES INDUSTRY CONFERENCE (SOFIC)

The Operations Forces Industry Conference is an annual event and exhibition. It provides an opportunity for industry professionals to network, see the newest innovations in the field, and hear speakers from SOCOM. Hundreds of our largest defense contractors display cutting-edge armaments for land, sea, and air.

I attended the last several years, but this year, I noticed a strong influence of autonomous weapon systems in terms of a variety of drones. Some of the defense contractors present were from Israeli Military Industries (IMI) including General Zvi Fox (Ret.) and Colonel Reserve Itsik Elimelech (Ret.) current president, IMI Services USA. The entire event was amazing, and I really enjoyed seeing the exciting new technology available to our military. General Zvi Fox passed away a few years later. He was a true friend and a great Israeli patriot. When our family traveled to Israel we visited and had dinner with him, a very kind and delightful man. He will be missed by all his comrades.

FEBRUARY 21–23, 2017: GLOBAL SPECIAL OPERATIONS FORCES (SOF) SYMPOSIUM

The popularity and effectiveness of the STAR program continues to build relationships, and so it is not unusual that Anthony Weiss and I were invited to a multitude of events. Stuart Bradin, president and CEO of the Global SOF Foundation, invited us to participate in the Global Special Operations Forces Symposium in Innisbrook, Florida.

The SOF Symposium focuses on networking special operators throughout the world. This foundation helps transition special operators from military careers to civilian or defense contracting careers.

The STAR (SOF Transition Assistance Resource) has a similar purpose. We gather business executives and entrepreneurs within our community who then become mentors to our soon-to-be retiring special operators.

Attendees of the symposium came from all over the world. I was able to speak with Major General Mark Clark, president of Resolute Solutions Consulting and former chief of staff of SOCOM; Admiral Eric Olson, former commander of SOCOM; General Valter Virdi, Italian three-star general with SOCOM; and Admiral Kurt Tidd, four-star admiral and head of US Southern Command (SOUTHCOM).

I had previously met Admiral Tidd in 2011 when I and several civic leaders experienced a tailhook landing on the aircraft carrier, USS *Dwight D. Eisenhower*. Once aboard, our group had been personally greeted by Admiral Tidd. We had dinner on the carrier in the admiral's private quarters and afterward watched aircraft sorties taking off and landing throughout the night.

JANUARY 29, 2019: SOCOM MEDAL OF HONOR RECOGNITION DINNER

General Tony Thomas, head of SOCOM, wanted to host a special dinner for living and deceased Medal of Honor recipient operators in Tampa. He contacted me and said that SOCOM did not have a large budget but wanted the affair to be first class. I put together a list of our local business leaders and STAR civilians and asked them help underwrite the event at Palma Ceia Golf and Country Club (PCGCC). Every civilian was honored to donate and show support for these great American heroes. The event began at 6:00 p.m. for a social hour on the back deck of the club overlooking the golf course and watching the sunset.

At 6:30 p.m. the crowd headed into the beautiful ballroom for the presentation of the colors and national anthem. Each donor was seated at different tables giving them an opportunity to meet and get to know the inductees and their families. The event proceeded with the invocation and flag folding ceremony, followed by a very nice introduction by General Thomas, the commander and host for the event. The dinner was first class—a beautiful beef filet along with fine accompaniments. Dinner was followed by a movie describing the many accomplishments and assets of Special Operations Command.

Our guest speaker was retired four-star US Navy Admiral Eric Olson, who gave thirty-eight years of military service. He served in Special Operations units throughout his career, was engaged in contingency operations, and commanded at every level. His military career culminated as the head of SOCOM, where he was responsible for the mission readiness and deployment of all Navy, Army, Air Force, and Marine Corps Special Operations Forces. In this capacity, he led over 60,000 people and managed an annual budget of over ten billion dollars. His duties involved much interagency and international collaboration.

Admiral Olson gave a patriotic speech and described the many values that make our special operators so unique. For example, their mental toughness, dedication, education, reasoning capacity, training, and pride. He mentioned the SOCOM ethos, that humans are more important than hardware and you cannot mass produce special operators. After Admiral Olson spoke, each of the surviving seven Special Operations Medal of Honor recipients, as well as the families of those who were deceased, received a plaque to be placed in the hallways of SOCOM.

The list of Medal of Honor Commando Hall of Honor Inductees that night were:

Major General William Donovan, US Army
Major General Merritt Edson, US Marine Corps
Command Sergeant Major Bennie Adkins, US Army
Boatswain's Mate First Class James Williams, US Navy
Sergeant Gordon Yntema, US Army
Sergeant First Class Eugene Ashley, US Army
Master Sergeant Roy Benavidez, US Army
Colonel Williams Jones, US Air Force
Colonel Robert Howard, US Army
Sergeant John Levitow, US Air Force

Sergeant First Class Mervin Morris, US Army
Sergeant Gary Beikirch, US Army
Command Sergeant Major Gary Littrell, US Army
Captain Gary Rose, US Army
Master Sergeant Gary Gordon, US Army
Sergeant First Class Randall Shughart, US Army
Sergeant John Chapman, US Air Force
Staff Sergeant Robert Miller, US Army
Staff Sergeant Ronald Shurer, US Army
Special Operations Combat Medic Edward Byers, US Navy

The presentation was so emotional that everyone was teary-eyed at the description of why each of the inductees had earned the Medal of Honor. It was so patriotic to hear the brave acts that these men did to make a difference in saving lives or defeating the enemy. It was a beautiful gesture that each of the civilian donors received a Medal of Honor book signed by the surviving inductees who were present that evening. The event was very moving and particularly meaningful.

On February 2, 2019, I received this letter from General Thomas:

Dear Mark and Deborah,

On behalf of the men and women of the US Special Operations Command, I would like to personally thank you for your generous donation in support of our Medal of Honor Hall Induction.

Our SOCOM enterprise continues to face a complex and growing threat which our Soldiers, Sailors, Marines, and Airmen aggressively pursue on a daily basis. Taking time to recognize the heroism and honor displayed on the battlefield is not only important to the service members, but their families and the SOCOM community. We are proud of the work they do, and I am grateful for your continued support and interest in the United States Special Operations

Command and our mission.
Sincerely,
Raymond A. Thomas III
General, US Army
Commander

Thanks for all you do for TEAM SOCOM!! T₂

OCTOBER 25, 2019: MEDAL OF HONOR PATRIOT AWARD DINNER–ALL SERVICES

I was asked by Bobby Newman, local businessman, friend, and big supporter of our military, if I would sponsor a table for an important event, the Medal of Honor Patriot Award Dinner. The J. C. Newman Cigar Co. is American's oldest family-owned cigar manufacturer and still operates to this day in Ybor City, Florida. I was honored to be able to sponsor the table along with other STAR civilians including Anthony and Nancy Weiss, Doug and Maureen Cohn, Michael and Janet Kass, and David and Ann Rosenbach.

The event was held at the Marriott Hotel Water Street in Tampa. Over 950 attendees were honored to meet forty-seven of the seventy surviving Medal of Honor recipients. The Medal of Honor was established by Congress and signed into law by President Abraham Lincoln as the highest award for valor in action against an enemy force which can be bestowed upon an individual serving in the armed services of the United States. The medal is presented to its recipient by the president of the United States in the name of Congress. Since its inception in 1861, 3,505 individuals have been presented with the honor. Nineteen have received it twice.

The Medal of Honor Society was signed into legislation by Dwight D. Eisenhower in 1958 and is one of the most exclusive organizations in the United States. No amount of money, power, or influence can buy one's rite of passage into this elite circle, and unlike most any other organization, its members hope there will be no more inductees. Above all, the recipients share a love for the United States of America and carry the distinct privilege of wearing the Medal of Honor.

The event started with a cocktail hour at 7:00 p.m.. We were fortunate to work our way into the VIP reception, where we met most of the honorees as well as the present and past leadership of SOCOM and CENTCOM. Deborah and I really enjoyed meeting and speaking to Catherine Herridge, the FOX network military and Capitol Hill reporter (currently with CBS) who has an excellent reputation for researching every given situation thoroughly and reporting the truth. General Tony Thomas mentioned to me that "she is one of the finest reporters in the press who reports the truth because she verifies the source and follows up with a complete dialogue of the event." Catherine was approachable and receptive to hearing our questions and she was delighted that we were followers of her reporting.

Also in the room was General Joe Votel, who had recently retired as head of CENTCOM. Deborah and I had last seen him at his CENTCOM residence for dinner about six months earlier. He mentioned that he was enjoying the retired life outside Minneapolis, Minnesota. Former chief of staff of CENTCOM, General Jay Hood (Ret.) and his wife, Lynne, were there conversing with all the honorees as well. Jay and Lynne had become great friends of ours, as they had settled in Tampa after retirement. I also greeted General Karl Horst (Ret.), president of the Medal of Honor Society, along with his lovely wife, Nancy. Joe, Jay, Karl, and frankly all those men and women serving our country, are true American heroes and patriots for their dedication to this great nation.

The dinner began around 8:00 p.m. with the emcee for the event, Courtney Robinson of the local CBS affiliate 10 Tampa Bay WTSP introducing each Medal of Honor recipient as they walked on stage. The presentation of the colors was done by the US Central Command Joint Services Color Guard.

Sonya Bryson-Kirksey gave a grand rendition of the national anthem (Sonya sings for the Tampa Bay Lightning ice hockey games). Following the invocation by one of the Medal of Honor recipients, Gary Beikirch, Florida Governor Ron DeSantis addressed the crowd. Governor DeSantis was a Navy Judge Advocate (JAG), recipient of medals including the Bronze Star Medal, Medal of Honor Society president, and chairman of the Medal of Honor Convention in Tampa.

The dinner was a surf and turf of lobster and filet mignon. Later, the presentation of awards took place, first with the Distinguished Citizen Award given to a well-deserving, Bobby Newman. Bobby, with his dedication to the Southeast Guide Dogs, has assisted in giving over 200 military veterans a friend for life. These dogs have become the eyes, ears, and mental friends of our retired military who have suffered physical and mental challenges protecting our great nation. I was so proud of Bobby and his long dedication to our military.

The next award was presented to Catherine Herridge for her honest reporting of our military and politicians. The Bob Hope for Entertainment Award was presented to George Strait, one of the most prolific country western musicians. The Patriot Award was presented to General Joseph Votel (Ret.), former head of both, CENTCOM and SOCOM (a rare occurrence). I was fortunate to meet Gary Sinise briefly for a picture and explain our STAR program to him, as well as talking with and describing STAR to Governor DeSantis.

The event was over the top with so many civic leaders and our military leaders present. Deborah and I felt fulfilled to be able to help sponsor such a worthwhile cause. We discovered that through the week, the Medal of Honor recipients had gone to numerous high schools and briefed the students and described their journeys, each unique and appreciated. They expressed the importance of this country and encouraged them to go out and make a difference, that with prudence, patience, and perseverance, each of them could make a difference. What a great feel-good evening surrounded by America's finest.

APRIL 4–6, 2023: PARAGUAYAN PRESIDENT AND FIRST LADY VISIT TAMPA

In early March, I was asked if I could set up a special reception and dinner for approximately thirty- five people at Palma Ceia Country Club. I promptly reached out to the club and discovered they were fully booked for the evening of April 4 except for the Windsor Room, one of our favorites.

The following week, Deborah and I received an invitation to honor and welcome to Tampa President Mario Abdo Benitez of Paraguay and First Lady Silvana Lopez Moreira. General Bryan Fenton, head of Special Operations Command (SOCOM), hosted this very special evening, and we were very honored to attend.

As club member and unofficial liaison, I met with SOCOM protocol representatives to finalize the details for the evening including specifics on the venue, parking, and security matters, and to make sure all the requirements for a visiting head of state would be satisfied.

On April 4, 2023, Deborah and I arrived early at the club to make sure everything was in place. The SOCOM security, the Paraguayan security, and the United States Secret Service were all present and on task to assure the safety and protection of our international guests. At 6:00 p.m. everyone began to arrive: the Paraguayan family with their entourage, General Bryan Fenton and his lovely wife, Dawn, and the rest of the invited guests. We began the evening with cocktails and appetizers along the back patio overlooking the beautiful golf course. Bryan and Dawn introduced us to the Paraguayan leadership and their entourage, including defense minister, public relations team, Paraguayan ambassador to the United States, and numerous other representatives.

After forty-five minutes or so, we were called into the Windsor

Room for the private dinner. The room was filled with round tables and a podium. There were place cards at every seat. That is when I noticed President Benetiz would be flanked by me on his left and General Fenton on his right. I was surprised to have been invited in the first place, but then to be seated at the head table next to the president was unbelievable. Deborah was seated next to Maurizio, the president's son, then Dawn Fenton, and the first lady. Everyone was engaged in conversation. Since the president had been educated in the United States at Teikyo Post University in Waterbury, Connecticut, he spoke excellent English and was very familiar with our culture. President Benitez mentioned that he had been in talks with China about changing Paraguay's currency to the yuan and incorporating the Wuhan communication system into the country to encourage growth. Paraguay is surrounded by Argentina, Bolivia, and Brazil, all of which have aligned themselves with China. The president expressed his allegiance to the United States and to Taiwan. I was astounded hearing this, as I had not realized that China had taken their Belt and Road Initiative (a global infrastructure development strategy to invest in countries) to the Southern Hemisphere.

Just as dinner was about to be served, General Fenton went to the podium to welcome everyone to our community. He gave a rousing speech complementing the Paraguayan leadership and expressed our support of Paraguay. Then he invited me to the podium to say a few words. Stunned and honored, I came forward, welcomed them, and offered our Tampa hospitality to our new friends.

We had a delicious dinner and amazing conversation. The evening was quite extraordinary.

The following day I was asked if I could set up another dinner for that Friday night. I immediately reached out to a close family friend, Richard Gonzmart, the owner of one of the oldest Spanish restaurants in America, the Columbia Restaurant. When I described the situation and that we would probably need a table for seventeen people for dinner and entertainment he responded that he would make available any table I want for the Friday night dinner and flamenco dance show. That day, I went over to the restaurant and selected the front table for the evening.

Since I had also learned of the president's fondness for cigars, I thought it a perfect opportunity for him to tour a cigar factory. Cigar making was once a major industry here and Tampa was considered the cigar capital of the world. I called Eric Newman of the J. C. Newman Cigar Company, the last of over 150 cigar factories in Tampa, and asked if he would be available that evening before dinner to give a tour of the factory. Since it was only a few minutes from the Columbia Restaurant I thought we could work it all in and make the evening amazing. Eric and his wife, Lyris, were all set for us and the Paraguayan entourage. We planned on a 7:00 p.m. tour, an 8:30 p.m. dinner, and a flamenco dance show at 9:45 p.m.

In a last-minute change, the Paraguayan protocol called General Fenton's office and said the president was tired after his visit to the military bases in the Florida panhandle and wanted to meet up with us directly at the restaurant. General Fenton then contacted me and said that he and Dawn would still be joining Deborah and me at the cigar factory for the tour. When the four of us arrived, Eric and Lyris Newman met us at the factory entrance and proceeded to give us a very special tour. They made sure that several workers stayed late to demonstrate how they hand rolled their finest cigars and how the one-hundred-year-old machines still produced their standard cigars.

When we went down to the cellar of the factory, Eric mentioned that they had Paraguayan tobacco on the premises, and in honor of the president's visit, they had hand rolled a box of cigars for him. I was upset that the president was going to miss this opportunity, so I called the Paraguayan protocol and asked for them to at least drop by the factory on the way to the dinner at the Columbia since it was only a few minutes away. They agreed, and the entire Paraguayan team arrived at 8:45 p.m. with a Secret Service escort of over six cars. The Newmans graciously greeted the president and first lady and invited them into the cigar factory. We were all surprised that in spite of the lateness of the hour, they all wanted the full tour. Of course, the tour included a demonstration of the hand-rolled and machine-rolled cigars, followed by Eric presenting the president with a box of Paraguayan tobacco hand rolled in Ybor City in Tampa.

Though we were running late, everyone was happy. At 9:30 p.m. I received a call from the Columbia Restaurant to let me know that the show was about to begin in fifteen minutes. Immediately, I announced to everyone that we needed to head over to the restaurant right away so we could make the dinner and show. The entire SOCOM and Paraguayan entourages escorted by the Secret Service left for the Columbia Restaurant. Eric, Lyris, Deborah, and I followed. We all made it just in time to sit, place our dinner order, and watch the show. The flamenco dancers were fabulous, and the Paraguayans sang along with some of the Latin songs they knew. Even the president and the first lady got up and danced next to our table when the song "Volare" was played.

After dinner, I presented President Benitez with a box of the Newman's newest cigar, the American Cigar, as a gift to remember our city. It was a perfect ending to a welcome visit to Tampa with an evening of fine food and entertainment. Deborah and I were proud to be able to show our city to an international head of state and his family. And I was honored to be referred to as "the Tampa ambassador" by General and Dawn Fenton.

General Joseph Votel, me, and General John Mulholland

Colonel Eyal Rozen, Brigadier General Etay Virob, Brigadier General Boaz Hershkovitz, Deborah, Rabbi Richard Birnholtz, Major General Mickey Edelstein, General Joseph Miller (US SOCOM), and Major General Shai Avital

SOCOM demonstration

SOCOM demonstration

With General Joseph Dunford, chairman of the Joint Chiefs of Staff

Me and Deborah with General Joseph Votel and his wife Michele

General Bryan Fenton and his wife Dawn, President's son Maurizio, President Benetez, First Lady Silvana Lopez Moreira, me, and Deborah at Palma Ceia GCC

Dawn and General Bryan Fenton, Deborah, First Lady and President Benitez, Eric Newman and his wife Lyris at Newman Cigar Factory

CHAPTER 11

Sports, Antique Firearms, and Socializing with our Military Leaders

SEPTEMBER 6, 2009: GENERAL PETRAEUS AT THE TAMPA BAY RAYS GAME

Dick Crippen, president of the Tampa Bay Rays, invited General David Petraeus to throw the first pitch for the Rays vs. Tigers game. Dave brought Holly, and invited Deborah and me, as well as Tim and Anje Bogott. The Bogotts own one of the largest hotels on the west coast of Florida, the TradeWinds Island Resorts on St. Petersburg Beach. We were all guests of the Tampa Bay Rays and accordingly, we were in the owner's box, complete with air conditioning, television screens, food, drink, and desserts. We were honored to be there, and witnessed Dave throw a beautiful pitch to start our own Tampa Bay Rays major league baseball game. We enjoyed the company as well. Baseball is a great opportunity to socialize in between plays. Deborah spent a lot of time talking with Holly and Anje while the guys got to know each other better as well. The Tigers ended up winning the game 5–3 but Dave was the real winner, throwing a terrific pitch. We had a wonderful time.

MAY 26, 2012: GUN RANGE WITH AUSTRALIAN ANDREW "BOOMER" SMITH

Dr. Andrew "Boomer" Smith was a brigadier general in the Australian Army. He was kind enough to take a couple of the Coalition country representatives and me to the indoor gun range in St. Petersburg, Florida to demonstrate guns and ammunition from the 1700s to the present day. This was an amazing opportunity to shoot the guns, see how they operate, and learn how they became more accurate and efficient over time.

We started with a musket from the 1700s called the "Brown Bess" flintlock used by the British forces. The gun was propelled by black powder and shot a .695-caliber round ball. It did not have much of a kick and was pretty accurate. To load the black powder, you had to bite off the paper, pour the powder into the chamber, and use a cylinder to push the powder deep into the chamber. The problem in the day was that if it got wet, the black powder would not ignite.

The next gun was the Enfield Pattern 1853 musket. It used a .575-caliber minié ball, which was a cone-shaped cylinder with grooves on it for aerodynamic stability. It shot more accurately than the earlier musket.

Next, we shot the French Chassepot transitional breechloading rifle from the 1860s. The bullet was a very sophisticated cylindrical type with no cross markings. It was propelled by a charge of eighty-six grains of gunpowder. This gun had more of a kick than the previous two and did not require putting gunpowder into the chamber.

We then shot a Prussian Mauser Model 1871 single shot and Model 81/84 repeating bolt-action rifle. It was used until the 1880s, when rifles with smokeless powder replaced it. The Mauser was propelled by a charge of seventy-seven grains of gunpowder and the muzzle velocity was almost twice as fast as the earlier guns. The bullet was cylindrical but had three rings around it. This gun had a big kick when I shot it and was not too accurate. Plus, you had to cock the rifle each time you shot the gun.

The next gun was the Martini-Henry, which was a carbine short version of the first purpose-designed breechloader. It was adopted for general service with the British Forces and used from the late 1860s to 1890. It used a grooveless bullet and hence it was externally lubricated.

The final gun was a German 7.92 mm Mauser Rifle used from the late 1890s to 1950. The gun shot a fully jacketed bullet with a weight of 200 grams. The gun was smooth to shoot with little kick.

The entire demonstration was amazing because I was able to shoot a gun from each of those periods. It was incredible to get a feel for the accuracy and kick from each of the guns. This was a day I will always remember, and this helped increase my support of the new technology in weaponry.

NOVEMBER 11, 2016: A GOLF OUTING LIKE NO OTHER

What an experience! I played eighteen holes of golf on a cool autumn Friday with Major General George Smith, head of J5 (Planning), Major General Dean Milner of Canada, and Michael Reagor, J CIV, deputy assistant director of J5 at CENTCOM. We played the south course at MacDill Air Force Base. As anyone who has ever played this delightful sport knows, golf lends itself toward conversation.

During our round, Dean came up with a fun drinking game for us. Whenever someone shot a birdie he pulled out a flask and we would all take a shot of Woodford Reserve Bourbon. He was cracking us all up the entire time.

George was taking it all in and laughing along with us all but was mostly quite serious about his golf game. He is one of the finest military golfers I have ever played. He was either even or one over for the day. I think his handicap was three or four.

Michael was gracious in expressing his appreciation for all the work I had done for the military. He was very thankful in general but particularly grateful that as a member, I had been able to facilitate over 200 people in the ballroom at Palma Ceia Golf and Country Club (PCGCC) for the Annual J5 Christmas Party.

This was a fun-filled solid day with wonderful men who I am proud to call friends.

MARCH 5, 2017: A GOLF OUTING AT LIKE NO OTHER ... AGAIN!

I spent an enjoyable day golfing at Palma Ceia Golf and Country Club with Major General Dean Milner of Canada, his son, Derek Milner, and Brigadier General Paul Rutherford of Canada.

Dean is vice head of J5 (Planning) for CENTCOM. Derek had just enlisted in the Royal Military College of Canada. Paul was the director of general information management operations, which handles the cyber unit for the National Defense of Canada.

The Canadians really appreciate our Florida climate. At the time, Canada was at negative six degrees. As always, eighteen holes of golf lends itself to plenty of conversation. These included several personal and military conversations. Dean said that within the last twenty-four hours over twenty-five missions had attacked ISIS. He said, "We're doing a lot more now."

Paul said that cyberattacks from Iran, China, and Russia are major concerns to the western world. He is part of the cyber unit working with US Cyber Command. Derek was excited about the commencement of training school but acknowledged that he anticipated challenges because of the nature of military demands and expectations.

It was a great day spent with friends and who offer interesting insights into the challenges our military members face.

MARCH 21, 2018: PLAYING WITH THE NEW YORK YANKEES

Captain Jeff Cathey (Ret.) is a military liaison with Bank of America, which sponsors the New York Yankees when they come to Tampa. Jeff invited Admiral Joe Maguire (Ret.) and me to take two spots at the Yankees Training Facility and enjoy instruction, batting practice, and fielding balls with some of the Yankees squad.

I had known Joe previously, as he was a retired Navy SEAL who had dedicated his time in Tampa on the board of the Special Operations Warrior Foundation. This fantastic organization takes care of the education for the families of special operators who died in combat or Special Operations Command. Deborah and I also included Joe and his lovely wife, Cathy, for a Games and Trains Party.

The Yankees manager, Aaron Boone, gave us a nice briefing on the game of baseball. It has become so specialized—they take the pulse of their players; they work with their particular diets, athletic physical properties, and endurance; and then create a personal plan for each player designed to help them reach peak performance for every game. Manager Boone gave us some hitting and fielding instruction, and the pitching coach gave us some pitching instructions and allowed us to pitch to a catcher ninety feet away.

I had grown up as a catcher in Little League (elementary school age) and Senior League (junior high school age) and had a few skills to bring to the table. It happened that while in Senior League, I was catcher and my pitcher was Major League Hall of Famer, Wade Boggs. As you probably know, Wade went on to play for the Boston Red Sox and later the New York Yankees, where he won the World Series. He concluded his career by coming back home to Tampa and playing with the Tampa Bay Rays. Wade has been a lifelong friend and often told me I was his best catcher.

Joe and I went to each of the hitting, pitching, and fielding positions and enjoyed the day together. We had a great time reminiscing about our past days in Little League and how we had changed physically.

Six months later, Joe would go on to become director of National Intelligence and would testify on television about a whistleblower who had complained about comments the president had made to the Ukrainian leader.

Joe Maguire is a tremendous person and a true American hero, having given over forty years of dedication to this great country.

JANUARY 5, 2019: WESTERN DANCE NIGHT AT US CENTRAL COMMAND

Deborah and I were invited to a Country Western Dance Night by the commander of CENTCOM, General Joe Votel and his wife, Michele. We dressed up in our finest western wear, which we already had from a 2015 adventure where we herded 300 cattle for five days from the California border to Reno, Nevada. That had been an extraordinary experience, to say the least.

The charming western theme event was held at the Davis Conference Center at MacDill AFB, where the inside decor was westernized (without the cattle). There were about 150 attendees. The Votels were decked out in their western attire as well. It was a lot of fun and we thoroughly enjoyed CENTCOM families and civilian business leaders coming together in style. The Votels really know how to party!

On the gun range with antique rifles

With Vice Admiral Joe Maguire at a NY Yankees baseball practice

CHAPTER 12

Department of Defense Warrior Games

JUNE 22–30, 2019: A WEEK OF WARRIOR GAMES

The US Special Operations Command (SOCOM) hosted the 2019 Department of Defense (DOD) Warrior Games in Tampa. Approximately 300 wounded, ill, and injured service members and veterans participated in the competition. The athletes represented the United States Army, Marine Corps, Navy, Air Force, and Special Operations Command. Athletes from the UK armed forces, Australian Defense Force, Canadian armed forces, and armed forces from the Netherlands and Denmark, also competed.

Teams included active-duty service members and veterans with upper-body, lower-body, and spinal cord injuries, traumatic brain injuries, visual impairment, serious illnesses, and post-traumatic stress disorder. They went head-to-head in eleven sports including archery, cycling, shooting, wheelchair volleyball, swimming, track and field, wheelchair basketball, and for the first time in Warrior Games history, indoor rowing, powerlifting, and time-trial cycling.

The Warrior Games were established in 2010 as a way to enhance the recovery and rehabilitation of wounded, ill, and injured service members and expose them to adaptive sports. The games encourage them to stay physically active when they return to their local communities and inspire and promote opportunities for growth and achievement. Families are a significant part of an athlete's recovery and this year promised to have the most robust family program to date.

The opening ceremony on June 22, 2019, was very touching. Deborah and my mother, Barbara Rosenthal, joined me along with Nancy and Anthony Weiss and a nice crowd of over 15,000 Tampa Bay patrons to welcome our warriors. Jon Stewart, American comedian, actor, and commentator was the emcee and performed well to set the stage for the event. Each of the athletes walked or wheeled themselves on stage with their respective country's flag. After, the torch was lit by the mayor of Tampa, Jane Castor, and the commander of Special Operations, General Richard Clarke, they kicked off the competition.

On Sunday, the time trials for the biking took place on Bayshore Boulevard in Tampa. The distance was 4.2 miles with competitors in racing bikes, three-wheel racers, and tandem bikes. Every rider, even with their disabilities, was in top form. On the tandem bikes, the person in the rear was either blind or partially blind. It was such an emotional event to watch. Over 500 local Tampa Bay residents were there to hail the participants at the finish line. In the afternoon I went out to the University of South Florida and watched the track and field events.

One participant, 1st Sergeant Michael Landry from Camp Pendelton Wounded Warrior West, representing the Marines, won four gold medals and one silver. These included the 100-yard, 200-yard, 400-yard, 4 x100-yard, shot putt, and discus. After that was the finals of the tennis. In particular, watching the doubles matches played in wheelchairs was fascinating. There were over 1,000 local attendees to witness these true patriots competing again.

On Monday, I went over to the Tampa Convention Center to watch archery, weightlifting, and basketball. The most amazing was the one-armed archer who pulled back the bow with his teeth. He shot two bullseyes (10 on the target) and one 9 (next ring after the bullseye) while I was watching him. What a spirit he had!

Later, my friend, Nick Zambito, and I watched the weightlifting and the basketball competition. I was emotionally taken when the weightlifter from Great Britain with no legs participated and lifted over 200 pounds. The crowd went wild when he lifted the weights over his head. Also touching was the Marine, Durrell Jones, who lifted 302 lbs. over his head. The basketball was also very interesting as the participants had incredible dexterity as they pushed their wheelchairs and bounced and shot the balls.

On Tuesday, we went back to the convention center to watch the wheelchair basketball and the wheelchair rugby. All of the competitors were so enthusiastic about representing their respective services. The crowd really appreciated all the athletes and clapped for both teams as they competed.

On Wednesday, I went back to watch basketball and more rugby and a bit of the stationary rowing machines. One of the winners in the event had one arm and no legs. He was another amazing athlete.

On Friday, we did not go to the competition but later that night enjoyed celebrating Canada National Day at the Amalie Arena. Over 1,000 friends of Canada were present along with some of the athletes participating in the Warrior Games. We met some of the athletes that were going to perform on Saturday in the swimming events, so we decided we would go and support our Canadian friends. I had a nice talk with the chief of staff of SOCOM, Major General James Linder, along with his lovely wife, Laurie, and their friends. It was a nice celebration and included a video and a band playing popular songs. Plenty of food and moose milk was served to all the guests.

On Saturday, Nick and I went to watch the swimming at the Long Aquatic Center in Clearwater. We had just arrived to see one of the Canadian women that we had met the night before swimming in the finals of the 100. She ended up winning the event along with two others. She even came up to Nick and me and gave us both a hug after her victory.

We then watched some of the more severe wounded warriors participating in the event. One of the swimmers had just one arm and no legs and showed what a determined patriot he was as he completed the meet. I was teary-eyed watching as each of these handicapped participants gave their all to finish the race. These military stars were truly incredible. I happened to see General Tony and Barb Thomas and the new commander General Richard Clarke, there to give their support. I was honored to witness this great event.

On Sunday, I was invited to sit in the Bank of America box at Amalie Arena, thanks to Captain Jeff Cathey, the head of military accounts for Bank of America. I brought as my guest, Nick Zambito, a WWII veteran, and we watched the closing ceremonies together. It was highly emotional as each of the branches of the military and the guest countries gave awards to the teams and the most dedicated and enthusiastic member of the team. After the awards were given, Commander Clay Pendergrass gave an incredible speech about each of these wounded warriors that have picked themselves up and are competing again in the Game of Life. The closing was passing the torch to San Antonio, Texas for the next Warriors Game and putting out the flame.

SEPTEMBER 15, 2019: SPEAKING ABOUT THE WARRIOR GAMES

My friend, Nick Zambito, along with Pastor Steven Kaufman of Good Shepherd Church, asked me to speak to their congregation about my history with the military, the STAR program, and the Warrior Games recently held in Tampa. I had prepared for the occasion by putting together a slideshow of pictures and video to describe the history of my involvement with the military and the Warrior Games.

I talked about the various social functions introducing the military leaders to the Tampa community as well as bringing the Tampa community to the military for briefings at MacDill AFB. I also discussed some of my military trips where I'd been able to learn more about our armed forces as well as assist in helping and promoting our incredible military.

Then I proceeded to show the highlights of the Warrior Games from the opening ceremonies to numerous athletic events to the closing ceremonies. Fortunately, in the crowd was Colonel Cary Harbaugh (Ret.), who was in charge of the Warrior Games. He added to my presentation by telling us all about how the finances worked and about the audience participation in Tampa.

My photos showed some of the most outstanding athletes and the competition. The crowd was very enthusiastic about learning what a great event this was for the city of Tampa. I felt good about educating the citizens of our city about how incredible our military is and sharing my passion with them.

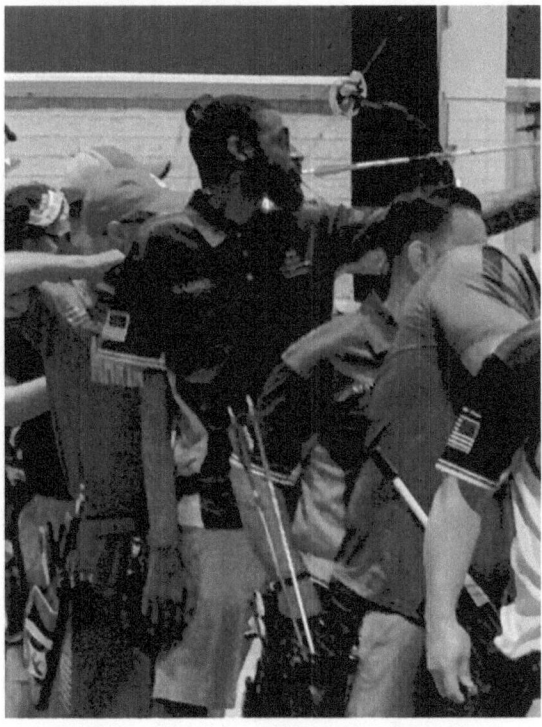

Member of the Wounded Warrior program shooting a bow and arrow with one arm

The wounded service member's impressive target

CHAPTER 13

Visit Aboard USS *Dwight D. Eisenhower* Aircraft Carrier

JANUARY 23–24, 2009: TRIP TO USS *EISENHOWER* AIRCRAFT CARRIER

As a public relations promotion, the US Navy invited ten business leaders to visit the nuclear-powered USS *Dwight D. Eisenhower* (CVN-69) for a 24-hour opportunity to witness the operation of one of the most highly technical Navy aircraft carriers. I was so fortunate to be part of the civilian group, which included retired Captain Jeff Cathey, Bank of America Senior Military Affairs executive who was one of the leading Navy pilots with over 1331 carrier landings, of which over 400 were at night, and Captain Jack Hanzlik, the director of public affairs for CENTCOM.

It might be helpful to explain that a captain in the Army, Air Force, and Marine Corps is the third officer rank; the captain in the Navy and Coast Guard is the sixth officer rank (one rank below admiral). Admiral is the Navy equivalent of generals in the other branches.

This ship was originally commissioned as simply the USS *Eisenhower*, without the "Dwight D." The full name was incorporated just prior to its commissioning in 1977. The first ship of its class, the USS *Nimitz*, does not include the full name, but the others of its class do. In practice, the ship is nicknamed the "Ike." The CVN-69 has an interesting etymology. "C" stands for *cruiser* since carriers were originally considered to be a type of cruiser, and often, early carriers were converted cruisers. The "V" is short for *volplane*, which means *glider* or *to glide* in French and denotes that it is heavier than air aircraft. "N" denotes *nuclear-powered*. The number simply means, the 69th carrier, starting with CV-1, the USS *Langley*, commissioned in 1922. The nuclear-powered craft is included in the count, rather than counting them separately from non-nuclear vessels.

The day before our passage on the aircraft to the carrier, Captain Jeff Cathey and I left Tampa for the three-hour drive to Naval Air Station (NAS) Jacksonville. We needed to arrive early to receive a briefing and directions related to our mission the following morning, promptly at 7:00 a.m. We arrived at NAS Jacksonville with our required long pants, jacket, and a change of clothes. It was colder than I had prepared for, but fortunately, Jeff had an extra flight jacket and offered it to me to wear. Clearly, the temperature at sea plus the wind factor on such a ship is rather severe in the heart of winter, even in Florida.

Captain Jack Scorby Jr., commanding officer of NAS Jacksonville, gave us a briefing in a large room on the base, gave us all the info about the risks involved, and provided us with an agenda for the twenty-four-hour visit. We were then given a flight helmet and an inflatable life preserver unit (LPU) with a chem light (chemical light stick), whistle, and fluorescent sea dye marker—in case of a water landing.

After the hour-long briefing, we all boarded a C-2A Greyhound Carrier Onboard Delivery (COD) plane. This is a twin-engine service plane used to ferry personnel, mail, supplies, and high priority cargo, such as replacement parts, from shore bases to aircraft carriers at sea. We boarded the plane, which had all twenty-six seats facing backward. The twin six-blade turboprop engines started up and off we went down the tarmac.

We flew straight east and then south for about forty-five minutes until we could finally see the *Eisenhower*. It was an incredible sight. Of course, I had seen photographs and videos, but that did little to prepare me for seeing this enormous ship in real life, especially approaching it from the air. It looked like a floating city with planes lined up on the deck. As huge as it was, it also felt too small to land on with the Greyhound. I had faith in the pilot and the ship's crew, but that didn't come close to erasing all the trepidation I felt as we sped toward the aircraft carrier.

We were instructed to lower our heads to our chests and warned to expect a quick jerk as the arresting cord stopped—I hoped—the plane. Sure enough, we suddenly heard the wheels screech, followed immediately by a strong jerking motion from the rear of our plane. We came to a rest—a complete stop—in less than five seconds. Nothing to worry about, just another day in the Navy. This amazing feat by the Navy has been happening for almost 100 years, since October 26, 1922, when Lieutenant Commander Godfrey de Chevalier flew his Aeromarine 39-B onto the flight deck of the United States's first aircraft carrier, the USS *Langley* while cruising off Cape Henry, Virginia.

Once the plane stopped on the deck, the rear ramp of the plane opened, and we all disembarked onto the deck of the carrier. When we arrived, the enlisted sailors saluted me because I was wearing Jeff's flight jacket; I promptly pointed to Jeff, and they correctly saluted Jeff instead of me.

We then went inside the carrier structure and were greeted by three public affairs officers who announced they would be our guides for the tour of the carrier—Lieutenant Beth Gauck, Lieutenant Junior Grade Phil Deroger, and Lieutenant Commander Dave Shepherd. They gave us a briefing about their floating city of over five thousand sailors and sixty-two aircraft, as well as the three galleys (cafeterias) on board.

We were then escorted to our quarters to drop off our carry-on bags. We were settled into groups of two on bunk beds that were normally used by the pilots. Each room was about ten feet by ten feet, with two desks, two chairs, a television, and a bunk bed. My roommate under me in the bottom bunk was former Air Force officer Owen Roberts, founder of Capital Formation Counselors, Inc., one of the most successful investment firms on Florida's west coast. The room was located just under the flight deck so, as each plane landed, the arresting cable would unwind and then wind up with the powerful noise of steam being released.

After setting up our rooms with our overnight bags and checking out the latrine with all stainless-steel fixtures, we were escorted to the galley to have lunch with the sailors. The three kitchens serve over twenty thousand meals a day with a kitchen staff of 197. Every two weeks they are reloaded with food and liquids. The menu for the standard mess hall is the same in each hemisphere of the world as delineated. That keeps this simple and logistically manageable.

We then headed up to the admiral's quarters at the top of the ship for a briefing. Admiral Kurt Tidd had amazing quarters, with a large office, dining area, and living area.

The admiral gave us a briefing on the Carrier Strike Group 8 that was his responsibility, including the submarines, destroyers, oilers, and other Navy ships as escorts. He mentioned that the sixty-two flying craft on this carrier included: E-2 Hawkeye AWACS (four), F/A-18 Hornets (twenty), H-60 Seahawk helicopters (seven), F/A-18 Super Hornets (twenty-four), EA-6B Prowlers (five), and C-2A Greyhound CODs (two). There are from seven to eight ships in Carrier Strike Group 8 besides the carrier: two Ticonderoga cruisers, one nuclear-powered submarine, one supply ship, and two or three Arleigh Burke-class Destroyers (DDGs). The *Eisenhower* carries 3.3 million gallons of jet fuel. With this arrangement of ships, they can cover the air and water bubble of five hundred miles.

From there we went to the bridge to meet the captain of the Eisenhower, Captain Dee Mewbourne. This is where the controls of the ship are located. We got to sit in the captain's seat and watch how these amazing young sailors navigate this phenomenal structure. The controls were all computerized and the speed of the aircraft carrier was upwards of thirty knots (equivalent to about thirty-five miles per hour on land) when traveling in the heat of battle. After the observing these pilots of the ship, we headed to the deck of the carrier to witness the pilots of the aircraft as they took off and landed as part of their training sorties.

We had helmets and goggles on and stood right at the arresting cables as the F/A-18 jets came in for their landings. This was an unimaginable sight to see, as the pilots had only a small margin to make the landing work. They had a choice of four arresting cables to aim for. The pilots landed on the deck with the plane at full throttle in case the arresting cable did not hold, or they missed it and they needed to take off again and go back around for another attempt. On this day, all the pilots aced their landings.

After leaving the flight deck we went back into the heart of the hangar and met with the handler, also known as the aircraft handler (ACHO). The handler is responsible for the arrangement of aircraft about the flight and hangar decks. It is important that this is done properly in order to avoid a "locked deck" where too many misplaced aircraft are positioned such that no more can land. The handler had a miniature scale model of the *Eisenhower*, with all the aircraft as they appear on the actual deck, with the color-coded ordinance, so he can maintain safety and security, at all times. He called the model of the ship the "Ouija board." It was a fascinating system—one I was happy to not have to manage.

After leaving the handler's office, we headed to the room under the arrestor cables. The huge control valve that absorbed the impact of the cables was impressive. Each pendant had its own engine system that absorbed and dispelled the energies amassed when a landing aircraft was arrested. Carriers use hydropneumatic systems, each weighing forty-three tons, wherein oil fluid is forced out of a cylinder by a ram connected to the purchase cable through a control valve. A major development in arresting gear was the constant runout control valve, which controls the fluid flow from the engine cylinder to the accumulator and is designed to stop all aircraft with the same amount of runout regardless of the weight and speed. It was mind-boggling.

After spending some time listening to the control valve filling and absorbing the cables, we headed to the one of the so-called Ready Rooms for one of the squadrons on board. Here each pilot is told his mission and the armaments he will carry into battle. Then, we were off to the dental office where each of the sailors receives dental care and has their dental records available in case identification is needed. The dental and medical operating rooms were immaculately clean and up to date for any surgery that might be required.

From there, we headed to the behind-the-scenes part of the galley where we witnessed the chefs preparing meals for the five thousand sailors. The massive kitchen equipment was so awe-inspiring, and the team of assistants worked as efficiently as the most intricate manufacturing factory. What was so amazing was the dedication and care that each cook took to serve the meals with pride. If only every restaurant worker could be that motivated.

After leaving the galley, we went to a lower deck of the carrier where the planes were stored and maintained. This was a huge deck with two large elevators to lift the planes up to the main deck on short notice. The operation here was as efficient as in the galley, with a similar pride of craftsmanship. After walking through the maintenance area, we headed to the rear of the ship—the stern. The jet engines for the aircraft were tested and stored at this location. Since the carrier is nuclear controlled, the only odor you smell for thrust is steam. The jet engines for the planes burn JP-8 jet fuel, so this is the only section of the carrier where we smelled the familiar odor of fuel.

We headed back to the maintenance area, where an F/A-18 fighter pilot let us sit in the cockpit of his plane and showed us the armaments that the plane could deliver. He also showed us how the bombs were released from the plane. The front of the bomb releases from the wing 1/100 of a second before the rear of the bomb. In that way, the bomb heads straight down and the plane is not in the path of the ordnance delivery, keeping the aircrew safe. A lot of actual rocket science went into the design of that mechanism.

By then it was time for dinner, so we all went upstairs to the admiral's dining room for a lobster fettuccine five-course meal. The food was delicious, and the captain and admiral were very entertaining. Once we were all stuffed, we went outside to the admiral's balcony and witnessed another group of sorties from these extraordinary pilots. It looked like a finely choreographed ballet, with each of the support team on the deck wearing different colored shirts—for example, handlers and directors in yellow, hook runners and maintenance in green, fuelers in purple, ordinance handlers and firefighters in red, plane captains in brown, quality control and medical in white, and chocks and chains in blue. The pilots continued repeated landings and takeoff until around 10:00 p.m. Our group had the opportunity to meet each of the pilots for ice cream afterward.

By that time, most of our group was tired and went to sleep, but I was so wound up that I walked around the carrier some more and even did PT (physical training) with a group of sailors. What a twenty-four-hour period we had a once-in-a-lifetime opportunity to witness. Also, I had the chance to see the massive anchoring system on the *Eisenhower*. The links each weighed 350 pounds and the anchor itself weighed 60,000 pounds—roughly the weight of five elephants. For comparison, this is about two and a half times the size of an anchor on a typical cruise ship.

At 8:00 a.m. the following day, we had a breakfast of eggs, bacon, grits, and hash browns with the sailors. After that fine meal, we said our goodbyes to the captain and admiral and headed to the COD for our preparation for takeoff.

As mentioned earlier, we were seated on the COD facing the rear of the plane. The pilot instructed us to tighten up our seat belts and put our heads down to our chest and be ready for a huge 4G pull, or four times the force of gravity. The plane was set on the steam catapult and zing—off we went. I have never felt a pull like this in my life as the plane shot off the deck. My ribs were pushing so hard into my chest I thought I was going to lose my breath (and my breakfast). After about ten seconds, the plane actually dipped since the catapult was faster than the propellers. Finally, the props took over, we stabilized, and we headed back to the northeastern Florida coast.

About forty-five minutes later, we landed at Naval Air Station Jacksonville with the most fantastic memories from this remarkable visit to the USS *Dwight D. Eisenhower*. Deborah would have to listen to each detail for many days to come. What stood out the most was that everyone we met, from the most junior seaman to the highest-ranking officers, had immeasurable pride in their work and in their membership in the US Navy. They knew they were serving their country and that their fellow sailors depended upon them, and they took that responsibility seriously.

F/A-18 Super Hornet aboard the USS *Eisenhower*

Admiral Kurt Tidd, me, and Captain Dee Leon Mewbourne

Flight deck of the USS *Eisenhower*

CHAPTER 14

Plunging Into the Sea Aboard the USS *Pittsburgh* Nuclear Submarine

APRIL 11, 2011: TAMPA TO CAPE CANAVERAL TO BOARD THE USS *PITTSBURGH*

Nine members of the Tampa community boarded Bob Franzblau's private jet and headed to Cape Canaveral to board the USS *Pittsburgh* (SSN-720), a nuclear attack submarine. We arrived at the jet port at Cape Canaveral around 9:00 a.m. and then shuttled to the docks on the far east side of the cape. Upon arrival at the docks, we met with another twenty or so civilians, among them was my University of Florida fraternity brother, Richard Schwartz.

We were briefed before entering the submarine as they were loading supplies and provisions for the trip. The USS *Pittsburgh* is a Los Angeles Class Submarine named after the Pennsylvania city. The sub has twelve officers and ninety-eight enlisted aboard. As we left the docks, the enlisted and the civilians went into the bowels of the sub while the head of the submarine, Commander Mark A. Savage, commander Navy Region Northeast, John Osterweil, me, and a marine guard stayed up on the conning tower.

The Coast Guard escorted us for about thirty minutes until we were deep enough to head down in the Atlantic Ocean. The wake the sub was making as we headed out to sea was enormous. The ride was very bumpy up in the tower, so I was glad when we were deep enough to dive. Obviously, it was time to go below, so we headed down into the galley of the sub.

Once we were completely submerged, the sub was cruising smoothly and with very little drag. We were all briefed again by the commander and given a baseball cap. The front of the cap said USS *Pittsburgh* and the back of the cap had our names on it. We were also each given a certificate with our name, date aboard USS *Pittsburgh*, and then signed by Commander Mark A. Savage. We were then served hamburgers with all the fixings. After two weeks at sea, typically all the rations are canned, so we felt privileged to have fresh food. After lunch, we toured the sub and were able to view the torpedo racks and the torpedoes. I was selected to set off a simulated torpedo wearing eyewear and a helmet. I pushed a button and a loud swish sounded and the sub shook.

It was a bit scary at first. We were able to see the rooms of the enlisted with the hot racks and desks for some of the leadership. The beds are called "hot racks" because they are always warm—as one group takes over command of the sub, the other group goes to sleep. This means that two people share the same bunk, just at different times.

The sub has the air very cool with added oxygen to keep everyone awake and alert as much as possible. The sub produces its own oxygen and fresh water. Also, the lighting changes for daytime and nighttime so the occupants are acclimated to the time of day. We were briefed on sonar and how the United States is the leader in the technology of tracking the ships and submarines of other countries. The submarine has a generator as a backup in case the nuclear reactor acted up.

We each had an opportunity to sit in the control seat and look through the periscope. The commander had us all sitting in the galley, which had secure seating as he directed the sub to dive. We witnessed a 600-meter dive at fifteen, twenty, and twenty-five degrees. We would dive and then surface and then dive again. It was impressive how the Navy team had such control over the seas.

We were out at sea for over twelve hours, and it was nice to get back to the surface. This was another memorable trip that showed the incredible technology and professionalism of our Navy. After the hatch was opened, we all exited and were transported to the Cape Canaveral tarmac. We boarded the jet and were back in Tampa by 5:00 p.m. What an incredible experience!

Photo of the USS *Pittsburgh* Submarine from the conning tower as we head out to sea

USS *Pittsburgh* submarine

Piloting the USS *Pittsburg* under the Atlantic Ocean

CHAPTER 15

Helicoptering onto the USS *Mesa Verde* Amphibius Assault Ship

MAY 2, 2009: TRIP FROM NAVAL STATION MAYPORT TO USS MESA VERDE

At 8:00 a.m. I met with Richard Schwartz, my University of Florida roommate, at Naval Station Mayport in Jacksonville, Florida. We were both looking forward to this unique experience.

At 9:00 a.m., Rear Admiral Joseph Kernan gave us a briefing at Mayport about our mission for the day. Admiral Kernan is the commander of the United States Fourth Fleet. A Naval Academy graduate and the son of a career Air Force pilot and Air Force nurse, the admiral spent most of his career as a Navy SEAL. He was part of the legendary SEAL Team Six, the counterterrorism unit that killed Osama bin Laden, and had assignments as commander of SEAL Team Two, as well as Naval Special Warfare Command, overseeing all the Navy SEALs. In his current position, he became the first Navy SEAL to serve as a numbered fleet forces commander. After his Navy career, he would serve for three years as under secretary of defense for intelligence.

I didn't know about the admiral's background at the time and only learned it later. In hindsight, it's funny to think that I could have asked him about the shiny, gold trident pin that was so prominently displayed on his uniform. It's probably a good thing because I would have been in awe and missed the details of the briefing he gave us.

The Fourth Fleet Forces is the Naval component command of the US Southern Command. It ensures freedom of the maritime seas. Its operating area is the Caribbean Sea and the oceans around Central and South America. All military vessels operating in this area fall under its responsibility. This includes ships, aircraft, and submarines. The Fourth Fleet Forces has five missions. These are peacekeeping, humanitarian assistance, disaster relief, traditional maritime exercises, and counterdrug support operations.

Our group of civilians totaled twelve. Tom Coughlin, coach of the Super Bowl champion New York Giants and his family were VIP guests. Coughlin was in the Navy before he coached football. We boarded three large Seahawk helicopters and headed southeast for about forty-five minutes. We landed on the USS *Mesa Verde* (LPD-19). The *Mesa Verde* is the third San Antonio-class amphibious transport dock ship of the United States Navy. The heavy winds made the landing of three Seahawks tricky, but the Navy pilots handled it like pros. I'm sure they have flown in such conditions hundreds of times—at least, that's what I told myself.

Several international officers greeted us. All were part of the coalition of countries that protect Caribbean nations. The officers gave us a short briefing on the main concerns in their individual areas. These concerns were primarily illegal drug transportation via fast boats, submarines, or aircraft. Hearing these stories directly from people whose lives are impacted by them made the problem feel more real and immediate, no longer an impersonal, faraway matter that could never affect me.

We then received a briefing in the ship's sickbay. This area contains two operating rooms and a twenty-four-person hospital ward. It can handle an overflow capacity of up to 100 patients. We saw the state-of-the-art equipment used for medical operations and for dental surgery.

Then, we headed to the rear of the ship for a ride on an LCAC—landing craft air cushion vehicle. We climbed aboard one of the two LCACs and into the cockpit. The LCAC was eighty-eight feet long and forty-seven feet wide. She had a huge air bladder underneath as well as two large fans on the deck for propulsion. The LCAC can carry a full platoon of US Marines along with an M1 Abrams tank, up to seventy-five tons, at speeds up to forty knots (46 mph) and distances of two hundred nautical miles. She can transport the entire load from the ship to land on any beach or coast. Armaments on board include two 12.7 mm (.50 inch) machine guns and gun mounts will support M2HB .50-caliber machine guns, Mk19 Mod3 40 mm grenade launchers, or M60 machine guns. It's an impressive craft.

The all-enlisted crew started up the LCAC and the air bladders began to fill. The ship lowered her loading ramp as the LCAC rose and the pilot started the two large fans. As loud as a jet, the fans pushed the LCAC out of the ship and into the sea. The LCAC hovered above the water and performed figure eights at almost fifty knots. It was an amazing ride, but I get seasick in my own bathtub. Coach Coughlin and I both turned white, but we kept our breakfasts down. Once we landed back on the ship, I felt much better.

The crew of the ship was very cordial and offered us lunch. After our meal, we reboarded the Seahawks and headed back to Naval Station Mayport.

This was an incredible adventure for Richard and me. The Navy sailors and Seahawk helicopter pilots were amazing!

Helicoptering to the USS *Mesa Verde* (we are in the helicopter in the foreground)

USS *Mesa Verde* (photo taken from our helicopter)

With Richard Schwartz aboard our helicopter as we prepare to land on the *Mesa Verde*

Me outside the *Mesa Verde* LCAC with Coach Tom Coughlin of the World Champion New York Giants and Richard Schwartz

CHAPTER 16

Aboard the Air Force Refueler KC-135 Over New Orleans

MAY 15, 2009: AIR FORCE KC-135 REFUELER TRIP

Colonel Lawrence Martin briefed us on MacDill Air Force Base (AFB), which is at the south end of a peninsula extending into Tampa Bay. Home to US Central Command (CENTCOM) and US Special Operations Command (SOCOM), it is the only base in the world to have the distinction of housing two combatant commands. A respective four-star general or admiral commands them.

MacDill also houses the 6th Air Refueling Wing and the 927th Air Refueling Wing. It has the infrastructure to support any flying mission in the Department of Defense inventory.

The 6th Air Mobility Wing, renamed the 6th Air Refueling (Wing ARW), is the "host wing" for the airbase and operates twenty-four KC-135R Stratotankers. It provides mission support to over three thousand personnel in its immediate command. It also has more than fifty mission support partners comprising over twelve thousand personnel.

The 927th Air Refueling Wing is an associate unit of the 6th ARW and is part of the Air Force Reserve Command. It has approximately one thousand part-time and full-time personnel.

There are two subunified commands headquartered at MacDill. One is US Marine Corps (USMC) Forces Central Command

(MARCENT), commanded by a three-star general. MARCENT is the Marine contributing and supporting to CENTCOM. The other is US Special Operations Command Central (SOCCENT), commanded by a two-star general or admiral and is the special operations unit contributing and supporting to CENTCOM.

Ms. Jennifer Campbell also briefed us about the base as it related to the city of Tampa. She reported that over sixty coalition country representatives have a presence on the base. They are part of CENTCOM and are involved in fighting terrorism around the world. More than twenty-five thousand people come on and off the base each day. This results in over six billion dollars of economic impact to the Tampa Bay Area.

Colonel Martin has a challenging job. He is the gatekeeper of the various heads of the many military entities on the base, while also commanding the 6th Air Mobility Wing.

Today, we would be flying on and learning about the Air Force aerial refueling aircraft, the KC-135. The mission was to travel west from Tampa on a KC-135 to a rendezvous near New Orleans. Once there, we would refuel six F-15 jets in flight, and then return to MacDill AFB. The open cargo deck of the plane would be very loud, so we would be wearing earplugs.

The refueler holds thirty-three thousand gallons of JP-8 jet fuel. Nine bladders in the wings and fuselage store the fuel. The challenge during refueling is to keep the plane balanced as fuel drains. This crew accomplishes this by using some of the fuel as ballast and shifting it around as necessary.

We commenced the trip around 1:00 p.m. and rendezvoused with the F-15s five hundred miles away about an hour later. The F-15s stationed themselves in formation off the left side of the tanker and waited their turns to gas up. When it was time, each plane would break formation and post up about a hundred feet behind the refueler. They would then close the distance to within a few yards of the KC-135. The boom operator would "fly" the boom to the location of the fuel port on the fighter's left wing. Once connected, refueling occurred in as little as fifteen seconds. Once refueled, the F-15 would post up to the right side of the refueler.

Looking out from the refueler window and seeing six aircraft there was surreal. We just never see planes that close in the air. The skill required to safely fly that close is beyond impressive. And, what it takes to fly just yards from our plane while refueling is something I would not have comprehended if I hadn't seen it myself. The turbulence from the large KC-135 must make it supremely difficult for the pilots of the much smaller F-15 to fly with such precision. On top of that, to think that we were passing flammable jet fuel between us is mind-boggling. These folks do it every day.

I was invited to go to the underbelly of the refueler, lay on my belly, and experience this delicate operation at close range. The F-15 was so close to us I could practically see the whites of the pilot's eyes.

Watching all six of the F-15s complete their refueling with not one pilot looking stressed is beyond words. They then headed back to their base, and we headed back to Tampa—mission successfully accomplished.

One of the KC-135 pilots shared with me that during the Iraq War, the United States had over 275 planes in the air at any one time. Refuelers, also called tankers, patrolled at various altitudes in a five-mile radius. Four tankers were on station at each elevation and up to five combat aircraft would line up for refueling at each tanker. The planes would then drop their ordinance and return to the tanker to queue up again. What an incredible feat.

What a day I had with the US Air Force—such professionalism, dedication, and hard work.

MARCH 11, 2010: KC-135 FLIGHT SIMULATOR AT MACDILL AFB

Lieutenant Colonel Tom Connelly and Tech Sergeant Michael Rodriquez briefed us on the flight simulator facility and the history of the KC-135. The KC-135 Stratotanker provides worldwide aerial refueling support and aeromedical evacuation transport. It provides these services to the Air Force, Navy, and Marines, as well as our allied nations. First delivered in 1952, the KC-135 is the first jet-powered air refueler in the US inventory. The last of its kind was delivered in 1965. It is one of the six fixed-wing planes with over fifty years of continuous service and is expected to fly well into 2040.

The plane has a wingspan of over 130 feet and is over 136 feet long. It can travel up to 530 mph at 30,000 feet and has a range of over 11,000 miles. The refueler can carry thirty-three thousand gallons of fuel in nine strategically located bladders. A typical crew consists of two pilots and a boom operator. It can transfer fuel through the boom at almost seven thousand pounds per minute (one thousand gallons per minute). The simulator itself provides the aircrew with qualification, requalification, and continuation training.

After the briefing, we went upstairs to the simulator. Once there we sat in the cockpit with all the actual controls and instruments. Refueling locations are different on each plane. Clear communication with the boom operator allows the pilot to sync up with the aircraft. This great experience made me appreciate the complexity of keeping our planes in the air for an unlimited time. I wouldn't have believed it, but I successfully refueled an A-10, F-15, B-1 Bomber, and an F/A-18! Simulated, of course!

NOVEMBER 20, 2013: KC-135 MACDILL AFB CONTROL TOWER

As part of the publicity of the air command at MacDill AFB, the base invited a group of Tampa Bay Area civilians to join them inside the control tower to see inside a KC-135 Refueler, and to try our luck in the KC-135 simulator.

Looking at the tarmac from the control tower was a unique perspective as we watched an actual KC-135 touch down and land. We then walked onto the tarmac, went inside the plane, and were given a briefing.

Then off we went to the KC-135 simulator. I had successfully refueled jets in the simulator a couple of year before, so I felt confident. This time too, I was able to refuel, but I had a problem with the landing. Unfortunately, my KC-135 went down in Tampa Bay.

It was a fun day meeting other Tampa executives and business leaders as well as our finest Air Force staff. I am always impressed with their professionalism and humility as they describe their important positions as well as the care they have in protecting us each and every day.

Ready to board the AC-130 Air Force refueler

Air Force F-15C (photo taken from the AC-130 refueler)

At the rear of the refueling plane

CHAPTER 17

Special Visit to Fort Pierce and Military Maneuvers at Coronado, Little Creek, Fort Bragg, Quantico, and Fort Campbell

OCTOBER 20, 2011: TRIP TO THE NAVY SEAL MUSEUM IN FORT PIERCE

Admiral Eric Olson, who was the first Navy SEAL to wear four-stars, was asked to bring some of his memorabilia to be donated to the Underwater Demolition Team (UDT) section of the Navy SEAL Museum in Fort Pierce, Florida. Eric asked me if I was interested in taking a trip, and of course, I said yes. We loaded up my SUV and off we went to the east coast of Florida.

Upon arrival, the museum staff greeted us. Outside the museum were many of the original boats, helicopters, space modules, and minisubmarines (minisubs) that the SEALs used. Eric was one of the original SEALs who experimented with the minisubs and rebreathing devices. The minisubs would be attached to the large submarine, then would detach close to the target area. He showed us numerous minisubs that he had been in and wrote the original script on how to perform with maximum efficiency.

We went inside the museum and proceeded to transfer Eric's items, including his uniform, from the car. The museum had set aside a special room for his relics. While in the museum, the admiral showed the staff and me a model of performing fast roping down a helicopter. He mentioned that the 1993 raid in Mogadishu by the United States military, aimed at capturing faction leader Mohamed Farrah Aidid, went awry when one of the operators who was fast roping down from a Black Hawk helicopter fell to his death. Then the locals started the battle, which he said was accurately depicted in the movie, *Black Hawk Down*. The admiral told us that the movie was very realistic in the action, however, the soldiers did not run down the streets to the soccer field as the movie showed at the end. Eric himself had gone to the soccer field for a purpose—to convince the Pakistani general, who was in charge of U.N. Forces there, to bring armored personnel carriers to the battle and pick up our special operators and remove them from the heat of battle they were encountering.

We also saw the lifeboat from the *Maersk Alabama* ship, depicted in the movie, *Captain Phillips*. The lifeboat was involved in the attempted hijacking that the Navy SEALs intercepted to rescue Captain Phillips. It was a memorable day spending time with Eric and listening to him relive his past experiences as a SEAL.

JANUARY 6–10, 2015: TRIP TO CORONADO, CALIFORNIA FOR BUD/S

As the president of the United States Navy League Tampa Bay Council, I was invited to travel to Coronado, California by Rear Admiral James Mulloy, the J-3 (Operations) at CENTCOM. I was to visit the USS *Stockdale* destroyer, an Arleigh Burke-class guided missile destroyer. Anthony Weiss and his wife, Nancy, joined me.

Also included was an invitation from Commander Clay Pendergrass, Navy SEAL at SOCOM, to visit the Basic Underwater Demolition/Seal (BUD/S) Training School in Coronado. Clay was a member of SEAL Team Two, One, and Seventeen, and Commanded

NAVSCIATTS (Naval Small Craft Instruction and Technical Training School). His decorations include the Defense Meritorious Service Medal, the Bronze Star, and the Combat Action Ribbon. Deborah and I have become great friends with him and his special family.

We coordinated the trip with both parties to visit the destroyer and the BUD/S school during our four-day visit. Admiral Mulloy connected us with the commander of the USS *Stockdale*, Commander Sean Grunwell to host us on the destroyer. Clay contacted Lieutenant Commander Kerry S. Jackson to host us at BUD/S on Coronado Island.

On January 6, Nancy, Anthony, and I flew from Tampa to San Diego and stayed overnight to be ready for our visit the next day. The following morning, we arrived at the gate of Naval Base San Diego and were greeted by the point of contact (POC) for the base, who escorted us to the USS *Stockdale*. We were welcomed aboard by Commander Grunwell and members of his crew.

The destroyer was very sleek with the most modern equipment. We toured the entire ship with numerous sailors including Lieutenant Keller, who explained each element of the destroyer, from the diesel engines and steering controls, the missile tubes and capabilities, to the joysticks that guide the missiles. We viewed the galley, the port, starboard, the offices, and the digs for the sailors. We sat in the captain's seat and even pushed a few simulator buttons. The ship was so impeccably clean, and everyone aboard was professional in their respective fields. We were impressed with the awesome capabilities of our Navy's Arleigh Burke-class destroyer.

Commander Grunwell had his team take a picture of us with him. He then gave us some mementos from the ship. After the tour, we took Lieutenant Keller out to lunch at his favorite seafood restaurant. Anthony and Nancy wanted to rest, so I drove them to the hotel. That evening we all headed to a nice restaurant in San Diego.

The following day, January 8, we toured the downtown San Diego, San Diego Zoo, the Sand Diego Model Railroad Museum (North America's largest model railroad museum), and Hotel Del

Coronado. After that, I dropped Nancy and Anthony at the hotel and then headed back to the base to look at all the ships in the slips. I had a little problem with some of the pictures I took but told the sailors that I was the president of the Navy League and only wanted them for my private use.

That night we invited Commander Kerry Jackson and three of his team members to join us for dinner at their favorite restaurant. The conversation turned to the problem of transitioning officers from the military into the civilian sector. Kerry mentioned he had numerous friends who felt let down when their time in the military was completed. They had led in the fight against terrorism but were unable to get a job as a civilian. They felt they had no networking skills other than what they knew within the military. They felt like a fish out of water.

Later, when Anthony and I went back to our hotel, we pondered about this issue. We wanted to figure out a way to help our finest transition. This was the beginning of our STAR (SOF Transition Assistance Resource) program to assist our special operators retiring from the military and entering the civilian world.

On January 9, we traveled from San Diego to the Naval Amphibious Base (NAB) Coronado to meet up with Kerry and his team again. We learned that the SEAL teams on the West Coast are odd numbers and the SEAL teams on the East Coast in Virginia Beach are even numbers. Many of the buildings on the base were very modern including the workout facility. We viewed the K-9 facility and the props that are used for the German Shepherds and Belgian Malinois. We then went outside to the docks to view the Navy pontoon boats and the new stealth fast boat. We boarded this gray-appearing speed boat with inboard/outboard motors and a large device at the rear of the boat. Then I was told to take over the command of the boat and take it for a ride. The boat was sleek and since it was a V hull, the boat handled extremely well. I took it to sixty knots and turned the wheel to see if the boat would respond well and I was pleased to find it smooth and responsive. The tabs on the sides keep the boat straight and stabilized. After I took the boat out in the bay for about ten minutes, Anthony took over and was not shy with the throttle. He drove the boat like he was speeding away from someone, and I had to hold on for dear life. We had a fantastic time!

After the commander parked the vessel, we went to the drydocks and viewed the maintenance department that maintained the boats. From there we headed to Gator Beach on NAB Coronado and the Phil Bucklew Center for Naval Special Warfare to view the museum of the history of the SEALs and see the human performance center. We also viewed the Naval Warfare Group 1 training ranges and then the locker room with all the equipment for each of the SEALs. Anthony and I both had the opportunity to handle the latest Navy SEAL guns and equipment.

We then went outside and were able to witness a new team perform their calisthenics, working on rebreathing equipment, and taking their rafts out to sea. We saw the area for the training outside and the bell that is rung when a SEAL in training throws in the towel. We read a sign that said, *The Only Easy Day was Yesterday*. We then went to the obstacle course where one of the team leaders demonstrated running through the entire course with speed, efficiency, and accuracy. We were amazed at his strength, dexterity, and the sheer will to complete the course. The day at BUD/S was so memorable and we were honored to witness the training of these incredible American warriors.

The next day we took Kerry to a local watering hole, Danny's, where many of the SEAL teams go to enjoy themselves. We were fortunate to meet a group of SEALs and we took care of their drinks. What an incredible experience we had in Coronado! On the plane back to Tampa, we discussed the previous evening and what we could do to assist the operators in transitioning.

DECEMBER 15-17, 2016: TRIP TO NAVY SEALS AT LITTLE CREEK, VIRGINIA

This trip was to the Naval Amphibious Base Little Creek, which is considered the major operating base of the US Amphibious forces for the Navy's Atlantic fleet. Anthony Weiss and I met up with Commander Brendan Leary, who showed us the operations of our Navy SEALS facility (Seal Team Four), training course, and amphibious boat base. The Naval Amphibious Base in Little Creek is one of the largest amphibious bases in the world.

We also traveled to the Honor Foundation, a transition institute unique to the Navy SEALS and Special Operations community. Joe Musselman, CEO and founder, invited us to the graduation. We met top-notch people about to enter the private sector. Interestingly, STAR and the Honor Foundation focus on the same end goal, which is the success and transition of our military forces into the private sector.

Finally, we were able to visit Norfolk Naval Station, which has the largest concentration of US Naval forces in the world, consisting of 75 ships, 14 piers, and 134 aircraft, and 6 aircraft carriers. Norfolk is the home of Naval aviation, commencing in 1911 when pioneers first piloted a plane taking off from an aircraft carrier.

Our trip to these locations reinforced my love and respect for those who serve and have served in our armed forces.

JUNE 6-8, 2017: US ARMY SPECIAL OPERATIONS COMMAND CAPABILITIES DEMONSTRATION IN FORT BRAGG, NORTH CAROLINA

The purpose of this exercise is to provide a clear understanding of the capabilities of the Army Special Operations Forces through a progressive, real-world, SOF integrated operation. At the end of the day, the observer experiences, through active participation and candid disclosure of knowledge, the strength and readiness of the Special Operations Forces.

Anthony Weiss and I were two of eighty-three military-involved civilians invited by SOCOM leadership. We flew from Tampa to Raleigh, North Carolina, rented a car, and drove to Fayetteville.

On Thursday, June 7, 2017, we boarded a bus to the headquarters building of the US Army Special Operation Command at the base at Fort Bragg. Our unique experience began when a simulation of an assault stopped us from entering. We were told to leave the bus, walk single file, and not to look left or right. We were escorted with armed Kalashnikov-rifled mock enemies into the headquarters building conference room. Although we knew it was not a real situation, we did experience a sense of being threatened in a real situation like that.

Upon arriving in the conference room, a uniformed officer immediately began shouting at us in French. Afterward, he spoke in English and explained, "You see, this is what we have to go through in unfriendly neighborhoods who speak in a foreign tongue. Our challenge is to overcome the language and cultural barrier." Next, the commanding general of the US Army Special Operations Command, Lieutenant General Kenneth Tovo, was introduced. We were welcomed and then explained that we would be witnessing some of the activities of engagement.

Next, we were led outside the building where leadership pointed out a monument to the 1,602 special operators who have died since its inception, December 1, 1989. We were then asked to look up and we saw seven Black Daggers parachute down to within 100 feet of where we stood. The ram-air parachute is a high-altitude low opening (HALO) style parachute. The parachuters warmly approached us, shook our hands, and we were then led to a bus. Within five minutes we arrived at a gun range and a building, wherein, upon gearing up with bullet-proof vests, helmets, and goggles, we climbed steps and oversaw how professional operators performed their duties under duress, like when a percussion bomb blew out a door or a C-4 charge blew out a door.

Thereafter, the skill and training of these Green Berets were confronted with "friendlies" and "enemies" in each room of the building. They were expected and as such, performed, making the distinction, and addressing the issue accordingly between the choices given. We were then invited to shoot an MP5 submachine gun and a Glock pistol at a gun range. Next, the bus transported us to another gun range where we were allowed to shoot one of three sniper rifles. Although I am not a skilled shooter, with guidance I was able to shoot my target, approximately a quarter of a mile (640 meters) away.

Following this, the bus transported us to a building where we were given MREs (meals ready to eat) just like the military when they are deployed, which was tough for us civilians. We then saw several weapons systems, such as grenade launchers, Grey Eagle drones, .50-caliber guns, as well as emergency rescue kits.

About fifty feet away, we were directed to bleachers, which oversee a two-story block compound-assimilation building. We watched how Green Berets approach a potential cityscape building and attack enemies using 4x4 all-terrain vehicles and modified pick-up trucks with a .50-caliber gun in the turret.

Later in the day, we took the bus to a made-up city comprised of about ten two-story masonry buildings. It looked like a scene in the news of a city in the Middle East. We climbed up the stairs of one of the buildings. Suddenly, we were under an assault, and although it was simulated, it felt profoundly real and even featured three helicopters racing at tree level. These helicopters included a Little Bird, a Black Hawk, and a Chinook. Next, to our surprise, disbelief, and astonishment, ropes were dropped from the helicopters and several Rangers (Special Operations raid forces) fast-roped down onto the rooftop of the buildings and engaged in a gunfight with "enemies." Afterward, all eighty-three of us boarded the helicopters and flew thirty minutes back to the main airfield at Fort Bragg. I was assigned to a Chinook. It was very fast and agile.

At the air hanger, we had a meet and greet with Lieutenant

General Kenneth Tovo. Anthony and I had the opportunity to describe our STAR program, which we continue to develop as we learn and experience the many operations through our trips. He was very pleased to hear about our work.

Dinner after the base was Italian at Luigi's. Anthony and I invited several special operators including Kirk Windmuller to join us. After the long day, I fell asleep easily. The following day we woke up and went to the Airborne and Special Operations Museum. The museum was fantastic, highlighted by the wreckage of the Black Hawk Super 61 helicopter, shot down and considered to be the vehicle that changed the campaign of Mogadishu. We then flew back to Tampa and returned to our nonmilitary world with a thorough appreciation of both.

MARCH 14–17, 2019: TRIP TO WASHINGTON DC AND QUANTICO

General Mickey Edelstein, the head military attaché from Israel to the United States, invited us for a visit. Anthony Weiss and I arrived at the Israeli Embassy at 3:15 p.m. and were greeted by a gentleman that handled the security detail. He was courteous and very thorough in checking each of our packages and our credentials. The Israeli Embassy is located on Embassy Row in Washington, DC. The building looks contemporary and is made of light tan brick.

We were greeted in the atrium by General Edelstein's assistant and then went up to his office, where he greeted us with open arms. I had met Mickey approximately seven years before at a SOCOM dinner for foreign special operators. That was the night I invited the entire table of Israeli operators over to the house the next morning for lox and bagels. About three years later, I took my family to Israel, where we met up with Mickey at the Gaza Strip at his command post. We enjoyed a great relationship, and I enjoyed supporting his successes in the Israeli IDF. We continue to stay in touch like family.

At our meeting at the Israeli Embassy, we discussed Israel in the current world. Shortly after our meeting, his assistant Michal noticed on her phone that a rocket had been sent over the border to Israel and they'd had to shoot it down with the Iron Dome. This was shocking to me that Israel faces this threat every day and the rest of the world is not informed of the aggression that their neighbors pose to them.

Since Mickey had been to my home in the past and had witnessed the Train Room and the history of trains, I made him a custom train conductor's hat with all his pins, and embellishments showing his achievements and battles he has fought in the past. I was able to do this thanks to Michal, who found all the pins in Israel and sent them to me. Mickey was grateful to have the conductor's hat as a keepsake. I mentioned to him that all the generals, admirals, and heads of state (including the prime minister of Israel from 1999 to 2001, Ehud Barak) also had one.

After that, we toured the embassy and discussed the important employees that operated there. This was my first experience in an embassy. Mickey told me that the Chinese Embassy was across the street and the Chinese had brought over 1,500 workers to build it. The building has six floors underground and includes many high-tech devices.

We left the Israeli Embassy and took pictures of all the others on the street as we headed toward the Army and Navy Club for dinner with Mickey and his lovely wife, Hadar. For over thirteen decades the Army and Navy Club has been a premier club in the United States. It is a home away from home for our country's military officers. The Club is known for its fine wine and food, along with an incredible library of unique military books. The most illustrious names in military and political history are members. We had a delicious filet and lobster dinner and enjoyed delightful conversation. Mickey and Hadar expressed that they had a wonderful experience living in the United States. They were returning to Israel in August. After dinner,

Anthony and I called it a night at the Hilton Arlington.

Retired General John Allen was gracious enough to set us up for a visit to Quantico, Virginia for a base tour. On March 15 we left Arlington after a nice breakfast and headed to Quantico. It took us approximately forty-five minutes with traffic to meet at the McDonalds at the entrance to the Quantico base. Upon arriving in the parking lot, we were greeted by Captain Britin Ellard, escort officer, Mrs. Tracey Ford, MCCDC chief of protocol, and a driver. We moved into their van and were briefed on the Marines facility with over twenty-five thousand people per day coming and going from the base, which boasts over thirty-three live-fire ranges. We were also given an itinerary for the day's activities.

We first went to the martial arts facility and were greeted by Staff Sergeant Kowtko, who gave us the history of the Marines and how they have modified their martial arts program to encompass styles from the Japanese, Koreans, and Chinese. The hallways were filled with pictures and weapons that had been used by the Marines from the First World War to the present. A listing of all the Marines and their regiments was posted in an organized panel on the wall. We then went into a room where three instructors gave us a complete demonstration of self-defense and offensive measures using knives, pistols, and rifles. I would not have wanted to face any of the three with their deadly techniques.

As we left the building, Staff Sergeant Kowtko mentioned that the Marines have always been the first to fight and have to be the best trained. Outside the building is a brick-lined entrance with the names of Marines who have given their lives for our freedom inscribed on each one. Seeing all those bricks was very emotional.

After the martial arts demonstration, we traveled to the K9 facility for a demonstration by the German Shepherds and the Belgian Malinois. We watched as the instructor with the dog walked up to a woman dressed in a thick leather one-piece protective outfit and gave us a few cases where the dog would attack the woman because of her running away or not following orders. The dogs learn to bring the enemy down to the ground by grabbing extremities rather than going after the head or neck. In addition to this, the instructors took the dogs around an obstacle course and showed the versatility of the dogs. It was all very impressive, and the trainers were in total control of their amazingly well-behaved dogs.

From the K9 facility, we traveled to the General Davis Center for a briefing about the history of the Marine Corps. The National Security Act of 1947 directed the Marine Corps to conduct the seizure or defense of advanced naval bases and other land operations to support naval campaigns. In addition, they are responsible for the development of tactics, techniques, and equipment used by amphibious landing forces. The Marine Corps is an integrated combined arms organization of complementary air, ground, and logistics components. After discussing the different assets, the mission and organization structure was detailed with leadership by Lieutenant General H. Berger, who is the four-star commandant of the Marine Corps. This was a 101 course to educate us on the Marine Corps.

After the lecture, we traveled to the officers' club for lunch with Major General Mark Wise, deputy commanding general of the MCCDC, along with four of his lead officers. The lunch was delicious and included a great discussion about our STAR program and its assistance in transitioning into the civilian sector through networking. After lunch, we exchanged business cards and Anthony and I left a positive mark on each of the officers as we assured them the same success in the civilian sector as they have had in the military.

After lunch, we headed to the HMX-Hangar for a briefing on the Marine Corps job as the sole provider of the president's travel by helicopter and the vice president's travel by Osprey. We watched a movie about the history of the president's helicopter and then we walked into the hangar, where we viewed numerous Ospreys that are used for the vice president, secret service, and foreign dignitaries.

Then the hangar door opened, and we headed toward one of

the Ospreys that was on the tarmac. We boarded it and were given earplugs, a headset, goggles, and a sound system. The pilot, Captain Josh Twenter, and Major Patrick Johnson demonstrated to us the incredible versatility and possibilities of the Osprey. It can go up like a helicopter and then off like a plane or go down the runway as a plane and then stop midair. The ride was amazing around Virginia and Washington DC.

After we landed and walked into the hangar, we were guided outside to another hangar where we had a major security check. This hangar was for Marine 1, the president's private helicopter. We had the opportunity to sit in the president's seat and then take a picture next to the presidential seal on the helicopter. It was an incredible experience. We left the hangar and purchased all types of souvenirs at the gift shop.

After this remarkable experience, we headed for the MCU building, where we listened to my dear friend and brilliant retired four-star general, General John Allen, give a one-hour lecture to over 1,500 Marines. The lecture was very enlightening about the history of technology in warfare and how today's technology is so cutting edge that future wars may be guided by computers and drones. The title of the lecture was "Hyper War—conflict in the time of zero time-lapse."

After the well-received lecture, Anthony and I had dinner with General Allen at one of his favorite restaurants, the Globe and Laurel. We each had a nice prime rib dinner with a delicious piece of pecan pie a la mode. We then headed back to the Hilton after a full day of activities with the Marine Corps.

On March 16, 2019, Anthony Weiss and I headed back to Quantico from Arlington for the graduation ceremony, parade, and commissioning of the Marine Corps Officers Candidate's School. The event was held at a huge, paved area called Brown Field. Approximately 250 candidates marched into the area divided into two groups, Charlie Company and Delta Company. The cannons fired as the candidates marched along with a small Marine Corps band. The national anthem was played and then the Marine Corps marched in perfect unison. The commanding general, William F. Mullen presided over the event and presented awards to the most outstanding candidates. We were honored to be sitting in the VIP tent along with past graduates and other military leaders.

The legacy of Officer Candidates School in the Marine Corps is rich in history and honor and dates back over 125 years to the present-day home of Brown Field in Quantico, Virginia. The current road to a commission as a second lieutenant in the Marine Corps at Officer Candidate School begins with one of several programs: the Officer Candidates Class, the Platoon Leaders Course, or the Naval Reserve Officer Training Corps. Each course is a screening process with the mission to educate, evaluate, and screen individuals for the leadership, moral, mental, and physical qualities required for commissioning as a Marine Corps officer. The event was emotional and memorable and brought tears to my eyes. We left Quantico that day with a greater understanding of our US Marines.

Anthony and I traveled from the base to the National Museum of the Marine Corps. The museum building was shaped at an angle to represent the planting of the flag on Iwo Jima. This museum is perhaps one of the finest I have ever seen depicting the history of the Marine Corps. From standing on the masts of the great old wood schooners to the latest equipment in the world, the Marines have always carried the burden of being first to protect our great country. One of the memorable items in the museum was the pair of original flags that were planted on Iwo Jima and the story behind them. Raising the flag on Iwo Jima is an iconic photograph taken by Joe Rosenthal (no relation) on February 23, 1945. It depicts six United States Marines raising a US flag atop Mount Suribachi during the Battle of Iwo Jima in World War II. The photograph was first published in Sunday newspapers on February 25, 1945. Once the Marines reached the top of the mountain, the 800 ships around the island began sounding their horns. The taking of the island was supposed to take four hours but inevitably took four days of fierce fighting.

Joe Rosenthal was at the top of the hill loading his camera and began taking pictures as the second flag (which was larger than the first flag) was being raised. He didn't even have time to adjust his camera as he began snapping pictures of the raising. After this happened, he handed the film to an enlisted marine, who immediately sent it to Guam for development. Then Joe Rosenthal had all the Marines on the hill pose for another picture with the flag standing vertical and he had time to adjust his camera and make sure the pictures would come out right.

The *New York Times* printed the iconic picture of the men raising the flag in the heat of battle. Joe Rosenthal had not seen the picture until then and was amazed it turned out so well. The second set of pictures he took never made the press. Joe Rosenthal's signed original picture, his camera, and the two flags are displayed in the museum. The museum gift shop was fantastic and had everything you could imagine about our great Marines.

From the museum, I took Anthony Weiss to the airport for his return flight back to Tampa. He was so grateful to have accomplished so many items on his bucket list. I traveled alone from DC to Rockville, Maryland to stay with Itsik Elimelech's family. Itsik is the president of Elbit, formerly (IMI) Israeli Military Industries, for the United States. Since it was the Sabbath, he could not drive. We had a delicious lunch thanks to his talented wife, Naomi, at their lovely home.

After lunch and a nap, we walked to Itsik's Orthodox Sephardic Temple and had an abbreviated evening service. I was honored to open the Ark and present the Torah to the readers. That evening we had a nice dinner at a delicious steak house. The next morning, I woke up and we had an excellent breakfast and then headed to DC to catch my plane back to Tampa. On my way to the airport, I drove by and photographed the Washington Monument, Capitol Building, and the Executive Building. What an incredible three days I had just experienced.

JANUARY 18-21, 2022: FORT CAMPBELL TRIP

The word had been getting out about our STAR program—a broader description as well as the details of the program is forthcoming near the end of this book. At any rate, Anthony Weiss and I continued to spread the word and build the program. In that spirit, we were invited to travel to Fort Campbell to visit the 5th Group, 101 Airborne, and 160th Night Stalkers from the Army and to give a briefing on the STAR program to the military as well as the civilian business leaders of Nashville, Tennessee.

The first night Anthony Weiss and I had dinner with Mike Thomas, who is the son of General Tony Thomas (Ret.), Command Chief Warrant Officer Al Porupski, and Chief Warrant Officer Josh Birch at The Local Restaurant. We had a great time discussing each of the men's plans after the military. Mike Thomas had been accepted into medical school and was excited about his future.

On January 19, we went to the 5th Special Forces Group Airborne headquarters and met with the command team headed by Colonel Brent Lindeman, Command Sergeant Major Josh King, and Command Chief Warrant Officer Al Porupski. They then took us to the Hall of Heroes and Museum as well as Gabriel Field, which shows the history and memorializes the fallen soldiers of the 5th Special Officers Group. Then off to the J. Tack Locker to speak to an instructor on how the Green Berets are taught to communicate with Air Force aircraft.

Next, we were taken to the gun range where we observed training of the Green Berets conducting rifle marksmanship training with 5th Special Forces. Special Forces weapons instructors provided us with a safety class on how to properly fire the M4 rifle weapons system. In addition to firing the rifles, Anthony sent off a smoke grenade and a percussion grenade.

That night we went to Edwards for a steak dinner with five operators who were in the 5th group and one 160th special operations aviation regiment. It was a delightful evening of good food and good conversation.

Then the next day Amy Marohl, transition coordinator for the 160th, took us around to Grimm Hall, where they had a simulator for the MH-47G Chinook and the Blackhawk which are flown by the 160th. We both piloted the simulator for an hour to try out our skills in refueling the helicopter with an AC-117.

From there, we went to the Allison Aquatics Training Facility to witness the training that prepares the soldiers in the event of a water landing. It teaches them to remain calm if the plane or helicopter crashes into the ocean. This $5 million pool simulator was incredibly realistic. It was exciting to witness an operator go through the exercise. Roughly 2 percent of all helicopter flights land in the ocean and this exercise will save lives in the future.

We then headed to Nashville, where we stayed at the new Hilton hotel in the downtown area. Upon our arrival, we were greeted by General Scott Brower (Ret.). He, along with four civilian business leaders, took us to the Predators Hockey game. We enjoyed an enthusiastic full house and a 5–2 victory over the Winnipeg Jets.

After the game, I went to Nashville's downtown area, which was packed with Southern eateries, honky-tonk bars with live music, and stores selling Western wear. Each eatery had a band and all of them were packed, even on a Wednesday.

On Friday, we met at the Chamber of Commerce of Nashville with General Brower and eighteen civilian business leaders to give a briefing on our STAR program and how to adapt it to the Fort Campbell and Nashville area. It went very well. We made time for questions and answers after our presentation. Anthony and I felt great knowing that we were making a difference in the Nashville community by exposing them to STAR and how it could be utilized in their community.

Visiting the Naval Amphibious Base Coronado—Don't ring the bell!

The USS *Stockdale*

US Army Chinook at Ft. Bragg (now Ft. Liberty)

Anthony Weiss and me with HMX-1 (Marine One) at Quantico

In front of the vice president's Osprey (Sikorsky VH-3A) at Quantico (Marine Two)

Sergeant Major Josh King, Commander Colonel Brent Lindeman, me, Anthony Weiss, Chief Warrant Officer 4 Josh Burch, and Chief Warrant Officer 5 Allan Porupski, presentation of a Sword from the 5th Group at Fort Campbell

Fort Campbell Allison Aquatics Training Facility for helicopter landings at sea

CHAPTER 18

US Air Force Special Operations Visit to Hurlburt Field, Duke Field, Eglin Air Force Base, and Tyndall Air Force Base

Thanks to Air Force Command Sergeant Gregory Smith, on June 4, 2019, Anthony Weiss and I took off for Pensacola, Florida to view four Air Force installations, which included Hurlburt Field, Duke Field, Eglin AFB, and Tyndall AFB. We had met Greg at SOCOMs 30th Anniversary Dinner in Tampa the prior year. He had mentioned that anytime we want to visit the Air Force Special Operations Command, we had an open invitation.

Air Force Special Operations Command or AFSOC is an Air Force major command and covers the air component of United States Special Operations Command. AFSOC is organized into three active-duty wings, one reserve wing, one National Guard wing, one active-duty overseas group, and one active-duty overseas wing. The mission is to organize, train, and equip airmen to execute global special operations. The missions across the world include agile combat support, aviation foreign internal defense, special tactics, command and control, precision strikes, information operations, intelligence, surveillance, reconnaissance, and specialized air mobility.

AFSOC employs uniquely equipped aircraft that are operated by highly trained aircrews to conduct precision strike; mobility;

intelligence, surveillance, and reconnaissance (ISR); and information operations (IO) missions. The missions may be manned or unmanned. AFSOC's primary method of dealing with a threat is the use of detection avoidance navigation, so most of their missions are at night and at low levels. Some of the aircraft used are the AC-130U and J gunships, MC-130H Combat Talon, CV-22 Osprey, C-145A Combat Coyote, and the MQ-1B Predator and MQ-9 Reaper Drones.

So off we went to Pensacola for our visit to Hurlburt. We arrived at 8:30 a.m. at the gate and were greeted by Command Sergeant Smith. Then we arrived at the 1st Special Operations Wing and Greg gave us a briefing on the history of the Air Force Special Operations. He mentioned that the command's ancestry began in the wars in Burma during WWII, then to Asia, and then to the attempted rescue in Iran.

We walked along a corridor that also served as a museum of the history of the command. We were then taken into Major General Becklund's office for a briefing of the 492 Special Operations Wing. He mentioned that the command began from the 482 Group that was activated on August 20, 1942, at the United States Army Air Force station 102, Alconbury, Huntingdonshire, England. Before that time, the Army had handled all Air Force activities.

The United States Air Force Special Operations School is located at Hurlburt Field to provide training in leadership development, force protection, warfighting, security cooperation, theater engagement, culture, and language, and also includes the Defense Language Institute. This training turns airmen into air commandos by screening each of the applicants and finding the best position for their capabilities in the overall operations.

From there we headed to TGI Fridays for lunch with Greg. At lunch, we discussed our STAR program and the possibility of the base handling a transition program for officers nearing retirement. After lunch, we headed outside to the tarmac where we were greeted by the Air Force special operators from the 4th Squadron who were in charge of the new AC-130J Ghostrider. The plane was awesome and had two guns projecting out of its left side. We were fortunate that the team of nine invited us to enter the plane and get a firsthand view of this amazing aircraft. We saw the 30mm gun along with the 105mm, and the AGM-176 Griffin missile tube inside the aircraft. The 30-mm bullet is the size of a coke bottle, and it can be fired at a rate of over twenty per minute. The 105mm shoots a shell weighing over 40 pounds each and shoots over ten per minute. The shells can have a delayed fuse or go into the ground and then explode. The shells can also be programmed to explode fifteen meters above the ground and explode with a spray of over 150 square meters. The technology is amazing. The team had air conditioning piped into the craft just for our comfort that day.

Next, we were shown the latest V-22 Osprey that is in the Air Force Special Ops control. The Osprey was very different from the vice president's HMX-1 that we had seen a few months earlier. It had no seats in it and was able to be refueled in the air.

We then went into a simulator that was a 180-degree half-round dome. This simulator allows a ground operator the flexibility to radio in commands from a ground area for bombing raids of the drone, F/A-18, an A-10 Warthog, or any other plane in the area. The operator can see the target and the plane and give directions for the bombing raid and also directions of the craft, so they do not fire in the direction of friendlies. This was an incredible simulator that at the cost of $2.5 million saves so much more because you do not need to fly actual aircraft or use ammunition and will decrease the chance of accidents. This also gives the operator a lot more experience to be able to perform under pressure when a real event occurs.

Next, we went into the Ghostrider simulator and tried to land the large airship. It was not a pretty scene when Anthony and I crashed the plane as we attempted to land it. Then we viewed some of the training facilities, including the pool, weight room, and classrooms. This was a very good introduction to this very special air command.

After the tour, I went back to the outdoor museum to take

pictures of the numerous early air commander planes. It was interesting to see the progression from the Second World War to the current gunships and surveillance planes. We then met with Command Sergeant Smith again, Jeff Taylor (combat controller) and Sean Aiello (military intelligence) for dinner at a local restaurant, the Old Base Steamer, located in Fort Walton Beach. We had a nice dinner but more importantly, we made some great new friends.

The following day, we traveled to Duke Field, which is home to the nonstandard aviation operation, the Combat Aviation Advisors (CAA). We were greeted by ten operators in charge of the Air Force's Blue and White C-145 and C-146 Skytrucks. These nondescript planes are the transportation for our operators in lands where the government or civilians are not friendly, or are unaware Americans are performing operations in their country. This is a way that operators can be dropped off or can parachute into remote areas or small airfields to perform their duties and missions.

We sat in a C-145 plane and received a briefing about all the possible content layouts that are available for the plane. It was very interesting to learn about all of the teams who provide the assets for the operators to perform their mission. We then went inside the facility and received a very informative briefing. The Special Operations Activities include unconventional warfare, foreign internal defense, and security force assistance for the CAA operators. Each applicant for the organization is tested and placed in the position they are most qualified for. The four phases of the training for the CAA operators include tactical field skills, ops training, cultural language, and functional specific training. The core values are trust, maturity, competence, and commitment.

From there we traveled to the US Army 7 Special Forces Group (Airborne) located at Duke Air Force Field. We met with Colonel Michael Ripley, the deputy commander of the US Army Training and Doctrine Command of the 7th Special Operations Command. We had lunch with him and his associate at the dining hall, which was completely empty except for us. We had a nice lunch and discussed our STAR program with him and the possible assistance our program can add to his retiring warriors.

After lunch, we went back to his office, where we were given a professional briefing on our Army's finest. Their principal tasks include stabilizing or destabilizing the targeted regime, with local partners providing the main effort. Our forces maintain a small or no footprint in the country. These missions are typically of a long duration and require extensive preparation, the effects of which are better measured in months or years. They require intensive interagency cooperation, and sometimes the Department of Defense forces may be subordinate to Department of State or CIA operators. We can have at any one time over 2,400 operators downrange. The typical Detachment Alpha includes a commander, assistant commander, operational sergeant, assistant operations and intelligence sergeant, two weapons sergeants, two communications sergeants, two engineering sergeants, and two medical sergeants for a total of twelve to a team. The briefing was well done, and I was impressed with the amazing top Army team. Michael was very warm and cordial to both Anthony and me. We were so proud to know him.

As we were driving back to our hotel, we passed Eglin Air Force Base. We decided to make a U-turn and attempt to enter the base with our MacDill AFB passes. Fortunately, we were able to enter and drove around the massive base. It is home to the maintenance and management of the most sophisticated Air Force planes. Since Hurricane Michael destroyed much of Tyndall AFB, almost all of the F-22 and F-35 planes were moved to Eglin AFB. We drove around until we spotted each of the planes in the hangars. They are amazing technical achievements.

We then stopped at a hangar and entered, not knowing what to expect. We met two gentlemen who had just started lifting weights. Fortunately for us, one of the men was in charge of maintaining the F-15 planes, and he stopped what he was doing, greeted us, and agreed to take us to his hangar with two visible F-15's being worked on. It was so nice seeing the F-15 on the ground as I remembered a few years earlier refueling that plane with a C-135 refueler out of MacDill AFB. The plane looked so much different on the ground than it appeared in the air under the KC-135 refueler. We learned that the F-22 has taken the place of the F-15 and the F-35 has taken the place of the F-16.

After that experience, we headed to the Air Force Armament Museum. There were numerous planes, helicopters, and armaments on the exterior of the museum, including the SR-71A Blackbird spy plane and the Mother of All Bombs (MOAB), which was dropped in Afghanistan in 2017. Inside were numerous planes, guns, bombs, and even one of the unused Fat Man Nuclear Bombs from the Hiroshima bombing (just the shell, of course).

In the museum was a history of the Tyndall Base Bombing Range located near Panama City, Florida. The base was named after Francis Tyndall. He was a fighter pilot during WWI and was credited with shooting down four German planes behind enemy lines in 1918. Tyndall died in 1930 in a plane accident while inspecting an Army field. Anthony and I left the base with a greater understanding of our fantastic Air Force. We went back to Fort Walton Beach and had another dinner at the Old Base Steamer.

On June 7, 2019, we left our hotel in Fort Walton Beach around 9:00 a.m. to make our two-and-a-half-hour drive to Tyndall AFB. We drove through areas in Panama City and Mexico Beach where the destruction was still visible from Hurricane Michael. Most of the area had been decimated by the CAT 5 hurricane in 2018. Very little reconstruction had been done since the hurricane had hit over eight months earlier. Upon arrival at Tyndall, we noticed that all the housing, schools, hangars, and most of the buildings were destroyed. We arrived at the base, which houses the 325th Fighter Wing of the Air Combat Command, First Air Force 53rd Weapons Evaluation Group, Continental NORAD, and the Air Force Civil Engineer Support Agency.

The base commander, Colonel Brian Laidlaw, an F-22 pilot, hosted our visit. He took us around the base and showed us the ongoing activities and the devastation to the facility. He said he had met with President Trump at the base on May 8, 2019, to discuss the reconstruction and the budget to repair the base and said he was very impressed with President Trump's knowledge of costs and efficiency in the reconstruction concept. He was glad that the president cared about the base and how to rebuild it as efficiently and cost-effectively as possible to bring the base back online in the shortest amount of time.

After giving us a briefing at his office, we mentioned that we would like to see NORAD and some of the F-22 Raptors that were on the base along with the drones. He was very gracious and happy to accommodate our request. We had a nice lunch at the base cafeteria and then we headed to NORAD headquarters for the continental US. We were greeted by Lieutenant Colonel Brian Murray, who is the commanding officer of the Canadian Detachment at Tyndall. He escorted us into one of the only buildings to avoid damage from Hurricane Michael. The security was tight, so no recording devices or cameras were allowed. The secure room was a massive open room with about fifteen rows of staggered seating. When fully filled with operators, approximately one hundred people could fill the room. We walked to the top of the room and were greeted by approximately ten officers who manned the operation at the time. The NORAD 601st Air and Space Operations Center had opened on June 1, 2007, as a response to the September 11, 2001, attacks.

The state-of-the-art facility allows the Air Force to protect America's skies from attack, as well as provide lifesaving relief during natural and man-made disasters. The high-tech, sixteen-screen data wall in the media-based theatre is reminiscent of a space-age control center. The facility houses theater battle management core systems that the Joint Forces Air Component commander uses to task and retask feeds to pilots, navigators, and air battle managers, allowing them to make better-informed decisions. It also employs, through its Western and Northeastern Defense Sectors, the Battle Control System Fixed program to collect input from a network of radars to alert operators of airborne activity in the continental US airspace and surrounding waters. We could watch on the screen as all the commercial aircraft around the US were shown on one of the two large screens. The other screen showed the air traffic in Washington DC.

According to the briefer, if a plane goes off its predetermined flight path, the FAA will notify them. NORAD will be contacted if the plane does not respond. If after a certain period the plane will not abide, NORAD will send in military planes to escort the civilian plane down. According to our briefer, this had happened sixty times in the last year. If the plane still won't abide by the military escorts, then a call goes straight to the SECDEF (secretary of defense) on the hotline to ask if the plane should be shot down. This would be the final decision of the president. Along with the operators in the facility were military JAGS to make sure the protocol is correct.

Lieutenant Colonel Murray was kind enough to answer all our questions. Since the room was not restricted to those with top-secret clearance only at that time, Anthony asked what the difference would be between what we were seeing and what would be shown to those with higher security clearances. He mentioned that the top-secret screens would show all of the military aircraft and our leadership in the sky in addition to civilian aircraft. We left the facility with a very good understanding of NORAD and the importance of its team to our national security. From there Brian drove us along one of the three runways, showing us a lot of the devastation from the hurricane as we traveled to their existing facility.

Unfortunately, we could not see an F-22 Raptor since it was being painted in a sealed clean-room hangar. Brian did take us to the third runway, which houses the mothballed F-16, now converted into unmanned drones that are used for target practice for the F-22 and the F-35. The F-16s are controlled remotely and act as enemy fighters flying along the Gulf of Mexico as the F-35 and F-22 pilots test out the latest weapons systems. The planes are shot down over the Gulf and then retrieved by barges.

It is brilliant to use a fighter jet that was mothballed and sitting in the desert rotting and convert it into a drone that we can practice real-life missions on. Base commander Colonel Laidlaw was a true professional gentleman. He went above and beyond when he showed us his base and the importance of Tyndall to the Air Force.

With Anthony Weiss in front of an AC-130J Ghostrider Gunship at Hurlburt Field

F-15 Eagle in Hanger at Eglin AFB

Mother of all Bombs at the Armament Museum at Eglin AFB

CHAPTER 19

National Naval Museum: America's First and Last on the Moon

MAY 13, 2010: TRIP TO PENSACOLA TO VISIT THE NATIONAL NAVAL MUSEUM

Our group of nine Tampa Bay community leaders boarded fellow Tampan and businessman, Bob Franzblau's jet and headed up the coast. Bob is best known for purchasing Thompson Cigar Company in 1960 and transforming the struggling business into one of the largest cigar mail-order operations in the country, even surviving the Cuban embargo. During the flight, we could see the remnants of the oil slick created by the Deepwater Horizon oil spill. It was a disaster the likes of which we had never seen. The Coast Guard played a major role in the successful response to that ecological tragedy.

Devoted to the history of naval aviation, the National Naval Aviation Museum is located at Naval Air Station Pensacola. Its mission is to select, collect, preserve, and display historic artifacts relating to the history of naval aviation. This history includes that of the US Navy, the US Marine Corps, and the US Coast Guard.

We arrived at the base around noon. Escorted to the rear of the museum, we saw aircraft being rebuilt and restored to their original condition. Then we toured the new facility being built to look like the interior of an aircraft carrier. This great addition to the museum became the National Flight Academy. This is an immersive experience for seventh to twelfth graders that inspires interest in STEM education. STEM includes science, technology, engineering, and mathematics.

After the visit to the new facility, we toured the museum itself. We viewed the 150 planes and spacecraft positioned on the ground or hung from the ceiling. It was incredible to see the history of naval aviation.

We were then taken from the museum to a small reception and greeted by honored guests: astronauts Neil Armstrong and Gene Cernan. These two great men were, respectively, the first man and the last man to walk on the moon. Anticipating this meeting, I had purchased a globe of the moon from the Tampa Museum of Science and Industry. I greeted Neil Armstrong and showed him the globe. I also showed Neil a picture of where I was going to hang it in the Train Room. He immediately took command of the globe and showed me where he landed Apollo 11. I had him put an X on it to mark the spot.

I asked Neil, a Navy pilot with seventy-eight combat missions, what his biggest fear was on the mission. He told me he was confident he could land the lunar module anywhere after making so many landings on aircraft carriers. He also mentioned he was not concerned about running out of fuel even though the lunar module only had fifteen seconds of fuel remaining when it touched down. He chuckled and said his greatest fear was that he might slip on the steps of the module as he walked down to the lunar surface, and that the whole world would be watching on television. Neil was so excited to have my globe in his possession that he walked around to show everyone where he had landed. He knew every detail and every landmark on the moon and was delighted to share his stories.

I next handed the globe to Gene Cernan. I asked him what special thing had happened to him on that final journey to the moon. He mentioned that he carved his daughter's initials on the moon, and since there is no weather there, the initials will likely stay there forever. Gene signed my globe and wrote, "Last on the Moon."

After the event, our group of nine had a nice dinner then headed back to Tampa. It was a memorable day meeting our finest astronauts and American heroes.

Astronaut Neil Armstrong showing us where he landed on the moon

With Astronaut Gene Cernan, last man on the Moon

Naval Museum banquet honoring the first and last on the moon at the National Naval Museum in Pensacola, Florida

CHAPTER 20

United States Army Military Academy at West Point

SEPTEMBER 18–20, 2019: TRIP TO UNITED STATES MILITARY ACADEMY AT WEST POINT

On Monday at 9:00 p.m. I received a text from a friend, Michael Kass. Michael was a civilian member of our STAR group, a successful businessman, and an attorney at law in Tampa. He mentioned that his VISTAGE business group had planned a trip to the United States Military Academy at West Point and one of their team was unavailable to go on the trip. VISTAGE was established in 1957 and is considered the world's most trusted CEO coaching and peer advisory organization.

I was so excited about the opportunity, as it has always been on my bucket list, especially since I have had the honor of knowing many of the graduates like General Steven Hashem, General David Petraeus, General Tony Thomas, General Joseph Votel, and Colonel Hal Walker. Colonel Rolfe Arnhym (Ret.), a graduate from West Point in 1953, put together the itinerary for the two-day visit with as much sightseeing, briefing, and interacting with students and professors as possible.

We left at approximately 10:00 a.m. from the St. Pete-Clearwater International Airport in Michael's Lear Jet with Jody Haneke, CEO of a website design company, Chris Mc Laughlin, operating principle of four Keller Williams realty offices in Tampa and Lakeland, Corey Miller, president of Miller General Contracting, Dr. Jim Norman, president of a Thyroid/Parathyroid Center, and Marcus Reyes, CEO of a plumbing and HVAC company, and Rolfe Arnhym, a graduate of West Point in 1952 and the CEO of Vistage Florida. We arrived at New York Stewart International Airport around noon. From there, a van took all of us to the West Point campus, about twenty minutes away.

We settled down at the Thayer Hotel on the campus, a three-star hotel, where most of the visitors to the campus stay. Colonel Sylvania Thayer, called the father of West Point, served as the superintendent from 1817 to 1833. Despite all the obstacles he faced in molding the academy, Thayer's superintendency is marked by unparalleled achievement. He implemented strict disciplinary standards and a course of academic study. His emphasis on honorable conduct gave rise to what has become the ethos and spirit of West Point, now embodied in the hallowed words: duty, honor, and country.

We each went to our room and discovered that almost all the rooms had a picture of a famous or successful graduate with a brass plate describing their successes. In each area of my room were personal pictures of the graduate with family members and honors. I contacted Dave Petraeus and told him I was there. He mentioned that there was a room dedicated to him and that I should ask for it. I checked with the front desk, but unfortunately, since this week was Alumni Week and Branch Week for the freshman (plebes), Dave's room (#314) was not available. I sent Dave an email about not being able to get the room and he responded, "Nice to know that it is still in demand."

My room was the General Fredrick Franks Jr. Room. He graduated in 1959 and was the captain of the baseball team. He was wounded in the Vietnam War and became the first active-duty Army general amputee since the Civil War. He coauthored the New York Times Bestseller, *Into the Storm*, with Tom Clancy, and was appointed by West Point's president and chairman of the Battle Monuments Commission in 2001 to serve on the board of trustees of the US Military Academy. The room was very nice with family pictures and mementos and a sign-in book.

After settling down in our rooms we began our West Point and The Long Gray Line tour and briefings. We started with a nice lunch at Herbert Hall with the vice president of development, West Point Association, Ms. Kristin Sorenson, and the senior director of major gifts, West Point Association, Mr. Mike White, a 1982 graduate of West Point.

While having sandwiches, we were given a PowerPoint presentation about the new facilities. Some would be paid by government and some with private fundraising. Unfortunately, the United States government would not cover all the costs to update the most prestigious military academy in America. I was surprised to learn of this problem. We need to give these amazing men and women all the best of facilities, faculty, and technology so they stay at the top of their game.

Each year over 12,000 high school students vie for 1,100 spots at the academy. Academic grades, national testing of SAT and ACT scores, congressional letters of recommendation, varsity sports participation, and extra activities, are all considered in the admissions process. The briefing was an eye-opener for me as I realized that many of the finest all-around students in America are enrolled at this beautiful facility in upstate New York.

After the lunch and briefing, we took a tour of the campus with the Grad Insider Tour Company. We toured the football practice field, the Mickie Football Stadium, the Kimsey Athletic Center, the church, the Cadet Uniform Factory, the superintendent's home, the Plain, tennis facility, intramural facilities, the Jefferson Library, the Garrison Mess Hall, the Hayes Gym, polo pool, and numerous dorms for the cadets. The honor code for every cadet is sacred— *a cadet will not lie, steal, or cheat and turn in anyone that does.* The classes are broken down as follows: 1,100 students in each grade totaling 4,400 students in total, plus approximately 60 foreign students. The freshmen are called plebes, the sophomores are called yearlings, the juniors are called cows, and the seniors are called firsties.

We then moved on to other parts of the campus. The Mickie Football Stadium has a lot of history in its 37,000-seat facility. Future plans include expanding the side on the reservoir and adding club seating. The West Point Cadet Chapel is a Protestant church built in gothic revival architecture style in 1910. It houses the largest chapel pipe organ in the world and features 23, 511 individual pipes. The Cadet Uniform Factory was a unique tour as they have been making uniforms with over 249 pieces for each cadet for the last 100 years. The factory uses more than 50 miles of material and 2,500 miles of thread each year to dress the Corps of Cadets. The seamstresses have a unique talent adding all the detail to each uniform.

In the past 100 years, little has changed about the gray uniforms, which led to graduates of West Point being called the Long Gray Line. The pants and coats are still made of wool, and in an age where so much of manufacturing has been automated, the majority of the work is still completed by hand at the Cadet Uniform Factory at West Point. It's interesting that the cadet uniforms of both men and women, have tails at West Point. Supposedly, the Radio City Rockettes in New York City got the idea from the seamstresses at West Point.

We drove past the homes of the 60th superintendent of West Point, Lieutenant General Darryl Williams and the commandant Curtis Buzzard, responsible for the administration, discipline, and military training of cadets at the academy. I was so fortunate the next day after lunch to meet Lieutenant General Williams and when I shook his hand, I passed him one of my STAR coins. He in turn, passed me his three-star, very impressive large coin which read *Live Honorable, Lead Honorable, Demonstrate Excellence, DUTY, HONOR, COUNTRY*. I mentioned that I had heard he was doing a great job with America's finest. He was very honored to hear that.

We then went by the Plain, which is the parade field for West Point. The Plain rises approximately 150 feet above the Hudson River and is the site of the longest continually occupied US Army garrison in America since 1778. In its early years, the entire academy was located on the Plain and it was used for varying activities ranging from drill and mounted cavalry maneuvers to an encampment site for summer training to a sports venue. Currently, the Plain refers to the parade field where cadets perform ceremonial parades. We noticed the statue of General George Patton addressing his men on the Plain.

We then traveled to the varsity tennis courts and the varsity football practice field. We then went into the area where the dorms and the Jefferson Library are located and noticed a plaque on the opposite building along with a canon on each side of the entrance. The plaque read *The Civil War 1861–1865*. The small gun had fired the first shot of the Civil War in the West at Vicksburg several days before the attack on Fort Sumter in April 1861. The large gun had been part of the left ridge of Captain Elder's Battery 5 First US Artillery and fired the last shot at Appomattox on April 9, 1865.

We went to the top floor of the library and viewed the Plain from there as well as the setup for cadets' Branch Week. That week marked the annual Branch Week at West Point where representatives from each of the branches met with cadets to talk about their branches and answer questions. For plebes and yearlings, the week is geared toward educating them about their options. Cows, on the other hand, are expected to spend the week talking to branches that interest them and begin narrowing down their preferences.

Here is a typical list of branches: Air Defense Artillery, Adjutant General, Armor, Aviation, Chemical Corps, Cyber, Engineers, Field Artillery, Finance Corps, Infantry, Military Intelligence, Military Police, Medical Service, Ordinance/EOD, Quarter Master, Signal Corps, and Transportation Corps.

The real pressure falls on the firsties, who have until Monday at 11:00 p.m. to finalize the rankings that will be used to place them into branches. Branch Week marks their final opportunity to ask questions, explore the branches, and make sure they know which ones they prefer. There are seventeen possible branches to select from for men and fifteen for women. The women have the option to opt out of infantry and armor. The higher the cadet's ranking in the class, the better chance they have of getting their first choice.

In the Jefferson Library was an exhibit of all the United States Military Academy Class Rings. They even had the class rings of General Douglas MacArthur, General Dwight D. Eisenhower, and General Omar Bradley. An exhibit in the library showed the origin of the Military Academy. After the War of Independence, never again did America's leaders want the Army to have to rely on foreign military ingenuity. President Thomas Jefferson's decision to officially establish the academy in 1802 sparked a national push to build a cadre of Army officers trained as engineers. As the nation expanded its western boundaries, those officers played pivotal roles. By recruiting men from all across the nation, West Point made history by becoming the first national military and engineering college.

Before the establishment of the military academy, during the Revolutionary War, the harsh winter of 1777–1778 froze the Hudson River, allowing elements of the Connecticut militia under the command of General Samuel Holden Parsons to march westward across the river. They first occupied West Point on 27 January 1778, making it the longest continually occupied post in the United States.

George Washington considered West Point to be the most important military position in America, stationing his headquarters there in the summer and fall of 1779. The Great Hudson River Chains and high ground above the narrow S curve in the river enabled the Continental Army to prevent British Royal Navy ships from sailing upriver and thus dividing the colonies. After his victory over the British Army at the Battle of Yorktown, Washington kept the Continental Army garrisoned nearby at New Windsor at the New Windsor Cantonment until the official end of the war. West Point was a strategic location since the Hudson River became very narrow and there was a large bend at that point. The British were trying to establish a location north of New York to take over the northern areas of the Continental States.

Before the Civil War, many of the graduates had to decide if they were going to fight for the North or the South, such as, General Robert E. Lee. He decided to fight for his home state and fought for the South. Despite the many successes of West Point graduates in the Civil War, the postbellum years presented new challenges for the Academy as Southerners returned, hazing practices escalated, and the first Black cadets were admitted. The Academy survived the difficult times, but there was little innovation or growth. Fortunately, this period would be followed by years of reform and review that saw the institution evolve and mature.

From the Jefferson Library, we viewed the dorms, many of which are over 100 years old. Of course, there is no air conditioning, and the temperature during our visit was in the high 70s in the middle of the day. From there we went to the Mess Hall Garrison. This was the most amazing dining hall I had ever seen. The main wall in the dining hall had a mural of all the battles in the history of the world. Six dining rooms intersect in the center with an elevated platform, and 4,400 cadets have meals at the same time in this facility. They have twenty minutes to eat their meal and clear their tables. This was an amazing facility for our finest.

From the dining hall, we traveled to the athletic facility called the Arvin Cadet Physical Development Center. Inside, the large Hayes Gym is used for performing the required obstacle course on the first level and track on the mezzanine. Also, included are three swimming pools, basketball courts, and racquetball courts. Since Douglas MacArthur's tenure as superintendent, every cadet is required to participate in either an intercollegiate sport, a club sport, or an intramural sport (referred to as "company athletics") each semester. We watched as both men and women practiced the obstacle course in order to achieve their required times. This ended our tour for the day, so we went back to our rooms to prepare for our dinner at the Thayer.

At dinner, we were joined by chief of staff of West Point in 1991, Colonel Mark Bieger; director of strategic resource planning and integration in 1994, Colonel Greg Boylan; director of Army staff in 1976, Lieutenant General Bill Grisoli, Colonel Fred Meyer, Department of Civil and Mechanical Engineering in 1984, and Miguel Gutierrez, in charge of student transition for all West Point graduates.

The dinner was very engaging with many of the norms and values of West Point being discussed. After dinner, Miguel Gutierrez and I had a nice talk for over an hour about the transition of our finest into the civilian world. I explained that our STAR program had been assisting for over four years, and later, I sent him all the ideas and the two-year calendar we had constructed with the assistance of SOCOM. I invited Miguel to come to our STAR 50th Dinner the following month at Palma Ceia Country Club. The day was amazing, and I returned to my General Frederick Franks Jr. Room.

We had a full day planned, so we were up early the next day to have breakfast at 7:30 a.m. On the wall in the Thayer Hotel lobby was the Cadet Prayer from the US Military Academy: *Make us to choose the harder right instead of the easier wrong and never to be content with a half-truth when the whole can be won.*

Our first stop after breakfast was at Lincoln Hall for a briefing by Colonel Mark Bieger, class of 1991, on strategic planning and integration. Then we went on to the Combatting Terrorism Center for the state of terrorism briefing directed by Mr. Brian Dodwell along with two colleagues. The areas of terrorism to worry about are on the African Peninsula, he said, where we have dictators and communist leadership, and the inhabitants are persecuted and lack food, clothing, and shelter. These oppressed people often feel they have no choice but to join fanatical groups like ISIS. In addition, in the future these areas will lack fresh water, which is an issue that could become a world problem.

After the briefings we had lunch at the West Point Club. During lunch, we were fortunate to have a West Point student, Cadet Sergeant Kim Caccama, from New Jersey, give us a very good description of what it was like on the first day of class and what a typical day at the academy is like. She is a mile swimmer and also does the butterfly on the varsity squad. I was so impressed with her maturity, etiquette, and professionalism in describing her life at West Point. I gave her my STAR challenge coin after lunch, and she was so grateful that she followed up with a thank-you email. We also had an ethics briefing by Dr. Richard Schoonhoven, of the Department of English and Philosophy. He discussed how to deal with death and injury during war and how to deal with it mentally afterward.

After lunch, we had a briefing from Colonel Pat Howell, class of 1992, from the Modern War Institute. We discussed the speakers who speak on current events at the Academy and how to send out information on the internet. Next, we went to the admissions building and discussed admission standards as mentioned earlier, determined by academic grades, national testing of SAT and ACT scores, congressional letters of recommendations, varsity sports participation, and extracurricular activities.

After a full day of briefings, we went to the Plain, listened to the leaders of each of the seventeen branches, and viewed all the military aircraft, guns, cyber equipment, trucks, and parachute practices. There were Black Hawk helicopters along with an Apache. We walked around the Plain and noticed the statues of General Douglas McArthur and President Ulysses S. Grant facing the Plain. We then went to the waterfront and took pictures of the monument at Trophy Point. This is a memorial for the lost Northern soldiers during the Civil War, which totaled 2,230.

Trophy Point is a scenic overlook of the Hudson River Valley at West Point, New York. It has been the subject of numerous works of art since the early nineteenth century. It is the location of Battle

Monument, one of the largest columns of granite in the world. After taking pictures with the group, we went to the West Point Museum to learn about the history of the campus and buy some souvenirs from the gift shop.

On the wall was inscribed the following:

> *The United States Military Academy's mission is to educate, train, and inspire, the Corps of Cadets so that each graduate is a commissioned leader of character committed to the values of Duty, Honor, and Country and prepared for a career of professional excellence and service to the Nation as an officer in the United States Army.*

After that, we went back to the hotel, where I worked out a little bit in the workout room and then got ready for our final dinner at the Thayer. The guests for dinner included Mr. Mike White, the academic director (AD), class of 1982, and Colonel Abel Young, the deputy AD. We had a nice conversation discussing sports scholarships and the athletics that students can select. We had completed another big day full of insight and discovery.

Our final morning was set up to meet at the Kensey Athletic Center, which is the home of the weight training and the athletic museum. We met with Coach Swanson, nicknamed "the Satin," who gave us a briefing on the weight room programs. Each of the 1,100 athletes has a personal weight program that he puts together to help them achieve individual peak performance. Coach Swanson was proud of the new weights totaling over thirty-five tons with each barbell stating *BEAT NAVY!* In addition to the weights in the room was a health-food bar for proper nutrition.

We then went upstairs to the athletic museum, which was well detailed, from displays about the original star football players, to the three Heisman trophies, to the Commander-in-Chief's Trophy, which Army has kept for the last three years after beating both Navy and Air Force in the same year. It's interesting to note that Coach Mike Krzyzewski (class of 1969) played under Coach Bob Knight. Both ended up being coaches for Duke and Indiana in later years. Also, a former assistant coach for the tennis team included the great Arthur Ashe.

This was an incredible two days at West Point, and we learned so much about these hallowed grounds. We even learned some of the bugle notes of trivia here at West Point. Some interesting facts are that there are 340 lights in Cullen Hall, which was built in 1869, and the reservoir has seventy-eight million gallons of water. We then traveled to the Stewart International Airport and headed back to Tampa.

The Cadet Chapel at West Point

Washington Hall, the dining hall (mess hall) at West Point

With the superintendent of West Point, Lieutenant General Darryl Williams

Corey Miller, Chris McLaughlin, Marcus Reyes, Michael Kass, Rolfe Arnhym, me, and Jody Haneke on the tour of West Point

CHAPTER 21

The Star Program
SOF Transition Assistance Resource

JANUARY 2015: ORIGIN AND DEVELOPMENT

After leaving the Navy SEALs at Coronado in January of 2015, Anthony Weiss and I discussed the hardships that Special Operations Forces (SOF) experience when they transition into the civilian sector. Anthony researched the existing programs throughout the nation and found that the Honor Foundation and Your Grateful Nation were two existing programs geared for operators and that they are tailored toward specific trades.

We then began our collaboration to put together a blueprint for soon-to-be retired operators with a foundation of prioritizing networking with successful, well-established professional and entrepreneurial civilians. This would come to be the next phase in my passion to assist these great American patriots. Our model would be to introduce and connect each operator with one or more successful local business leaders and shadow them and their business environments. This would introduce and open them to an array of career options, all with the guidance and support of these generous civilian leaders.

In August of 2015, I contacted General Tony Thomas and explained our program. I had already recruited civilian business leaders, many of whom supported military balls and wounded warrior foundations, who were very excited to participate in STAR. General Thomas was "all aboard" and invited us and our STAR participants to MacDill AFB and use one of their conference rooms, namely the William "Wild Bill" Donovan Room, head of the Office of Strategic Command, and regarded as the founding father of the CIA and Special Operations. General Thomas was very enthusiastic and totally supportive in helping us launch our program. Since then, every head of SOCOM has openly promoted the STAR program for soon-to-be-retiring special operators.

The details of the program for operators are as follows:

1. We want badged (served at least four missions in the heat of battle) operators who are within two years of retiring and plan to live in the Tampa Bay Area.

2. Each month we have a nice dinner hosted by a civilian and comprised of fifteen operators and fifteen civilians. We keep it small to create an environment of interaction and build enduring relationships. An evite is sent out and operators sign up so we can pair them with a different civilian business leader each time.

3. Operators can then shadow a business leader for a day and learn about his or her business operation and gain a greater understanding of the culture of their business sector.

4. We put operators in touch with Nancy Lane (a local volunteer) who then helps them establish their LinkedIn network connection, which ties them into the working and social world, both military and civilian.

5. We connect operators with Tampa Bay Job Links, a local organization founded by Blossom Leibowitz, which guides them in building a proper resume and trains them on how-to-give a two-minute elevator pitch to market themselves. Blossom

offers this service and her staff, namely Sheila Solomon Rudd, free of charge and is genuinely happy to serve our operators.

6. Operators are motivated to attend as many dinners as possible to maximize their exposure to the business community. And by the time their retirement paperwork is processed, they have the necessary tools to transition smoothly and feel confident about the civilian sector.

Civilian business leaders are expected to be passionate about the military, generous of heart, and genuinely committed to assist these special operators. The details for civilians are as follows:

1. Each civilian business leader must have a high degree of integrity and keep all shared information confidential.

2. Civilians must be willing to commit time and energy toward friending, partnering, and assisting operators in a manner they can count on.

3. Civilians are asked to spread the word and recruit other business leaders for the program.

4. Civilians are required to host, at their expense, one very nice dinner for fifteen operators and fifteen civilians.

Originally Anthony and I scheduled and coordinated the monthly dinners, arranged for the civilian hosts, helped facilitate the venue when needed, and led the speaking portions of the dinners. We would give a brief introduction about STAR, then we would open the floor by inviting each person to describe their backgrounds and hopes for the future (about two minutes per person). This would give everyone an opportunity to pair off with the person we had matched them with as a starting point, then reach out to others with whom they felt a connection, shared a common interest, or felt curious about. This would effectively be the beginning of networking and connecting military members with civilians.

Here is a typical STAR dinner evening timeline:

5:30–6:00—Social Networking

6:00–6:05—Introduction and Overview

6:05–6:30—Business Partner Introductions

6:30–7:00—Operator Elevator Pitches

7:00–7:30—Dinner and More Networking

7:30–8:15—Panel Discussion with Moderator

8:15–8:30—Closing Remarks

As STAR evolved, we set up a board to oversee the general goals, discuss lessons learned from previous dinners, and modify the program month to month as needed to produce the best results. As the program evolved, we encouraged service members, both retired and active, to participate in a leadership role. That way the program could be further strengthened by operators encouraging operators who all speak the same language. Past board members include Colonel Frank Anello (Ret.), Colonel Michael Arndt, Master Sergeant Troy Daland (Ret.), Lieutenant Colonel Brian Howard (Ret.), Captain Tony Hudson (Ret.), Master Sergeant Joe Lurz (Ret.), Colonel Michael Moad, Colonel Jeremiah Monk (Ret.), Colonel Brad Osterman (Ret.), Sergeant Major Matt Parish, and Captain Andrew Roemhild (Ret.). And special thanks to our first emcee, retired IBM executive, Vijay Lund, as well as Cordes Owen for establishing our STAR website, (tampastarnetwork.com).

As of the writing of this book, our 100th STAR dinner is scheduled for December 2023. Our current board consists of our emcee, Arch McClellan, retired Marine; Anthony Weiss and me, cofounders; Cynthia Rogers, resume and elevator pitch expert; Brian Zuckerman, entrepreneur and small business expert, Nick Daugherty, embedded in SOCCENT (Special Operations for Central Command); Josh Anderson, embedded in SOCOM (Special Operations Command), and Noel Boeke, head of programming.

These are some of the comments we've received from operators who transitioned successfully out of the military utilizing our program:

☆ "I recently retired from the Army after a successful and rewarding twenty-five-plus-year career as a Special Forces Green Beret colonel with leadership, planning, and management skills in diverse elite global organizations. In my last role on active duty as director of strategic planning at United States Special Operations Command, I led a twenty-five-plus member team that provided the chairman of the Joint Chiefs of Staff, secretary of defense, and National Security Council with groundbreaking plans, approaches, and options to counter our nation's most dangerous and complex threats. Through STAR, I learned of an opportunity that matched my expertise and skills. I now proudly serve as a key member of the corporate planning team as senior planning consultant, supporting the director of planning in the development, management, and execution of Moffitt Cancer Center's strategic plan to further its mission of contributing to the prevention and cure of cancer. The STAR formula works!"—Dan, Retired Colonel, Special Forces

☆ "I'm a retiring SEAL captain with a twenty-nine-year military background that has included various leadership roles throughout the SEAL teams, including stateside and overseas assignments, several deployments, and some challenging combat leadership positions. STAR helped me focus on what's next by introducing me to key community members in several industries. Two STAR mentors, in particular, opened my eyes to the benefits and excitement associated with a small start-up. As a result, I have taken a path I would never have considered before STAR."—John, Retired Captain, SEAL

☆ "I am a retired Army Special Operations aviation colonel with a diverse background in operations, resourcing, and acquisition. Through STAR I discovered how to market my passion for leader development, resulting in multiple business opportunities. Ultimately, I found a role working with high-net-worth individuals to develop strategies to achieve personal and financial goals for a leading financial group based in Tampa."—Joel, Retired Colonel, 160th SOAR (Night Stalker)

☆ "I'm a retiring Army colonel with twenty-seven years of service, approximately half of which were in the Special Operations community. The vast majority of my experience is in operational planning, synchronization, and management with some focus in strategic planning. I lacked knowledge on how or where I could contribute to the civilian sector. STAR showed me how while introducing me to a network of business leaders and mentors in the Tampa area. As a result, I landed a job in a very successful financial services company as an operational manager in its equity research, sales, and trading division."—Shawn, Retired Colonel, Ranger

☆ "I'm a recently retired Green Beret colonel with nearly three decades of experience in global special operations and commanding bases overseas. The dedicated mentors at STAR opened doors to opportunities I wouldn't have had access to. Transition was challenging, but through STAR I found a VP role shaping the operations and strategy of a *Tampa Bay Times* Top 20 Workplace."—Ed, Retired Colonel, Special Forces

☆ "The value of the STAR program isn't about job offers—it's about giving our teammates the opportunity to take a step back, reflect on what they've done in service to this nation, and start to understand how valuable that leadership experience can be to different elements of corporate America. This transitional step can be intimidating, and STAR is making a real difference. My next chapter is lined up, well-defined, and Tampa-based as a result of STAR. I cannot thank its members enough!"—John, Retired Captain, SEAL

☆ "Through STAR I discovered how to market my passion for leader development, resulting in multiple business opportunities and my next career."—Joel, Retired Colonel, 160th SOAR (Night Stalker)

☆ "I can't say enough about what the STAR program is doing for transitioning senior leaders in the Special Operations community or what it has done for me in the process."—Shawn, Retired Colonel, Ranger

☆ "The dinners were central to my transition, both informative *and* fun. The job shadow experience confirmed for me that I could easily adapt to the civilian world and fit in; I came away with the impression that all team rooms are generally the same, and this was helpful for me. I can't say enough good things about STAR and all the people and elements that make it up; start early and get all-in, just like you've done your whole life."—Kent, Retired Captain, SEAL

MAY 25, 2017: STAR GROUP VISIT TO SOCCENT

We set up a visit to Special Operations for Central Command (SOCCENT) at MacDill AFB for twenty-five participants in our STAR program. Marine Colonel Andy Milburn would be briefing us on his area of responsibility, which included twenty Middle East countries.

We then went outside and witnessed the team parachuting right next to the building. After each team member landed, they carried their parachutes to the building and hung them up in a very high, large room so they could stay aired out and dry. The facility has room to repair the parachutes along with a parachute simulator, which several of us tried. We then enjoyed a nice lunch that was hosted by our STAR group. The tour and parachuting teams were amazing. These special operators for Central Command make a big difference in the Middle East.

OCTOBER 29, 2019: STAR'S 50TH DINNER CELEBRATION

Our STAR program achieved the milestone of over four years of STAR dinners for our special operators and civilians. Since we felt the fiftieth should include graduates of the program and their spouses, we set up a special evening at Palma Ceia Golf and Country Club's Ballroom. We had over eighty-seven attendees.

Present were the many officers who had transitioned successfully into the civilian sector. We all enjoyed great food and libations and watched a video testimonial from many of the operators. It was all very meaningful and gratifying.

At a prior event, a Medal of Honor dinner, I'd had the opportunity to meet and speak with Governor Ron DeSantis about the STAR program and the success we were having with SOCOM and CENTCOM retirees. He had been very impressed. I naturally invited him to attend our fiftieth STAR dinner. Although he was unavailable, he did send Danny Burgess, a representative from his office. Danny is an Army Reserve captain and was recently appointed the executive director of the Florida Department of Veterans Affairs. He was very impressed with our program and mentioned he would let the governor know about it. He enjoyed the evening and said the

STAR program is quite amazing.

Also present was Miguel Gutierrez, a West Point graduate, class of 1980, in service for five years, who then went back to West Point to become the director of career services at the West Point Association of Graduates. He assisted graduates in transitioning into the civilian sector after they completed their military careers. Miguel was impressed with our program and said that he hoped to replicate it at West Point.

Each of the participants at the event had fond memories of their experiences with STAR and many were compelled to speak that evening and share their stories. The event was a total success with the "graduate" operators and their spouses being very fulfilled and appreciative of their civilian business partners.

JUNE 8, 2021: STAR'S 70TH DINNER AT DONATELLO ITALIAN RESTAURANT

At this dinner, I was partnered with Command Sergeant Major Mark Baker of the 160th Army Night Stalkers (SOCCOM). We had a wonderful dinner and I learned that Mark and his family had been in in Fort Campbell, Kentucky for the last two years, and they now lived in Tampa.

The following day, I had lunch with Mark at Palma Ceia Golf and Country Club, and we discussed his forthcoming transition into the civilian sector. He said his dream was to one day own an RV park between Orlando and Tampa and have a small shopping center with a convenience store and laundry facilities. Throughout lunch we discussed a multitude of topics including real estate, insurance, and construction. I then brought him to my office I walked through the many military photographs I have having on the walls that document many of the experiences described in this book. One picture with General John Mulholland caught Mark's eye. General Mulholland was his superior officer in Afghanistan overseeing Mark's top-secret missions.

After Japan's premeditated bombing of Pearl Harbor on December 7, 1941, America promptly responded with the Doolittle Raid, also known as the Tokyo Raid, on April 18, 1942. Likewise, after the September 11, 2011 attack on the United States, America moved to retaliate on Afghanistan. As humble and selfless as Mark was in describing his role as an Army Night Stalker with the elite 160th immediately following 9/11, he shared that his group had flown Boeing CH-47 Chinooks into Afghanistan to attack the Taliban, as depicted in the movie, *12 Strong*. On that mission, Mark wore the pin (wings) of the roommate of flight attendant Sara Low, who had been killed on 9/11 on his missions and his crew members would rub the pin before each mission for luck.

Sara Low had been a flight attendant on American Airlines Flight 11 from Boston to Los Angeles on September 11, 2001. Her plane was hijacked and crashed intentionally into the North Tower of the World Trade Center. As a response to this ghastly deed, her roommate Karyn Ramsey, also a flight attendant, pinned her own flight attendant wings on Sara's father, Mike Low, at Sara's memorial service. The wings were incredibly symbolic of Mr. Low's love of and pride in his daughter and her career and wanted to honor her. He asked a friend at the Pentagon to help him send Karyn's wings to the US campaign in Afghanistan. And so, Sergeant Mark Baker ended up with the privilege of pinning Karyn's wings on his uniform when he went on his missions to Afghanistan.

"After a mission brief, the task force public affairs officer read a letter from Mike Low, which explained his desire for Karyn's wings to be worn in combat. Afterward, she asked if anyone would volunteer to wear the wings and I volunteered," he explained. "I wanted to honor the love between a father and his daughter."

The wings never left Baker's side and even became part of a permission ritual for his helicopter crew. A crewmate would pin the wings on Baker's uniform and the whole crew would rub the wings for good luck before they left on a mission. He wore the wings on his uniform during twenty missions, totaling more than one hundred helicopter flight hours conducting combat and resupply missions across Afghanistan.

On May 21, 2002, Night Stalkers presented the wings back to Mike Low in a ceremony held at Fort Campbell, Kentucky. From there, the wings were sent to the National September 11th Memorial and Museum for permanent display. Sergeant Baker said knowing the wings will be on display makes him proud. "I am proud to have worn the wings, of my involvement in the War on Terror, of all the men and women who fight to protect our freedom, and of the way America prevails when faced with adversity," he reflected. "The wings being on display brings closure while declaring, 'we will not forget.'"

AUGUST 10, 2021: STAR'S 72ND DINNER AT URBAN STILLHOUSE

When one of the top corporations in American, General Dynamics, offered to host a STAR Dinner, we jumped at the opportunity to bring STAR to yet another level of success. Our special operators would truly have great exposure and experience huge support in transitioning into the civilian sector with General Dynamics behind them. We were very excited.

The venue was the Urban Stillhouse Distillery and Restaurant in St. Petersburg, Florida, and included over fifty-five attendees. General Dynamics had invited fifteen members of their leadership and spouses to meet and greet our special operators. The facility was the brainchild of two retired Army special operators, Mark Nutsch and Scott Neil. The building is over 16,000 square feet with numerous bars and tables on two floors with a feeling of warmth from fireplaces and gas lights, and over 300 brands of bourbon for their clientele. General Dynamics had reserved the entire restaurant for the night. The evening began as all do, with a social hour of libations and conversation between the fifteen special operators and the civilian business leaders. STAR's emcee, Arch McClelland, began the evening by honor STAR's founders, Anthony Weiss and me, then with introductions of the leaders from General Dynamics—vice president, Lloyd Peace, and senior vice president of marketing and community involvement, Tim Bagniefski. They each briefed us on the company.

General Dynamics armaments and logistics headquarters branch in St. Petersburg is the largest producer of bullets and artillery in the country. They believe that the company's corporate value is the quality of its people. Following this, we were honored to have Mark and Scott give a rousing briefing on their transition into the civilian sector and the fits and starts they'd had in eventually making a success of the Horse Soldier Whiskey brand and the restaurant.

Mark Knutsch and Scott Neil were Army Green Berets of the 5th Special Forces Group that participated in our retaliation after 9/11. They rode horses into the mountains of Afghanistan and with the Northern Alliance, laser spotted pockets of Taliban, and had B-52s carpet bomb them to submission. The movie, *12 Strong*, depicted the incredible actions of these men who were brave enough to attack the Taliban with a ratio of five thousand to one and take over Mazar-I-Sharif, a large stronghold of the Taliban. They were true heroes in the service to our great nation.

In addition to each telling their story, we had invited Mr. Brian Ford, COO of the Tampa Bay Buccaneers. He had arranged for the Lombardy Trophy to be brought to the venue and placed it strategically so that all attendees could take a picture with it. As the COO, Brian has made a successful career with Tampa Bay Bucs during his tenure. He oversees all aspects of the team's day-to-day business operations and community involvement. He has made it a point to support our current military and veterans and we are so honored that he has taken an interest in supporting our STAR program.

The food for the event was delicious and each of the operators gave their two-minute elevator pitch and then the civilian business leaders followed. After the event was over, Scott gave all attendees a tour of the facility, which includes three private dining rooms, an outdoor patio, three bars, an upstairs dining room, the "Library" and the "Man Cave." The evening was truly memorable.

Anthony Weiss, General Richard Clarke, and me at a STAR dinner

CHAPTER 22

Military Honors Treasured

MARCH 19–23, 2011: OUTSTANDING PUBLIC SERVICE AWARD

On January 30, 2011, Deborah and I received a letter from General Petraeus as follows:

> *Dear Mr. and Mrs. Rosenthal:* Mark and Deborah,
> *I will travel to Washington DC for a Congressional hearing in mid-March. While there, Holly and I would be honored if you could join us on Friday afternoon, March 11 (changed to March 19). If you can join us I will arrange for a tour of one of DC's important sites and a brief ceremony, followed by dinner at a restaurant together with some other partners from Tampa.*
>
> *We sincerely hope that you can make it. Holly and I very much appreciate your friendship and all that you do for our troopers. We would like to be able to recognize you in a small way (unfinished business from CENTCOM days), and my DC trip presents an opportunity for us to do that.*
>
> *Please know that I am also inviting Dr. and Mrs. Scott Kelley and Mr. and Mrs. John Osterweil to join us for the occasion and for recognition. It would be great if we could all get together again over dinner to catch up.*
>
> *If you can make it to DC, please email Mary and Ed in*

my front office ... and they can help coordinate. Holly and I look forward to seeing you.

With best wishes from Kabul,
David H. Petraeus
General, United States Army
Commander
Hope you'll be able to make it! All the best.

On March 19, 2011, Deborah, our son, Jason, and I flew to Washington DC (our daughter, Jennifer, was in Hong Kong for a study abroad semester for her studies in interior design). Still, I was not quite sure what Dave was planning for us. We stayed at the Ritz Carlton Hotel. General Jay and Lynne Hood were also present along with the Osterweils and the Kelleys. We all had a very nice dinner with the Dave and Holly Petraeus. The following morning, we were escorted to the Capitol Building for a tour of the facility. On the balcony of the Speaker of the House, John Boehner, we had our picture taken with the Hoods. We were then escorted to a small room to join Dave, Holly, and their staff. After greeting everyone, we were then seated, and Dave proceeded to brief us on the reason we were selected to be there. We were about to receive a very distinguished award. Issued by the chairman of the Joint Chiefs of Staff, Admiral Mike Mullen, Dave presented three levels of the Outstanding Public Service Award to me, Scott, and Jill Kelley, and the highest level going to John Osterweil.

As I stood up next to General Petraeus, he pinned the medal on me while his assistant read my citation:

> In recognition of outstanding public service to the United States Central Command, the MacDill Air Force Base community, and the Department of Defense from 31 October 2008 to 31 May 2010. Mr. Rosenthal distinguished himself by exceptional service while supporting the

mission of the United States Central Command, building a positive relationship, supporting community outreach, and advancing various military endeavors. Mr. Rosenthal's selfless contributions demonstrated his true patriotism and a sincere sense of personal responsibility to build and enhance the command. He worked tirelessly supporting countless Soldiers, Sailors, Airmen and Marines injured in combat at the James A. Haley Veterans Administration Medical Center in Tampa, Florida. His advocacy and sympathy for the families helped the Veterans Affairs Leadership improve and personalize care for injured personnel, and his support of the Fisher House at this facility is legendary within the community for improving the lives and morale of our wounded warriors. He is a strong backer of the Central Command Family Day Picnic, showing his appreciation in ways that make the event better and more enjoyable for all. He contributes to the success of service balls through fundraising and other contributions and supports the efforts of the Wounded Warrior Foundation. His enthusiastic commitment to the military and Central Command, in particular, coupled with his sense of responsibility, served as an example to his fellow citizens and a beacon to all military personnel in the Tampa Bay Area. His support of countless community programs exemplifies his caring leadership and is characteristic of his devotion to service and those who serve. Mr. Rosenthal's contributions are in keeping with the finest traditions of public service and reflect great credit upon himself, the United States Central Command, and the Department of Defense.

I was numb and in awe after receiving this award from perhaps one of the greatest American generals of all time. All the volunteer work I do for the military is out of the goodness of my heart and my respect for our incredible military. I felt very flattered and extraordinary pride for being the recipient of this award, and I felt deeply that the award was not just for me, but for my wife and all her work as well. This award is an honor me and my family will always treasure.

After the awards ceremony, the Petraeuses invited us all out to dinner. That was such a memorable event that it gave me even more reason to be as supportive as I could for the greatest military in the world.

On February 14, 2011, I received a beautiful letter from commander of CENTCOM, General James N. Mattis:

> *Dear Mark,*
>
> *Congratulations on receiving the Outstanding Public Service Award. It is a significant honor and reflects the phenomenal work you've done on behalf of Soldiers, Sailors, Airmen, and Marines operating out of the US Central Command headquarters and in the region.*
>
> *Your partnership has been felt through your selfless work supporting our Family Day Picnic, service balls, and the local Wounded Warrior Foundation. I know your time is valuable and I appreciate how much of it you have devoted to these efforts. I know I speak on behalf of every member of CENTCOM when I say—there is no better friend.*
>
> *Again, congratulations and thanks for taking care of our service members and their families. All the best and I look forward to spending more time with you and Deborah once my schedule clears.*
>
> *Sincerely,*
> *James N. Mattis*
> *General, US Marines*

MARCH 23, 2011: AS A SPEAKER AT THE JESUIT COMMENCEMENT EXERCISES

I was invited to speak at the Jesuit High School Commencement Exercises before the entire school and describe my volunteer work with MacDill Air Force Base, specifically, the Central and Special Operations Commands. They especially asked me to speak about receiving the Outstanding Public Service Award, issued by the chairman of the Joint Chiefs of Staff, Admiral Mike Mullen, and presented in the Capitol Building by General David Petraeus. This invitation to speak was a very special honor since I had graduated from Jesuit in 1975. I was proud that they wanted me to share this very special honor and my perspective on it with the entire school and faculty. I expressed that the truly greatest satisfaction in life is giving. And I related this tenet, this manner of living life, with the values we learn through the Jesuit teaching.

Six values that are known as the principles of the Jesuits are:

- *Magis*: Meaning "more." This is the challenge to strive for excellence.
- Women and Men for and with Others: Sharing gifts, pursuing justice, and having concern for the poor and marginalized.
- *Cura Personalis*: "Care for the individual person." Respecting each person as a child of God and all of God's creations.
- Unity of Heart, Mind, and Soul: Developing the whole person and integrating all aspects of our lives.
- *Ad Majorem Dei Gloriam* (AMDG): Living our lives for the greater glory of God.
- Forming and Educating Agents of Change: Teaching behaviors that reflect critical thought and responsibility.

I felt like I relayed each of these values to the audience of over 600 students and professors. It was an honor to go back to the school that had taught me such great values and ethics and made me the person I am now. Partnering the values of my Jewish foundation, I can honestly say that the strength of my successes—in business and in life—were solidified during my four years at Jesuit High School. Sharing my past and present with these students was truly a realization of my journey and a treasured honor in my life.

After the speaking engagement, I received a nice note from Father Richard Hermes, S.J., president of Jesuit High School, congratulating me on receiving the Outstanding Achievement Award.

JUNE 8, 2012: AS A LIAISON IN SAVING A LIFE

On September 6, 2009, at the Tampa Bay Rays baseball game where General Dave Petraeus had thrown the first pitch, Deborah and I had met Tim and Anje Bogott. Owners of the Tradewinds Resort Hotel in St. Petersburg, they are very involved in the community, and became acquainted with the Petraeuses as well. We were later invited to their home for an amazing party which included Dave and Holly and featured as guest of honor, Elie Wiesel, Holocaust survivor, and his wife Marion. Most of the guests were from St. Petersburg, so we made some new acquaintances. Shortly thereafter, the Petraeuses hosted a small dinner party at their home at MacDill AFB. Included at the table of twelve were Tim and Anje, as well as Elie and Marion Wiesel. We later had Tim and Anje at a Games and Trains Party.

A couple of years later, I was contacted by Tim Bogott about a very disturbing situation with his daughter.

Tim told me that their daughter was in Europe for a college semester abroad. She and her friend had gone to the Greek Islands for a weekend break when a tragedy occurred. Their daughter's friend had been attacked by a Greek sailor and she—not he—was being held in detention on one of the islands. She was in a cell with both men and women and felt her life was at risk. Their friend's parents were terrified. It seemed they had no recourse, influence, or legal authority to help their daughter. Tim thought that perhaps Dave could help. I gave him Dave's personal email address and suggested he explain the situation and to please keep me in the loop. At that time Dave was the director of the CIA. Sure enough, Dave provided Tim with impeccable guidance. He gave him the names of specific ambassadors and military leaders connected with Greece and instructed Tim to contact them and say that he was in communication with the director. Thankfully, both Tim and Anje's daughter and her traumatized friend were returned to the United States within twenty-four hours. I was glad I could act as a liaison to help in this frightening situation—not a perfect end result, but certainly a great remedy under the circumstances. I treasure the ability to have a positive impact and doing the right thing and I know Dave does as well.

MAY 23, 2013: AN HONOR PRESENTED BY GENERAL KARL HORST

As the president of the United States Navy League Tampa Bay Council, I set up a briefing by General Karl Horst, the chief of staff of CENTCOM under General James Mattis for eighty civilians. During the briefing, General Horst and Rear Admiral Matts Fogelmark of Sweden surprised me by calling me up to the stage.

General Horst and Admiral Fogelmark presented me with a certificate of appreciation for my volunteer work with the Coalition of fifty-nine countries who make up part of CENTCOM in the fight against terrorism. The Coalition was set up after 9/11 and has been a very active group in consulting and working together to fight terrorism around the world ever since.

As mentioned previously, I am passionate about having Coalition social events with local Americans, so they can experience our core family values. Our typical menu is barbecue—grilling hamburgers and hotdogs and having apple pie a la mode for dessert. This is a way to show Coalition families our simple American hospitality and our common love for family. Because of my involvement I became known as an honorary ambassador for the Coalition at CENTCOM.

To be presented with a certificate of appreciation is truly an honor I will treasure always. I will continue to work toward familiarizing our Coalition partners with our American family life.

MARCH 26, 2014: OUTSTANDING CIVILIAN SERVICE MEDAL PRESENTED BY ADMIRAL WILLIAM MCRAVEN

Admiral Bill McRaven and his wife, Georgeann, invited Deborah and me and our family and friends to Special Operations Command for a special event. I was unsure about the specifics, but I was so happy that everyone could come to see the state-of-the-art facility and witness the professionals at SOCOM. My mother, Barbara, Marvin Aronovitz, Deborah, and I were greeted by the McRavens and escorted up to the admiral's office.

We discussed our families and the trips we had taken with our children throughout the United States and around Europe. The McRavens are the most down-to-earth and sincere couple.

Later, we were escorted down the hall to the Donovan Room where we were greeted by about fifty military and civilian attendees. Among the civilians present were Mark and Arlene Reese and Richard and Sharon Schwartz, my college and long-time friends from college. Admiral McRaven had me sit on the stage along with him and then asked me to stand up and had his spokesperson read the following:

Mr. Mark Rosenthal distinguished himself by exceptionally

meritorious service and dedication to the United States Special Operations Command from August 2011 to March 2014. Mr. Rosenthal serves as a bridge between the Tampa Bay community and the Headquarters, bringing over 250 business and industry leaders to the Command and enforcing the importance of Special Operations. As president of the US Navy League, he provided tremendous support through community and business involvement, as well as successfully executing the Tampa Navy Balls. Through his direct efforts and support, Special Operations Command successfully executed an invaluable visit by former Prime Minister Ehud Barak, greatly enhancing an important international relationship. Mr. Rosenthal's personal efforts to ensure the successful community integration of Foreign Liaison Officers and their families are a cornerstone of the Command's global network. His tireless efforts and endless support to the Command's many initiatives make him a true teammate. The exceptional accomplishments and contributions of Mr. Rosenthal along with his service to our nation reflect great credit upon him and the United States Special Operations Command.

After hearing this I burst into tears. I had never been acknowledged like that ever before and was so proud to assist our military without ever needing any recognition. My heart and soul had been to assist and to promote the finest military in the world. I was given the microphone and was a bit choked up. I said that my mother had raised me to be a giving and kind person, and that my high school, Jesuit, had instilled in me the mantra of "Men for Others."

During my life, I came to interpret these values by being a positive civilian spokesperson that promotes and supports our fine military. I acknowledged my incredible wife, Deborah, who is the backbone of our family, and has instilled in me the confidence to keep my head high and take care of our family and our military in every way I can. I also mentioned my beautiful children, Jennifer and Jason, who have made our lives complete. I acknowledged my high school and college friends that had come to witness this great event. Finally, I commented on Admiral McRaven as being the most incredible leader SOCOM had ever known. This was a day I would never forget and is an amazing honor to treasure.

APRIL 14, 2014: LETTER OF CONGRATULATIONS

I was honored to receive the following note from General James Mattis:

> *Dear Mark,*
>
> *I've heard that you will be recognized by my old shipmate, Admiral Bill McRaven, and I want to add my congratulations. No one is more deserving of this honor and their recognition gives me the greatest of pleasures!*
>
> *With my best wishes,*
> *Semper Fi,*
> *Jim Mattis*

I was taken aback by his thoughtful letter of acknowledgment. It brought a tear to my eye and a fire to my soul to continue to work on behalf of our military heroes.

General David Petraeus presenting me with the Outstanding Public Service Award

With Admiral Michael Mullen, head of the Joint Chiefs of Staff, who signed the Outstanding Public Service Award

Rear Admiral Matts Fogelmark of Sweden and Major General Karl Horst presenting me with the Honorary Ambassador's Award of the Central Command Coalition

Admiral Bill McRaven presenting me with the United States Special Operations Command Outstanding Civilian Service Medal

Admiral Bill McRaven, Barbara Rosenthal, Jason, Deborah, me, Jennifer, and Georgeann McRaven as I received the Outstanding Civilian Service Medal at SOCOM

CHAPTER 23

Military Retirement and Change of Command Ceremonies

APRIL 21, 2011: RETIREMENT OF MAJOR GENERAL STEVEN J. HASHEM

Deborah and I first met Major General Steve Hashem and his delightful wife, Martha, at a social event at Special Operations Command in 2009. Steve and I became very close friends as we socialized often and played many rounds of golf together. Steve was a formidable golfer and had extensive experience in all areas of the military. I always enjoyed conversations with my dear friend.

General Hashem's career began as a graduate of the United States Military Academy in 1974. During his senior year at West Point, he won the light heavyweight boxing championship. He served in active duty for over ten years in a variety of leadership and staff positions in Europe and the United States. Prior to his first break from the military, Steve earned a master's degree in international relations from the University of Pennsylvania, along with a degree in Corporate Policy from Wharton School of Business. He worked for General Electric (GE), Martin Marietta, and Lockheed Martin in a variety of Senior Operations Management positions during his break from the military.

In 1985 Steven began his Reserve Career as a Battalion

Operations Officer in numerous areas, including being mobilized in Operation Desert Storm in 1991. From 1993 to 1996, he was assigned as commander, 404th Civil Affairs Battalion, and in 1998 he was appointed deputy commander for the Combined Joint Civil-Military Task Force during Operation Joint Guard in Bosnia- Herzegovina.

From 2004 to 2005, General Hashem relocated to Tampa to become director of Special Operations at the Center for Knowledge and Futures (SOKF) and the president of Joint Special Operations University. After going back to the civilian sector working as a private defense contractor in Philadelphia for five years, he returned to Tampa in 2010 to become the director of the Coalition Coordination Center at CENTCOM.

On April 21, 2011, Deborah and I witnessed our first Military Retirement Ceremony for General Hashem. It had such an impact on me since I knew Steve as a close friend, but I had not been entirely aware of his incredible military career until his life history was described during the ceremony. The venue was the Davis Conference Center at MacDill AFB and was at full capacity with 90% military and about 10% family and friends. Deborah and I were honored to be invited. The military sequence of events was new to us, so we had a unique admiration of this special military practice.

The stage awaited the official party. Once they walked on, everyone in the center stood to greet them. Then an Army enlisted man sang the national anthem which was followed by a beautiful invocation. Next came a narrated slide show presentation of General Hashem's career. Once the slide show concluded, the head of the Coalition, Brigadier General Praestegaard, provided some very nice remarks about the impact General Hashem has had on the 59 Coalition Countries based at Central Command (CENTCOM). Next, the current head of CENTCOM, General James Mattis, gave a rousing speech about the impact General Hashem had made during his illustrious career in the Military. The Award Ceremony was followed by a presentation by General Mattis of the Retirement

Certificate, the Retirement Letter from the president of the United States, and the Retirement Letter on behalf of the head of the Army. General Mattis then presented a special gift to Martha Hashem and expressed many accolades about Steve's very dedicated wife. Then came the very moving farewell remarks by General Hashem. Steve's speech thanked a multitude of people who were part of his life and included many of those present for the event. After Steve's speech, the Soldier's Creed of Army Values was read, and a recording was played of the singing of the Armed Forces Medley. The event was both enlightening and moving. At the reception that followed, Deborah and I congratulated Steve and Martha and thanked them for all they do for our country.

JULY 21, 2011: RETIREMENT OF MAJOR GENERAL MICHAEL D. JONES

The Retirement Ceremony of Major General Michael Jones, chief of staff of CENTCOM, was held at the Vince Auditorium at MacDill AFB. His last active-duty assignment was as the chief of staff for CENTCOM, first under General John Allen and then under General James Mattis, all overseeing the wars in Afghanistan and Iraq, as well as the US military activity throughout the Middle East and Southwest Asia.

Previously, General Jones served as the director of operations for CENTCOM. Other general officer assignments include commander of Civilian Police Advisory and Assistance Team in Iraq, deputy director of strategic plans and policy (J-5) for the Joint Staff in the Pentagon, and assistant division commander of the 1st Cavalry Division in Iraq.

General Jones was a career armor officer and served in a variety of command and staff assignments, including the operations officer (G-3) of both, the 1st Armored Division and the Multi-National Division North in IFOR in Bosnia. He also served at the US Army

Armor School as an armor tactics instructor and returned to command the Armor Leader Training Unit for the US Army and Marine Corps. Other key staff positions include director and chief of staff of the Army Staff Group, executive assistant to the director of the Joint Staff, and commander, 2-67 Armor.

The ceremony included the many military traditions with General Mattis presiding and eloquently describing Mike's great military career and accomplishments over his thirty-four years of dedicated service to our country. The event was wonderfully attended with family, friends, military leaders, and related associates. We were honored to attend.

AUGUST 8, 2011: CHANGE OF COMMAND AT SOCOM

The secretary of defense, Leon Panetta, officiated the change of the leadership of Special Operations Command from Admiral Eric Olson to Admiral William McRaven. This was a rare command change since these incredible leaders were both the only four-star SEALs in the Navy. Deborah and I were honored to be invited. The event was held at the Davis Conference Center at MacDill AFB in Tampa. The venue was at full capacity with 90 percent military personnel and 10 percent civilian business leaders.

Admiral Olson gave a very impressive speech by emphasizing that each special operator is a highly important asset to SOCOM. In fact, he said that the leadership of our operators is more critical than even our hardware. Once Eric completed his speech, both admirals stood up, and the SOCOM flag was passed from Admiral Olson to Admiral McRaven. Admiral McRaven gave a very complimentary speech thanking Admiral Olson for his incredible dedication and for making a difference in the ethos of SOCOM operations.

As a civilian, I especially appreciated the ceremonial flag

transferring command from Admiral Olson to Admiral McRaven as the official formality of the event. The leadership of CENTCOM, commander General James Mattis and deputy commander Admiral Robert Harwood were present along with former CENTCOM deputy commander three-star General John Allen. Also present was the commandant of the Marines Corps, four-star General James Amos.

After the event, there was a reception to congratulate Admiral Olson and his family and a wonderful social of military leadership with one another and with civilians. General Allen introduced me to General Amos, who presented me with his challenge coin, which I cherish to this day. Deborah and I enjoyed the event and were excited for the Olsons, a beautiful end to an extraordinary career. They decided to make Tampa their permanent home and we are delighted to have such wonderful friends in our community.

AUGUST 31, 2011: RETIREMENT OF GENERAL DAVID H. PETRAEUS
ARMED FORCES FAREWELL TRIBUTE

Deborah and I were in New York City when, at 5:30 a.m. on August 31, 2011, we headed to Pennsylvania Station to catch the Amtrak Acela Train to Washington Union Station. We arrived in DC at 9:00 a.m. and viewed the beautiful main hall with its vast dome ceiling. Washington Union Station was one of the country's first great union railroad terminal. Designed by Daniel Burnham, the station opened on October 27, 1907, and was completed in April 1908.

We then caught a cab to the Joint Base Myer for the outdoor ceremony for our friend, General David Petraeus. Our cab dropped us off near the bleacher area overlooking the immense grounds for the ceremony. Approximately 1,500 guests arrived for the event on a beautiful Virginia Day at Summerall Field. We could see from a distance all the dignitaries coming in for the event in their black SUVs with their security escorts—head of Central Command, General James Mattis; deputy secretary of defense, Ash Carter; chairman of the Joint Chiefs of Staff, Admiral Michael Mullin; director of the CIA, Leon Panetta; deputy director of the CIA, Michael Morell, along with numerous other dignitaries.

At 10:00 a.m. the ceremony began with the Joint Services (Army, Navy, Air Force, and Marines) marching in different formations. Then the flag bearers from each service were lined up in formation and the national anthem was played. General Petraeus then walked throughout the lined formations of men and women in uniform inspecting and greeting each of the groups. Next, General Petraeus, along with Admiral Mullen, and Ash Carter, sat in the covered staging area to view the procession of the military. Deputy Secretary Carter and Admiral Mullen each gave remarks about the incredible career of General Petraeus.

General David Petraeus was the head of the NATO International Security Assistance Forces from 2010 to 2011. He was the commander of US Central Command from 2008 to 2010. He served for nineteen months as the commanding general of the Multi-National Force–Iraq overseeing the surge in Iraq. Prior to this tour, he commanded the US Army Combined Arms Center in Fort Leavenworth. He developed the Army/Marine Corps Counterinsurgency Field Manual and corresponding changes to Army training and leader development. Prior to this, he served for over fifteen months as the first commander of both the Multi-National Security Transition Command–Iraq and the NATO Training Mission–Iraq, directing the Train and Equip Mission.

That deployment to Iraq followed his command of the 101st Airborne Division, where he led the Screaming Eagles during the fight to Baghdad and throughout the first year of Operation Iraqi Freedom. His command of the 101st followed a year deployed on Operation Joint Forge in Bosnia, where he was the assistant chief of staff for Operations of the NATO Stabilization Force and the deputy commander of the US Joint Counter-Terrorism Task Force-Bosnia.

General Petraeus, after graduating from his class with high honors at West Point, he also earned an MPA and PhD Degree in International Relations from Princeton University's Woodrow Wilson School of Public and International Affairs.

After the speeches describing the many accomplishments of General Petraeus, the four joint forces marched about the field in a large procession while the orchestra played the "Armed Forces Medley" representing each of the military branches. Following the ceremony, everyone walked over to Henderson Hall and greeted and congratulated General Petraeus and his family. This was the most ornate military event Deborah and I had ever attended. The Petraeuses were very appreciative that we joined them in this final farewell tribute, and we were quite honored.

NOVEMBER 14, 2011: RETIREMENT OF LIEUTENANT GENERAL DAVID P. FRIDOVICH

Deborah and I were honored to be invited to the Retirement Ceremony of deputy commander of SOCOM, Lieutenant General David Fridovich, at the Davis Conference Center at MacDill AFB. Admiral Eric Olson, the commander of SOCOM, officiated the ceremony and gave a beautiful description of Dave's many accomplishments.

General Dave Fridovich received his undergraduate Degree from Knox College then went on to receive his master's degree in political science from Tulane University. After graduating, he was commissioned into the Army as a rifle and reconnaissance platoon leader, company executive officer, and light infantry company commander with the 172nd Light Infantry Brigade in Fort Richardson, Alaska. In 2000, he commanded the Combined/Joint Special Operations Task Force in Operation Joint Forge in Sarajevo, Bosnia-Herzegovina. In 2005, Dave was appointed commander of Special Operations Command-Pacific. In 2010, he was appointed deputy commander of the US Special Operation Command (SOCOM).

Many of General Fridovich's missions were clandestine, so they could not be mentioned, but he spent much of his time in most parts of the world with a talent of influencing non-aligned countries to consider Western World values versus terrorism. He was so talented and persuasive, it could be said that he abetted in the prevention of military issues abroad.

We were so excited for Dave and Kathy as they transitioned into the civilian sector. Deborah felt a particular pride in her former Nova High School classmate's life-long military achievements and wished him a healthy and happy retirement. Since we both knew that his strong discipline and work ethic was extraordinary, we did not expect him to rest to much in retirement; rather, we knew he was more inclined to continue to accomplish great deeds and further his good work for the betterment of our people and our country (and we were right).

DECEMBER 27, 2012: RETIREMENT OF CAPTAIN TODD SCHAPLER

I first met Captain Todd Schapler during a Navy League function in Tampa. He was a strong supporter of the Junior ROTC (Reserve Officers' Training Corps) and participated and volunteered in the work the Navy League performed. I did not know at the time that he would later be instrumental in my becoming the president of the Navy League Tampa Council.

Todd is a graduate of the University of Washington where he earned a bachelor of arts degree in foreign affairs and Russian studies. He also earned a master's degree in business administration and is a certified project management professional.

Captain Schapler began his career at Cecil Field, Florida, and deployed to the Mediterranean Sea and the Caribbean Sea on the USS *John F. Kennedy* nuclear aircraft carrier. In 1992, he was assigned to the USS *Dwight D. Eisenhower* aircraft carrier, where he was the anti-submarine/anti-surface warfare and tomahawk land attack missile strike officer. He was also a naval aviator and flew the S-3A/B Viking in his active-duty career. In 1994, he was assigned as the department head in the VS-21 in the South Pacific aboard the USS *Independence* aircraft carrier.

Between 1999 and 2005, Captain Schapler went into the Navy Reserves, where some of his assignments included tactical support in Italy and Afghanistan. Later in 2005, he reported to CENTCOM where he served as the chief of operations. He was then selected as the CENTCOM liaison officer to the International Security Assistance Force (ISAF) in Kabul, Afghanistan. In 2007, he was called back to active duty at CENTCOM as deputy chief of current operations and joint operations center chief, where he directed the team responsible for monitoring and reporting all operational developments throughout the Central Command area of responsibility (the Middle East).

In addition to setting up briefings for our community leaders to CENTCOM, I often coordinated briefings for our Navy League volunteers as well. After the briefings in the main auditorium, Todd would invite our group into the Joint Operation Center (JOC) Room, as it was called, to see the big screen displaying what was going on in the area of responsibility (not the top-secret parts), mainly the Persian Gulf, Afghanistan, and Iraq. Todd would further brief us on how the satellites and drones provided the most up-to-date information on our operations, so that we had an edge, day and night, on the enemy.

The retirement ceremony was held in the JOC Room with a full house of friends and military leaders who Todd had deployed with during his career. The official party arrived, which included a large contingent of his family from Washington State. The ceremony began with the national anthem, followed by the invocation. Next,

Rear Admiral (RADM) Simon Cullen of the Royal Australian Navy gave some remarks about the many attributes and accomplishments of Captain Schapler and then presented awards on behalf of his shipmates. This was followed by the reading of the retirement certificate, the retirement letter from the president of the United States, and official presentations to his wife, Sandra. Then Todd shared some special experiences about his career in the Navy.

The ceremony was followed by a very nice reception. I was honored to be present and grateful for the opportunity of knowing him and enjoying our camaraderie and friendship during his stay in Tampa.

MARCH 22, 2013: CHANGE OF COMMAND AT SOCOM

General James N. Mattis invited Deborah and me to join a very select group of Tampa Bay business leaders to witness him as he relinquished command of Central Command to General Lloyd Austin.

General Mattis earned a bachelor of arts degree in history from Central Washington University in 1971 and a master of arts degree in international security affairs from the National War College of National Defense University in 1994. He enlisted in the Marine Corps Reserve in 1969 and was commissioned a second lieutenant through the Naval Reserve Officers Training Corps in 1972. During his service, General Mattis was considered an intellectual among the upper ranks. In 1972, as a lieutenant, he was assigned as a rifle and weapons platoon commander in the 3rd Marine Division. Upon promotion to lieutenant colonel, he commanded Battalion 7th Marines, one of Task Force Ripper's assault battalions during the Gulf War. In 2001, he led the 1st Marine Expeditionary Brigade as its commanding officer upon promotion to brigadier general in Afghanistan. It was as a regimental commander that he earned his nickname and call sign, "CHAOS," an acronym for Colonel Has

Another Outstanding Solution. Later, he was given a new call sign "Mad Dog" because of his many unique and sometimes controversial quotes. As a major general, he commanded the 1st Marine Division during the 2003 invasion of Iraq and the Iraq War. He played key roles in combat operations in Fallujah, including negotiation with the insurgent command inside the city during Operation Vigilant Resolve in 2004 and participation in planning the subsequent Operation Phantom Fury. He would continue his active duty and later, in 2010, he became the commander of CENTCOM at MacDill AFB in Tampa where he oversaw the wars in Iraq and Afghanistan.

Deborah and I saw him on several occasions at his home on the base. He was a true proponent of engaging the local community and connecting us with the military. He was a lovely host. We would all socialize with food and drink and then he would request our attention and enlighten us with a brief synopsis of the Middle East. Deborah and I got the impression that he was kind of a modern-day General George Patton—he was "old school."

Now, in 2013, he planned to retire. Officiating the change of command ceremony at Hangar Three of MacDill AFB was the Honorable Charles T. Hagel, the secretary of defense. Secretary Hagel described the incredible leadership General Mattis gave to CENTCOM and the military community. After the event, a reception was held at the Davis Conference Center. I was honored to meet some of the top generals in our military along with the new head of CENTCOM, General Lloyd Austin, and his lovely wife, Charlene.

APRIL 28–30, 2013: RETIREMENT OF GENERAL JOHN R. ALLEN

Deborah and I were invited to General John Allen's retirement ceremony at Annapolis, Maryland, the home of the United States Naval Academy. This was an amazing honor since we considered

John and Kathy Allen close friends from our shared time in Tampa.

Prior to the event, Ms. Anna Ward, the secretary to the commandant of midshipmen at the US Naval Academy, contacted me. She had worked for then-Colonel Allen when he was commandant there. She told me that General Allen had reached out to her to help coordinate a tour of the Naval Academy for us. Ms. Ward connected us with Mr. Don Nelson, in charge of security for the Naval Academy.

On April 27, we flew to Baltimore, Maryland, stayed the night in a hotel and then headed out the next morning for Annapolis, about forty-five minutes away. The city of Annapolis is very quaint with a Bostonian feel.

Annapolis was the capital of the United States from November 26, 1783, through August 13, 1784. The city has an interesting history. In the statehouse, the oldest in the nation still in legislative use, General George Washington resigned his commission before the Continental Congress on December 23, 1783. Also here on January 14, 1784, Congress ratified the Treaty of Paris to end the Revolutionary War, and on May 7, 1784, Thomas Jefferson was appointed minister plenipotentiary. It was from the statehouse, that on September 14, 1786, the Annapolis Convention issued the call to the states which led to the Constitutional Convention, which as we all know, took place in Philadelphia, Pennsylvania in 1787.

Mr. Don Nelson greeted us at the gate of the Naval Academy. He then drove us all around the grounds for a grand tour. The Naval Academy is located right on the bank of where the Severn River and the Chesapeake Bay meet. Of the five US military service academies, it is the second oldest and educates officers for commissioning primarily into the US Navy and the US Marine Corps. The 338-acre campus is located on the former grounds of Fort Severn in Anne Arundel County, thirty-three miles east of Washington, DC, and twenty-six miles southeast of Baltimore. The entire campus (known to insiders as "the yard") is a national historic landmark and home to many historic sites, buildings, and monuments. It replaced

Philadelphia Naval Asylum, which served as the first US Naval Academy from 1838 to 1845, which is when the Naval Academy formed in Annapolis.

Mr. Nelson took us around the beautiful campus of red brick buildings. He took us into the campus chapel and synagogue. I read this quote in the synagogue from Uriah P. Levy's last will and testament of 1862:

> I give, devise, and bequeath my Farm and Estate at Monticello in Virginia, formerly belonging to President Jefferson . . . to the People of the United States for the sole and only purpose of educating as practical farmers children of the warrant office of the United States Navy whose fathers are dead. I consider Thomas Jefferson to be one of the greatest men in history, author of the Declaration of Independence and the absolute democrat. He did much to mold our Republic in a form in which a man's religion does not make him ineligible for political or governmental life. I would rather serve as a cabin boy in the American Navy than as a captain in any other service in the world.

We toured numerous buildings on campus, which has such an amazing history, and then Mr. Nelson and his wife, Carol, invited us for a delicious lunch at the famous Alley Restaurant on campus. Around 2:00 p.m. we headed to the indoor gymnasium for the ceremony. The original plan was an outdoor ceremony on the grounds with marching formations, but since it was raining that day, the ceremony was moved indoors. I can only imagine the quick planning that had to take place to adjust to the logistical changes.

The list of invitees was the who's who of American military leaders, including four-star General David Petraeus; four-star Admiral Bill McRaven; four-star General James Mattis; four-star General Martin Dempsey, chairman of the Joint Chiefs of Staff;

four-star Major General Charles Bolden, administrator of NASA and astronaut; and three-star Lieutenant General James Clapper, director of national intelligence. What an all-star cast!

Four-star General James F. Amos, the thirty-fifth commandant of the Marine Corps, officiated the ceremony along with United States secretary of the Navy, Ray Mabus, as well as General Dempsey. The ceremony was very emotional as General Allen, after thirty-eight years of service, received all his certificates and accommodations from the top leaders in the country, including the president of the United States. Then the commandant's own Marine Corps Drum and Bugle Corps band played numerous patriotic songs as they marched around the gym in a formation of troops with their fixed bayonets. It was a once-in-a-lifetime experience to witness the retirement ceremony for one of the greatest generals of our time.

After the ceremony, there was a reception area where all the attendees socialized and congratulated John and Kathy for their incredible dedication and service to our great country.

Later, the Allens had a family dinner at Ruth's Chris Steak House and invited Deborah and me to attend. We were flattered to be included with their special family. The sixteen of us celebrated together as one happy family that night and it reminded us of the closeness of our friendship during those years they lived in Tampa. We saw them quite often back then and had many special times together.

The next morning, the Allens invited us to join them at Chick and Ruth's Deli in Annapolis. This famous deli has a midshipman or a high-ranking military leader lead in the Pledge of Allegiance each morning. What a delicious breakfast in such a patriotic place! This was an incredible ending to an unforgettable experience at the Naval Academy in Annapolis. We said our goodbyes and were sad to leave.

JUNE 12, 2013: CHANGE OF COMMAND OF THE US COAST GUARD

As the president of the United States Navy League Tampa Bay Council, I was honored to be invited to the change of command ceremony for the St. Petersburg Sector of the US Coast Guard. The ceremony is a time-honored tradition, formally proclaiming the continuity of the authority of the command. It is a formal ritual, conducted before the assembled company of the command, as well as honored guests and dignitaries.

The change of command itself is a transfer of total responsibility and authority from one individual to another. The ceremony has its basis in naval regulations that require all hands to muster at the time of turning over command. The regulations state the officer about to be relieved shall read their orders of detachment and turn over the command to their successor, who shall read their orders and assume command.

The ceremony started with the arrival of the official party with Captain Sheryl Dickinson, commander of Sector St. Petersburg, being relieved by Captain Gregory Case, the presentation of the colors, and the singing of the national anthem by Craig Sappo. Then came an inspection of the honor platoon by Rear Admiral William D. Baumgartner, the commander of the 7th Coast Guard district headquartered in Miami, Florida. He is responsible for all Coast Guard operations in the Southeast United States and the Caribbean Basin, including Florida, Georgia, South Carolina, Puerto Rico, the US Virgin Islands, and over fifteen thousand miles of coastline. In addition, the 7th District shares operational borders with thirty-four foreign nations and territories.

Admiral Baumgartner gave a briefing on the many achievements of Captain Sheryl Dickinson, including drug interdiction and saving lives on the seas. The ceremony for the Execution of Orders came next followed by the remarks of Captain Gregory Case. He spoke about his goals and aspirations as the new head of Coast Guard Sector St. Petersburg.

The ceremony was very memorable, and I was grateful to be included as a representative of the US Navy League. I was in the company of great leaders of the United States Coast Guard.

JUNE 27, 2014: RETIREMENT OF COMMAND SERGEANT MAJOR FRANK A. GRIPPE

Command Sergeant Major Frank Grippe was the highest-ranking enlisted leader for CENTCOM under commanding general Lloyd Austin, and a true American. Deborah and I were honored to be invited for his special day of retirement.

The event was held at the Davis Conference Center at MacDill AFB with a full audience present. The sequence of events was as we had experienced in the past with the arrival of the official party, the presentation of the colors, national anthem, invocation, remarks by General Austin, and the presentation of the retirement certificate and awards.

Frank gave a rousing speech thanking everyone for being there and sharing some of his incredible career experiences in the military. He was an Army Ranger who entered the military in Syracuse, New York, in April of 1981. He trained as a light infantryman and graduated from Airborne School at Fort Benning, Georgia. He had served in almost every possible position and most parts of the world during his thirty-three-year career.

Some of his awards and decorations include the Defense Superior Service Medal, Legion of Merit, Bronze Star, and the Purple Heart. I have kept in touch with Frank as he has transitioned out of the military and moved into the civilian sector in Tampa. He is currently executive vice president of government affairs for Neuro 20 Technology Corp.

AUGUST 15, 2014: CHANGE OF COMMAND AT JOINT INTELLIGENCE CENTER CENTCOM

The change of command ceremony is a simple, traditional event that is rich with symbolism and heritage. The key to the ceremony is the passing of the unit's colors. The colors represent not only the lineage and honors of the unit but also the loyalty and unity of its members.

The colors are the commander's symbol of authority representing his responsibilities to the organization. Wherever the commander is, there are also the colors. The custodian of the colors is the senior noncommissioned officer, who is the principal advisor to the commander.

The passing of the colors symbolizes the transfer of command and authority from the old commander to the new commander. Due to the reverence each of the ceremony participants feels toward the unit colors, they are kept over the left breast of the possessor, at all times during the transfer. The passing of the colors demonstrates to the members of the unit that the old commander has passed the mantle of leadership, and with this, also passes the loyalty of the unit to the new commander.

The outgoing commander of the Joint Intelligence Center at Central Command (CENTCOM) was Captain Frank D. Whitworth. I got to know Frank during my time in charge of the US Navy League Tampa Bay Council. I am proud to call Frank a friend. He is a great American patriot. The incoming commander was Captain Curt Copley.

The welcoming remarks were from Brigadier General Steven R. Grove, the director of intelligence for US Central Command. He gave a nice introduction and told the attendees what a wonderful job Captain Whitworth had done and said that he set high standards at the institution. Vice Admiral Mark Fox, deputy of Central Command, was the guest speaker.

Mark Fox worked with our team at the Navy League as we helped facilitate the 2014 Navy League Ball. Mark was super friendly and later in the year had his entire family over to see the Train Room. Mark is known for being the first commanding officer of Strike Fighter Squadron 122, the Navy's first F/A-18E/F Super Hornet squadron. In the Iraq War in 1990, he shot down the first Soviet-made MIG (operated by the Iraqis) since the Korean War.

Mark said that he shot the MIG with an air-to-air missile with no visual. Moments later, the parts of the plane he hit flew by him. This was the first air-to-air fight between an American Phantom jet and a Soviet MIG since the Korean War. Mark gave some very nice remarks about Captain Copley and included their previous military experiences. The event ended with both parties leaving after the boatswain's (a ship's officer in charge of equipment and crew) whistle was blown. I was honored to be able to attend this beautiful ceremony.

NOVEMBER 23, 2016: RETIREMENT OF VICE ADMIRAL SEAN A. PYBUS

Vice Admiral Sean Pybus, a three-star admiral, and deputy commander of Special Operations (SOCOM), retired after a thirty-seven-year career. His retirement ceremony was officiated by Admiral Eric Olson (four-star Navy SEAL and former head of SOCOM). This memorable event included the presence of Admiral Pybus's four children, all active-duty military, who each presented personal remarks about their father. This was very moving.

Current Special Operations head, General Tony Thomas, provided remarks about the accomplishments of Admiral Pybus as a sailor and a leader and talked about the many medals he had earned throughout his illustrious career. These include the Defense Distinguished Service Medal, Navy Distinguished Service Medal,

Legion of Merit, Armed Forces Expeditionary Medal, and the Navy Unit Commendation.

Sean was a graduate of the University of Rochester and was commissioned through the Reserve Officers Training Corps. He then went on to Basic Underwater Demolition/Sea, Air, Land Training in Coronado, California. He became a platoon commander for SEAL Team One, Two, and Six, and was deployed in many classified missions in Latin America, Europe, Asia, and Africa. He served as the assault squadron leader for the *MS Achille Lauro* cruise ship hijacking in one of his classified missions.

I am so proud and happy that Sean and his lovely wife, Patty, decided to retire in Tampa, and I felt privileged to attend the retirement ceremony of such a remarkable man.

JANUARY 6, 2017: RETIREMENT OF COLONEL DANIEL C. HODNE

Colonel Daniel Hodne was a special military leader because he had direct influence on the outcome of many of our military successes. He earned his commission from West Point Military Academy in 1991. He served as a Bradley fighting vehicle platoon leader and headquarters company executive leader. After volunteering for Special Forces training, he was assigned to the 5th Special Forces Group. He led operations throughout the Middle East and northeast Africa. He also participated in two combat tours during Operation Iraqi Freedom, as a Special Forces company commander and battalion operations officer.

While serving with the Joint Staff at the Pentagon, and after leading the coordination and staffing efforts that introduced "irregular warfare" into joint doctrine, he was chosen to be the sole Army strategist on the personal staff of the chairman of the Joint Chiefs of Staff in the Chairman's Action Group. In this capacity, he assisted two chairmen in formulating their best military advice to the president, secretary of defense, and Congress. He then led the Special Operations Plans Branch in the deputy directorate for special operations and counterterrorism for the National Military Command Center.

After his Pentagon assignment, he served as commander of the US Army Marksmanship Unit. Colonel Hodne completed his twenty-six-year military career as the chief of plans at US Special Operations Command (SOCOM)

I was honored to attend his retirement ceremony in the War Games Room at SOCOM. General Joseph Votel, commander of SOCOM, officiated the ceremony along with Dan's twin brother, Dave, as the assistant to the commander of CENTCOM. There was a map of the world on the floor of the room that looked like a giant iPad. Dan's duty had sent him to many parts of the world and accordingly, the map on the floor was illuminated with all of Dan's deployments.

Dan was one of our early STAR operators and he was very conscientious about following our guidance. He gave a very rousing speech about his history in the military and his love of country and family. The crowd of approximately 120 enjoyed the ceremony and then socialized afterward at a reception. I was honored to meet Dan's special family. We are very close friends to this day. Incidentally, with STAR involvement, Dan was hired by the Moffit Cancer Center and Research Institute shortly after his retirement. His background in strategic operations and planning proved very effective for Moffit and has influenced their entire ethos. He has been a total gamechanger for their 6,000-employee institution. Moffit is known for being one of the top eight cancer centers in America. Since first being hired, Dan has been promoted several times and is currently the chief of staff to the CEO.

MARCH 22, 2017: RETIREMENT OF CAPTAIN KENT PARO

The retirement ceremony of Captain Kent Paro took place at MacDill AFB. Vice Admiral Sean Pybus, deputy commander of SOCOM, officiated the ceremony.

Captain Paro completed Basic Underwater Demolition/SEAL(BUD/S) training in 1988 with BUD/S class 148 and was assigned to SEAL Team Three where he deployed as assistant platoon commander in support of Operations Desert Shield and Desert Storm. In December of 2000, Captain Paro was assigned as a Western Hemisphere action officer and then from 2001 to 2002, as the US Central Command branch head for the Joint Staff at the Pentagon. In May of 2004, he assumed command of SEAL Team Ten in Norfolk, Virginia, and led the deployment in support of Operations Enduring Freedom, Iraqi Freedom, and Joint Guardian. From 2005 to 2006, he served as the chief staff officer for Naval Special Warfare Group Two. From 2007 to 2011, he became a Navy Special Warfare officer detailer and went from Millington, Tennessee to Stuttgart, Germany. Captain Paro then served on the SOCOM command parachute team, the Para-Commandos, and rose from demonstrator to professional exhibition rating (PRO) and tandem instructor, performing for more than a million citizens around the country. From January 2012 to 2016, he was selected and served as the SOCOM Navy element commander. At Special Operations Command in 2014, Captain Paro was assigned as both director of program analysis and evaluation and assessment director for special programs until his retirement. His incredibly dedicated professionalism made a real difference in our Navy.

Admiral Pybus gave a terrific account of Kent's history with our military, giving him rave reviews as one of our best (details of his missions could not be revealed). However, he did mention that a particular mission was so top secret and so dangerous that he knew going in that there was a strong possibility Kent would not return.

The ceremony was well done with the US Navy Song, "Anchors Aweigh," sung at the conclusion.

Captain Paro was one of our first STAR SOCOM military leaders who came to our events and transitioned successfully into the civilian sector, becoming senior vice president of Grow Financial in Tampa.

APRIL 13, 2017: RETIREMENT OF CAPTAIN JOHN DOOLITTLE

As a cofounder of our STAR program as well as my involvement with the military, I was fortunate to get to know Captain John Doolittle and honored to be invited to attend his retirement ceremony at MacDill AFB. Officiating the event was Vice Admiral Sean Pybus, deputy commander of Special Operations Command (SOCOM). Admiral Pybus gave a beautiful tribute to Captain Doolittle's incredible service to this nation. He is a brilliant, down-to-earth military leader.

Captain Doolittle received his bachelor of science degree from the Air Force Academy in 1992. From 1997 to 2002 he was assigned to SEAL Team Two and conducted deployments throughout Europe, Africa, Kosovo, and the Baltics. In 2007, he reported to SOCOM in Tampa where he served in the Maritime Acquisition and Assessment Division. In 2009, he was selected for command of the Provincial Reconstruction Team in Ghazni, Afghanistan. His final command was in Tampa at SOCOM as the director for the preservation of the force and family (POTFF) task force.

It was an honor to attend this emotional ceremony along with his family, friends, special operators, and our STAR program participants. John, now retired from the military, is currently the chief revenue officer for KAATSU Global based out of Japan. KAATSU is the pioneer in the emerging blood flow restriction market.

JUNE 23, 2017: RETIREMENT OF COLONEL BRIAN K. FLOOD

Prior to the retirement of Colonel Brian Flood and as a member of our STAR program, Brian joined me for lunch and a visit to my office. As is our STAR model, soon-to-retire military members shadow Tampa Bay business leaders to get a sense of the fields they may have an interest in. I showed him the office and shared my experiences in real estate, insurance, and public adjusting. He appreciated the insight and perspective of these different sectors, and I was glad to share. When it came time for his retirement, I was flattered to be invited to the ceremony, which was held in the War Games Room at Special Operations Command (SOCOM).

Brian graduated from the United States Military Academy in 1992 and spent over twenty-five years serving this country. He was commissioned as an infantry officer upon graduation, and he went to Fort Polk in the 2nd Armored Cavalry Regiment and 1st Battalion 509th Parachute Infantry Battalion. In Panama, he served as the aide-de-camp to the commanding general of the US Army. After Panama, he commanded Headquarters Company 6th Ranger Training Battalion at Eglin Air Force Base. He then attended graduate school at Harvard (his first day was September 11, 2001), graduating Harvard University's Kennedy School of Government and the College of Naval Command and Staff. He was then assigned to the War Plans Division of the US Army staff at the Pentagon. Then he attended the US Naval War College in Newport, Rhode Island, where he earned a second master's degree and met his wife, Colleen.

Brian went to Fort Bragg where he served as the battalion operations officer for the 2nd Battalion. He then headed to Samarra, Iraq, where he served as battalion executive officer. Following his first tour with the 82nd Airborne Division, he was assigned to the Current Operations Division of Joint Special Operations Command (JSOC) and performed two additional combat deployments. From February 2010 until February 2012, Brian returned to the 82nd

Airborne Division and served as the battalion commander for the 5th Squadron, 73rd Cavalry.

In 2012 he returned to JSOC as the deputy chief of the Strategic Plans and Policy Division and deployed to Afghanistan to serve as the senior special operations liaison officer between the Special Operations Joint Task Assistance Force-Afghanistan and the NATO-led International Security Assistance Force (ISAF). He was then assigned to SOCOM in 2014 as chief of future operations (J35).

The event included several pictures of Brian throughout his career posted on screens around the perimeter of the room. Opening remarks were given by the head of Special Operations Command, General A. Raymond Thomas (Tony), followed by the award presentation, presentation of the presidential certificate of appreciation, flag ceremony, and then Colonel Flood's remarks. The ceremony ended with the singing of the US Army song, "The Army Goes Rolling Along." Afterward, there was a nice reception in an adjacent room.

That evening Deborah and I were invited to the Flood home to further celebrate his retirement. Brian took me into a room and showed me a wall covered with military awards and titles. He also showed me a few of the weapons he had used. He mentioned that on a Sunday in Iraq in 2007, he was outside the Green Zone protecting a group of people when he suddenly bent down, heard a shot being fired, and was spared being killed. The shot came from a sniper shooting at him and luckily, him bending down just at that moment prevented him from getting shot in the head. The bullet ricocheted off the sight of his weapon and he was fortunate to have only a minor injury. After hearing this, I realized the great risks our operators take to protect our country.

The party was very nice, and we enjoyed meeting Brian's friends and family members.

JULY 14, 2017: RETIREMENT OF COLONEL BRETT R. HAUENSTEIN

I met Colonel Brett Hauenstein through our STAR program, and he was a true star through and through. He is from Sioux City, Iowa, and has a very nice, relaxed personality. Brent was a brilliant leader at SOCOM. In 1989, he was commissioned into the Air Force and then went on to receive his master's degree from Embry Riddle Aeronautical University.

Brett became a helicopter pilot of the HH-1H Helicopter and then transitioned to the MH-53J Helicopter. He flew missions over Bosnia and Korea before returning to the United States to command the 23rd Flying Training Squadron where he was responsible for helicopter pilot training for the US Air Force. In 2016 he came to Tampa to become the chief of training and education (J7) for SOCOM. In this capacity, he oversaw training and education requirements and standardization throughout the Special Operations enterprise.

Colonel Hauenstein's retirement ceremony was held at the SOCOM University next to the Special Operations Command center at MacDill AFB. Lieutenant General Thomas Trask, US Air Force (vice commander of US Special Operations Command in DC) officiated the ceremony. General Trask is responsible for planning, coordinating, and executing actions with the Office of the Secretary of Defense, the Joint Staff, the services, and the other governmental agencies in the National Capital Region on behalf of the commander of SOCOM.

The ceremony proceeded in the traditional format. Brett gave a beautiful speech highlighting his twenty-eight-year career with an open letter that he included in the printed program. Below is what he wrote, which was so meaningful and characterized what a true patriot he is:

> *As I draw to a close 28 years of service, I reflect on the most important influences in my life and I am continually drawn*

to everything my family has done, and all I can say is that I have truly been blessed.

To my wife: After 28 years of marriage, you are still one of the strongest people I know and without your support, I would have never been able to go to work every day and give my all to the mission and my people. I never spent a single day worrying about the "home front" because I knew you had it all handled.

You stood tall through 15 moves, two of which we did by ourselves with a trailer and a couple of friends. You remained by my side while I spent hundreds of days a year flying all over the world and then enduring my absence for a year remote in Korea. I know you spent sleepless nights waiting for me to walk through the door at 3:00 a.m. and said a tiny prayer every time you heard a Pave Low flyby. You rode out hurricanes by yourself as I flew away from the aircraft so they would be safe from the storm. You patiently waited in recovery rooms after surgeries and pushed me through painful rehabs.

You were with me doing all the things a commander's wife was expected to do and selflessly went to every event I asked you to do, and you did it all with a smile. You were there when we lost friends and still managed to provide me the strength to carry on. I cannot express how much I love you: you are my best friend and confidant, and I would not trade the last 28 years for anything. I would not be the man I am today without you, and I look forward to another 28 years.

To my daughter: Haley, you continue to be an inspiration and one of my greatest blessings. You keep working hard and you are becoming a lovely young lady. A week doesn't go by without me feeling incredibly proud of the choices you make. You have an inner strength and someday you will see that as clearly as I do. You have shown me how resilient and tough a kid needs to be these days, and while growing up isn't always fun, I love seeing where your life is taking you each and every

> day. I can only dream of the things you will do in your life, and I cannot wait to see the woman you will become. Please know that I love you and will always be your biggest fan.
>
> Every time I counseled my young officers and NCOs, I had a list of proven advice to pass on: give 100% every day, take responsibility for your actions, remember that every job is what you put into it, and look out for your people, etc. The most important piece of advice I ever gave was for each person to remember that the day after you retire from the service, all of your accomplishments and all the extra time you spent away at work will largely be forgotten, but the one thing that needs to be forever is your family. I told them that if you do anything in this life, remember to protect and build those relationships. I am proud to say that after 28 years, I am thrilled to have Sandi and Haley in my life and can only hope that I have done right by them. —Brett

That letter in and of itself was very moving, as was the ceremony and the remarks overall. These words gave me a greater understanding of the thoughts, concerns, and worries our service members deal with as they balance the sacrifices of serving our country with the well-being of their families. It was my honor to attend.

SEPTEMBER 15, 2017: RETIREMENT OF COLONEL MARTY C. JONES

Officiating Colonel Marty Jones's retirement ceremony was Major General Robert Karmazin, who serves as the director of J7 Joint Special Operations Forces Development and has the dual responsibility of being the deputy commanding general for mobilization and reserve affairs at the US Special Operations Command (SOCOM) at MacDill AFB in Tampa.

Colonel Jones is from central Georgia and entered active service as a distinguished military graduate from Mercer University's ROTC program. He completed the Rotary Wing Aviator Course and qualified as a UH-60 assault pilot in 1991. He began operational assignments in Germany and then the 82nd Airborne Division at Fort Bragg, North Carolina, commanding assault helicopter platoons. In 2002, he was assigned to the Joint Readiness Training Center in Fort Polk, Louisiana, as the operations group aviation division senior operations observer/controller.

Colonel Jones served in Operation Iraqi Freedom and went on to command the 305th Military Intelligence Battalion in 2009. This is the Army's largest military intelligence battalion. In 2011, he moved to the newly formed US Army Special Operations Command in Fort Bragg to serve as their first G8, resources and requirements officer. He was deployed in Afghanistan twice as a duty commander. His most recent assignment was at SOCOM, J7, Joint SOF Development Directorate as the deputy chief of concept development and integration with primary duties as the director of the women in SOF integration team.

We were grateful that Captain Jones became a member of our STAR program for over a year. Upon retirement, he decided to go to the Department of Defense and move on to CENTCOM and work in the J-3 Planning Division. Marty and I have become great friends and bike together every weekend along Bayshore Boulevard in Tampa.

JUNE 1, 2018: RETIREMENT OF LIEUTENANT COLONEL BRIAN HOWARD

Lieutenant Colonel Brian Howard was the SOCOM liaison to our STAR program and a very special friend whom I was proud to mentor from a civilian perspective. He served over twenty-three years protecting our country.

Colonel Howard was commissioned as a Military Police Officer from North Georgia College in 1997. His first assignment was in Korea and then on to Fort Polk, Louisiana. After these deployments, he was sent as a detachment commander in support of Operation Iraqi Freedom II, III, and IV. A few years later he spearheaded the Bravo Company of Special Operations Battalion in efforts in Afghanistan, Iraq, and Kuwait.

After a successful command, Colonel Howard attended the Air Command and Staff College at Maxwell AFB in Alabama where he received a master's degree in military operational arts and science. He was assigned to CENTCOM and served as 4th Battalion's Operations Officer. He planned and facilitated 26 deployments and four ODB (Operational Detachment Bravo) level deployments. He then was assigned to SOCOM where he was a member of the J-35, which is future Operations Planning.

The ceremony took place in the SOCOM War Games Center. Major General Clayton Hutmacher, the chief of operations at SOCOM, officiated the event. As in all the structured ceremonies, the event began with the arrival of the official guests and party, national anthem, and invocation. Then General Hutmacher gave the opening remarks about the career of Colonel Howard followed by the award presentation, reading of retirement orders, and presidential certificate of appreciation.

Colonel Brian Howard then presented his remarks to the crowd, acknowledging all the people who had made a difference in his long career in the military. Brian was nice enough to recognize me and Anthony Weiss as cofounders of STAR and thanked us for assisting him in his transition from the military to the civilian world.

Afterward, there was a nice reception where I was honored to meet Brian's wife, Annette, and their two boys. The ceremony was a feel-good event and I wished Brian much success as he transitioned into the civilian sector.

JUNE 14–17, 2018: RETIREMENT OF MAJOR GENERAL DEAN MILNER

This was an unusual retirement for me to attend. On Thursday, June 14 at 8:00 p.m. I flew Air Canada to Toronto and then on to Ottawa for a special retirement ceremony for Major General Dean Milner. His position in Tampa was as the codirector of the J-5 (planning) at CENTCOM. Dean and his wife, Katrin, became great friends during their two years in Tampa. My son, Jason, and I biked with Dean and Katrin on Sundays when possible, riding along Bayshore Boulevard to and around Davis Islands, and then returning home for a total of sixteen miles. It was always a fun early morning outing while discussing what was happening in Tampa and around the world. Dean and I also played many fun rounds of golf in Tampa. At one point, we all happened to be in Miami at the same time, and we got together with our children (their two, Stephanie and Derek, and our two, Jennifer and Jason), and celebrated being together.

The trip to Toronto went well, but the leg to Ottawa ran an hour late. Once I arrived in Ottawa I took a cab to the Hilton Lac-Leamy Hotel in Gatineau, Quebec (about two miles outside Ottawa), arriving at 2:30 a.m. The manager of the hotel was surprised to see me. I asked him if he had saved my room since I had called in earlier about the late arrival. He left and went to speak to his advisor and came back with a room key. I asked if it was a nice room. He replied that the room was the finest in the hotel. I did not comprehend this at first but when I went up to room, I could not find the number on the door. I went downstairs and informed the staff that I could not find the room. The manager sent the bellman to escort me upstairs. As we walked down the hallway, he mentioned that my room number was not on the door and that my room was the "royal" room. When he opened the set of entry doors, I was amazed at the luxurious digs they had given me. I was sorry Deborah could not join me on the trip. She would have loved our very fancy penthouse suite with multiple rooms.

The entry foyer of the suite was massive, with a grand piano positioned in a room that I dubbed the den. A bar was over feet long near the kitchen, the dining room could seat twelve at a large table, and then there was a huge guest bathroom. When I finally entered the master bedroom, I was stunned to find how small the king-size bed looked in the enormous room that included fireplace, a set of reclining chairs, and his and hers office desks. The master bathroom had double sinks with marble everywhere. The shower featured a glass door with butted glass and so many showerheads that I could surely cover every inch of my body with a single flip of a switch. The elevated jacuzzi was three steps up and had a spectacular view of the entire city. I slept very well knowing that I was now "royalty."

The next day I woke up at 8:30 a.m. and headed over to Scone Witch Restaurant in Ottawa, a popular breakfast place, to meet with my old college roommates from the University of Florida, Richard Schwartz and Michael Kamenoff, and their wives, Sharon and Brenda, respectively. They happened to be in Canada and had taken a leisurely drive up the coast and were in Ottawa that same day, a pretty amazing coincidence. We had a nice breakfast together and then Richard and I went to view the parliament building, the Rideau Canal and historic lock stations, and the Fairmont Hotel.

The Rideau Canal, a great military engineering feat of the nineteenth century, opened central Canada to settlement and trade. The building of the canal brought thousands of people to the area, helping to shape the community of Bytown, known today as Ottawa—Canada's capital. The entrance locks mark the start of the 202-kilometer route linking the Ottawa River to Lake Ontario through a system of lakes and rivers. These are connected by channels, locks, and dams, all built by the working men of the day. The canal was completed in 1832 and today is an artery for recreational boating, a national historic site, and a UNESCO World Heritage site owned and operated by Parks Canada. In the winter the canal freezes and the residents ice skate for as many miles as they would like, making it the largest ice-skating "rink" in the world.

After saying goodbye to Richard, I took a general tour around Ottawa on the hop-on, hop-off bus service. Since I had just under two hours before the retirement ceremony, I seized the opportunity to hop on and off at every landmark I could and take in the beautiful country of Canada. I started at the National War Memorial and watched the changing of the guard at the Tomb of the Unknown Soldier. It was very emotional and demonstrated the great pride and patriotism of Canada. I then observed the many government buildings and embassies followed by the museums—War: Nature; Science and Technology; Aviation and Space; History; National Gallery; and Holocaust. I went along the Ottawa River to see the estates of the ambassadors and the prime minister of Canada.

I arrived back at my Hilton palace around 12:30 p.m., had a quick lunch buffet, and then I was picked up by Captain Ryan Merriman, whom General Milner had set up to assist me during my stay. Captain Ryan was a true Canadian patriot and will have an incredible career in the military.

When we arrived at the Army Officers Mess Building, we were greeted by the master of ceremonies, Retired Brigadier General Marty Frank, and his lovely wife, Margo. Brigadier General Marty Frank was the Deputy of General Operations for the US Army Alaska. He is a true gentleman and has transitioned to assist the Canadian military in construction projects throughout Canada.

I met so many nice Canadian civilians and military who were all amazing. There were approximately 250 people present for the ceremony including, of course, General Milner's entire family.

Since Brigadier General Frank was officiating, I told him that I had brought a special bottle of bourbon for Dean. He asked that I present him the bottle during the ceremony. This was unexpected, but I quickly prepared a short speech for this Canadian audience.

General Jonathan Vance, who is the chief of defense of the Canadian Armed Forces, gave Major General Milner a certificate from the military thanking him for his many years of dedication to the military, then other generals present gave traditional medals and awards for his service.

Then Brigadier General Frank called me up to the podium to present the special bottle of bourbon. I thanked all the generals present and all the Canadian civilians for their support and dedication to the military. Then I said, "The Moosehead beer is delicious; I am just hoping I can afford it after the tariff takes effect." The crowd enjoyed my comment, which was relevant to the discussions of the day between both our leaders. I then acknowledged Dean's family, parents, and children, and added that I knew his son, Derek, was very proud of his father and hoped to follow in his footsteps. I talked about what an incredible family he had and how we had become great friends with our biking, golfing, and social events through CENTCOM.

Then I said, "As you know, Dean is a bourbon connoisseur. I researched the industry and found a bourbon that would be fitting for the general. After 9/11, a team of special operators went straight to Afghanistan to respond to the terrorist attack. That is the team that the movie, *12 Strong*, portrays. Two of the twelve special operators, Mark Nutsch and Bob Pennington, transitioned into the civilian sector and started a bourbon company. They produced a few bottles of a select bourbon they aged eight years for special people. The bourbon is called Horse Soldier Commanders Select. The bottle is formed of the steel from the twin towers and autographed by Mark and Bob. Also, the label is pewter, and a special coin is attached to the bottle." I mentioned that no one is more deserving of savoring this special bottle than General Milner. "Enjoy it in good health. All the best on your retirement."

After the speech, the crowd gave me a warm applause and we all took a picture together. After the ceremony, a group of us went to dinner to a pub close by to celebrate.

On June 16, I woke up early from my palace residence and took a cab to the War Museum. It was an incredible museum that showed the history of all the Canadian military activities around the world. The museum had many relics of the WWII, including Hitler's limousine. Over fifty tanks from the United States, Canada, England, Russia, and Germany were present with all the details.

After the museum visit, I took a cab to the Sheraton Hotel Four Corners and met a large group of Major General Milner's Dragoon regiment. I learned that every two years all the surviving retired Dragoons have a reunion. They were just finishing up their board meeting when I arrived wearing a Canadian officer's hat. All the attendees found my choice of attire very humorous.

After the meeting, Dean, me, and two others headed for the links. We played golf at a military course called the Ottawa Highlands Golf Club in St. Barbara's. It was a beautiful golf course with rolling hills and evergreen trees that looked like Christmas trees. After our game, Dean and I took out the other team to have a celebratory beer at the bar.

From the golf course, Dean dropped me off at my hotel palace so I could change into a nice outfit for a riverboat cruise. I took him up to my room and he was amazed.

After changing, I grabbed a cab to Dean's hotel, we then went together in his car to the riverboat, which was a replica of a Mississippi paddleboat. We all boarded and enjoyed a nice buffet dinner with a DJ accompaniment. Over 150 of the general's family, friends, and Dragoons were present for the evening. The riverboat went up and down the Ottawa River until 11:30 p.m. It was a marvelous evening filled with great food, comradery, and libations. One of the highlights was meeting General Walter Natynczyk, who was the chief of defense and the head of the Canadian Space Agency.

On June 17, I woke up around 8:30 a.m. and realized I had left my passport in Dean's SUV. I called and thanked him for the incredible weekend and asked him to leave my passport at the front desk of his hotel. Luckily, I caught him before he headed home to Kingston.

I arrived at the Sheraton Hotel and picked up my passport and went across the street to the Canadian Museum of History. The museum was fantastic and included the origins of Canada, featuring many relics from the original Native Canadians and a great selection of totem poles.

After viewing the museum, I took a cab to the Yow Ottawa Airport to catch a plane to Toronto. While in Toronto, I had a three-plus-hour layover, so I took the local train to the center of the city and had a nice lunch atop the CN Tower. I returned to the airport about thirty minutes before departure and raced through customs to the airside. Thank goodness I had a Global Entry Card. I can thank my wife for getting those for us. As a result, I made it!

Seeing my Canadian friend, Major General Dean Milner, receive all the accolades he deserved for his dedicated service to our great countries was the icing on top of a great Canadian trip.

JUNE 29, 2018: RETIREMENT OF COMMANDER DARRYL C. ADAMS

I was honored to be included in the retirement ceremony of Commander Darryl Adams; we had a great relationship. I first met Darryl at the office of Major General Karl Horst (CENTCOM) in 2011. Karl was the chief of staff for General James Mattis, head of CENTCOM. Darryl was the acting executive officer to the chief of staff of CENTCOM. And as president of the Navy League Tampa Bay Council, Commander Adams and I discussed the logistics of the Navy Ball each year. He also became well acquainted with STAR and was a positive reinforcer of our program.

Darryl received his bachelor of science degree in landscape architecture in 1990. He was then commissioned into the Navy and performed initial sea duty on the USS *Saratoga* as a boiler maintenance and repair officer. In 1994, he transferred to the Naval Postgraduate School, in Monterey, California where he received a master's degree in national security affairs. Between 1997 and 1999, he served on the staff as a watch officer and intelligence exchange officer, participating in Operations Desert Fox and Southern Watch in Nairobi, Kenya.

In 1999, Darryl transferred to Tampa where he worked in Strategic Intelligence Programs, and as the executive assistant to the senior intelligence officer in SOCOM. In 2002, he transferred to the USS *Carl Vinson* supercarrier as the assistant intelligence officer. From 2010 to 2013, he returned to Tampa, where he served as the deputy chief, knowledge management branch, intelligence directorate, and executive officer to the chief of staff at US Forces Central Command. From 2013 to 2016, he served as the Joint Staff J32 mission manager to SOCOM to synchronize strategy and planning and integrate intelligence, surveillance, and reconnaissance.

After thirty years of service, Commander Adams retired from the military. Currently, he is involved in the Medal of Honor Foundation here in Tampa. I am honored to know Darryl during and after his military career and I am grateful for his dedication and service to this country.

OCTOBER 19, 2018: RETIREMENT OF MASTER SERGEANT JOSEPH F. LURZ

Master Sergeant Joe Lurz enlisted in the Marine Corps in 1998 and attended Marine Combat Training and Engineer School to become an electrical equipment repair specialist assigned to Camp Foster, Okinawa, Japan. In 2006, Sergeant Lurz was assigned to Marine Special Operations Company A of the newly established MARSOC (Marine Forces Special Operations Command) then deployed to the Philippines and Afghanistan.

In 2007, Sergeant Lurz was the element leader assigned to Marine Special Operations Team 8141 as part of Company D when he was deployed to Farah, Afghanistan. Upon returning from Afghanistan, he was promoted to master sergeant and served as training cell officer in charge of future operations. In 2014, he was deployed to the Special Operations Task Force in Helmand, Afghanistan in support of Combined Joint Special Operations. He was then assigned to SOCOM at MacDill AFB as the senior enlisted leader.

The retirement ceremony was held at the US Marine Corps headquarters at MacDill AFB. It was very moving and included many honored guests. Major Matt Lampert, retired USMC MARSOC Raider, who currently serves as a professional staff member of the Senate Armed Services Committee, officiated the ceremony.

After the ceremony, there was a reception for the event in Tarpon Springs at a microbrewery where we met Joe's family, friends, and fellow comrades who had served with him. Since Marine Special Operations is so small, most of Joe's teammates were able to attend the reception.

Joe is currently working as a managing director of consulting at the University of Charleston in South Carolina. Joe is an incredible leader, friend, and alumni of our STAR Program.

OCTOBER 26, 2018: RETIREMENT OF COLONEL ANDREW R. MILBURN

I first met Colonel Andrew Milburn at the Special Operations 30th Anniversary Dinner at the Tampa Convention Center. I invited him to join our STAR program as one of the few Marine Raiders who was posted at Special Operations for Central Command at MacDill AFB.

Colonel Milburn was born in England and knew he wanted to enlist in the military. Due to his impaired vision, he did not meet the criteria of being accepted in England. He then came to the United States, applied to the Marines and was accepted. Due to his determination and perseverance, he worked his way up to a Raider and a colonel in SOCCENT (Special Operations for Central Command). Colonel Milburn most recently served as commander of the Combined Joint Special Operations Task Force-Iraq in support of Operation Inherent Resolve. He was responsible for the Special Operations effort to counter ISIL (Islamic State of Iraq) in support of US allied and partner-nation objectives.

On October 26, Andy had his retirement ceremony at the SOCCENT headquarters at MacDill AFB. Major General Burke W. Whitman officiated and gave a rousing speech explaining all the incredible achievements of Colonel Milburn, performing flawlessly in Africa, South America, and Iraq.

The ceremony was very touching, with Andy's family all present. I was honored to be present and appreciated him giving a call out to our STAR program during his remarks. I read his book, *When the Tempest Gathers*, where he describes his experiences in the military. It is a fantastic read.

While STAR provided Andy with a good perspective of the civilian sector, his heart remained with the military. And so, he did what some do and found a way to combine the two. Andy retired from the military and now operates as an independent contractor on behalf of the United States. His company is called Mozart and he is currently assisting the Ukrainians.

APRIL 26, 2019: RETIREMENT OF CAPTAIN TRISTAN RIZZI

On this day, April 26, 2019, I witnessed another very memorable retirement ceremony of a great special operator. Captain Tristan Rizzi, a Navy SEAL for over twenty-five years, has made an incredible difference in our country's security, from heading Boat Team 22 for

Special Operations Command during the Iraq War to heading a provincial reconstruction team in Ghazni, Afghanistan.

His last position with SOCOM was as head of J-8 as the special programs assessment director responsible for managing all aspects of resourcing required to organize, train, and equip all Special Operations Forces, totaling more than $13.5 billion annually. The guest speaker was Vice Admiral Tim Szymanski, deputy commander of SOCOM who had some very nice remarks to share with us about Tristan's career. Then Tristan spoke and acknowledged the many people who had made an impact on his life. The ceremony was followed by an incredible singing of "Old Glory," while a flag was ceremonially folded, and then Tristan presented the flag to his wife. The entire event was very emotional.

Tristan Rizzi joined our STAR program during his last year in the military and was our point person at SOCOM for a year. He has now landed an incredible job in Tampa. He is president of Tocaro Blue, which offers intelligent vessel monitoring systems.

MAY 3, 2019: RETIREMENT OF COLONEL GLENN THOMAS

Colonel Glenn Thomas had his retirement ceremony at the Navy Operational Support Center at MacDill AFB. Among his many missions, most of which were classified, was as an Army Special Operations Green Beret in Operation Anaconda that headed into Afghanistan after 9/11. He was on the mission to find Osama Bin Laden and parachuted into Tora Bora with his team, including then seventy-eight-year-old Command Sergeant Billy Waugh. Billy believed that Osama Bin Laden had escaped through the valley of the mountain range just moments before the Americans had arrived.

Over 150 people were present at the event, including Billy. Master Sergeant Darrin Crowder, who was Glenn's superior officer on numerous missions, officiated the ceremony. This was another very memorable and emotional event for all to experience together with Glenn's family, friends, and comrades.

Along with the support and guidance of STAR, Glenn retired from the military and is currently a customer success executive (CSE) with Red Hat Company, an information technology company, and subsidiary of IBM.

MAY 3, 2019: RETIREMENT OF COLONEL JAMES MILLER

The retirement ceremony for Colonel James Miller was held at the Joint Special Operations University Auditorium. It was officiated by Lieutenant General Francis Beaudette, commander of the US Army Special Operations Command in Fort Bragg, North Carolina.

General Beaudette eloquently depicted the history of Colonel Miller's career in the Army. Jim went through ROTC at Bucknell University and then enlisted in the Army. His career of twenty-nine years in the military began in Germany where he headed the 51st Maintenance Battalion. Next, he was assigned to Bosnia for a year followed by deployments to Africa, Mali, and Ghana. In 2002, he was deployed to Afghanistan as head of Alpha Company in Operation Enduring Freedom. In 2005, he was assigned to the Joint Staff J-3 (Planning) as the deputy director for special operations at the Pentagon. He then returned to Afghanistan and then went on to Southern Command.

His last position was at SOCOM as the director of the joint acquisition task force tactical assault light operator suit. This is a research project to assist the fighting forces with lightweight body armor that will protect the body, and also assist the soldier in being able to lift and move large weights and transport them for a long distance.

The ceremony was very meaningful to all who attended including his many friends and family, who were supportive through his successful military career.

Following the ceremony, I spoke with General Beaudette and he reminded me that he was the assistant to Admiral Bill McRaven in 2014 when I had arranged to bring the tenth prime minister of Israel, Ehud Barack, to SOCOM to meet Admiral McRaven. General Beaudette was part of the team that had worked on the logistics for that special meeting.

The retirement ceremony was very moving as always, but more so when Jim acknowledged our STAR program and thanked us for assisting him in his transition into the civilian sector.

JULY 12, 2019: RETIREMENT OF COMMAND SERGEANT MAJOR PATRICK L. MCCAULEY

Today was a very special day for the McCauley family and our incredible command sergeant major of United States Special Operations Command in Tampa. Pat McCauley retired after thirty-one years of dedicated service to this country. The event commenced at 11:00 a.m. at the beautiful Davis Center overlooking Tampa Bay. The stadium seating venue was packed complete with 200 attendees in reserved seating. The attendees included three-star and four-star generals who had made an impact on Pat's career throughout the world. I felt very honored to be included in the ceremony.

The national anthem was beautifully sung by Ms. Ramona Storch. The invocation was warmly shared by Colonel George Youstra. Four-star General Tony Thomas (Ret.), former commander of SOCOM, provided remarks and military background of Command Sergeant Major McCauley. The general eloquently described Patrick's life story and enlightened us all about this extraordinary man. The introduction was well-done, and all the military players were acknowledged.

Command Sergeant Major McCauley enlisted in the Marine Corps Reserves in 1986 and was assigned to A Company, 8th Tank Battalion, 4th Marine Division. He transferred to the US Army in 1988 as an intelligence analyst. Upon completion, he was assigned to South Korea. In 1989, he was reassigned to Fort Riley, Kansas, where he served as personal security for the Noncommissioned officer in charge (NCOIC). From 1990 to 1994, he went into Special Forces and was assigned as a special forces communications sergeant. In 1995, Command Sergeant Major McCauley went from a team member to unit commander for Special Operations. From 1995 to 2015, he was team leader in many of the dangerous areas of the world from Central America to Bosnia to Iraq and then Afghanistan. He deployed multiple times in his career supporting Operations Enduring Freedom, Iraqi Freedom, and Inherent Resolve. From July 2016 to the present Major McCauley had been the command sergeant major to SOCOM and General Tony Thomas as commander.

After General Thomas's remarks, there were awards presentations by the head of the Army, General Mark Milley, including the traditional letter from the president of the United States. Pat McCauley began his speech by introducing his mother, who had given him his ideals of hard work, dedication, faith, and making a difference in the world. He next introduced his wife of over thirty years, Starla, who was the rock of the family. She raised their son and daughter selflessly and with all the same values Pat had been brought up with while he was on numerous missions around the world. Then he presented all the females in the family with flowers. It was very emotional as he made each presentation. Then off script, his daughter Alana got up and gave a tremendous tribute to her father. I was teary-eyed after hearing her eloquent description of their relationship and his dedication to this country. Pat then listed the many civilian and military people who had made a difference in his life.

It was so uplifting to hear the great stories and incredible people that were a part of his journey through the military. After his speech, his wife and children were given awards and certificates of appreciation.

Then came the amazing rendition of "Old Glory" by Mr. Evanelo Van Morris along with the SOCOM Honor Guard. The song, along with the video enhancement, was patriotic beyond words. After the flag folding, Pat presented the flag to his wife. The retirement ceremony ended with the playing of "The Army Song" and "The Ballad of the Green Berets."

After the ceremony, the McCauley's hosted all the guests for an after-party barbecue dinner on the base at the Harbor Bay Welcome Center. It was a great opportunity to congratulate the McCauley family. I had great conversations with the new commander of SOCOM, General Richard Clarke; retired commander of SOCOM, General Tony Thomas; and General Darsie D. Rogers, whom I had known as the head of SOCCENT (Special Operations for CENTCOM) along with the new Command Sergeant Major Greg Smith, as well as numerous other team members of the military community. Deborah and I had a wonderful time that evening.

JULY 15, 2019: RETIREMENT OF COLONEL CARY HARBAUGH

I took my dear friend, Nick Zambito (WWII veteran), to a unique retirement in the War Games Room at Special Operations Command. This was a very special event since Colonel Cary Harbaugh, a forty-one-year dedicated soldier who had run the US Special Operations CARE Coalition for six years, was going to say goodbye. Cary had been a dedicated, professional, caring leader, who gave each of the wounded 100 percent care and attention. He was the soldier's soldier.

Cary's wife, mother-in-law, and three daughters attended the event. His Army enlisted son, Robert (a sergeant first class), was on a special TV system located on a base in Afghanistan that allowed him to view the event.

General Tony Thomas officiated the event with his incredibly articulate style in describing Colonel Harbaugh's history in the military. He expressed how close the Harbaugh family was and mentioned some of the acronyms for the names each of the daughters and son have for each other.

As a native of Pittsburgh, Pennsylvania, he first served as an enlisted soldier and non-commissioned officer in Airborne and Special Operations units from 1978 to 1987. He graduated from the ROTC program at Ohio State University in 1987 and then he was off to deployment. He served on many missions, from Operations Just Cause, Desert Shield, and Desert Storm to Iraqi Freedom and Enduring Freedom.

In 2013, he began serving as the director of SOCOM's Warrior Care Program later called Care Coalition until 2019. The Care Coalition is the medical support wing of Special Operations that takes care of the special operators who are wounded, ill, and injured from the day they are inflicted to the day they die. According to Admiral Michael Mullen, the head of the Joint Chiefs of Staff, it is the only branch of the military that has complete care for its team members throughout their careers. Colonel Harbaugh took over control of the Care Coalition in 2013 and transformed it into the most prestigious care for our special operators available.

Additionally, Colonel Harbaugh hosted the 2019 Warrior Games in Tampa. The event was a total success, with the city of Tampa assisting in reducing the cost of the venues and support from Tampa's civilians. The event ended with Ms. Lara Sayre singing a beautiful Irish song, "The Parting Glass." After the ceremony, the attendees went to the Green Fields Irish Pub and celebrated with the Harbaugh family.

The event was attended by the current commander of Special Operations, General Richard Clarke, numerous members of both SOCOM and Care Coalition, many of Cary's friends and comrades, as well as Tampa Bay business leaders.

I consider Cary a very close friend of mine with whom I have had the honor of playing golf along his collegiate daughter Jesse "Mouse," who has a golf scholarship at The Citadel, the military college of South Carolina. In fact, in 2022 Cary invited me to serve with him as a member of the board of the Special Operations Warrior Golf Foundation. We sponsored five special operators who are also wounded warrior on a trip to Ireland playing four golf courses in seven days. This was a trip of a lifetime. We enjoyed the beautiful countryside, pristine golf courses, the warm hospitality of the Irish locals, and the comradery of a special group of guys on a mission to play golf and enjoy life. These incredible American special operators were Lieutenant Colonel Dave Hodges, Major Rob Kilmartin, Sergeant First Class (SFC) Peter Levola, Sergeant First Class Mike Morales, and Captain Van Wennen. Civilian hosts were Tom Gates, Art Werhoelter, and me.

FEBRUARY 28, 2020: RETIREMENT OF COLONEL CHARLES E. GETZ

Colonel Charles Getz, or as we called him in our STAR program, Charlie, had his retirement ceremony at the Surf's Edge Club at MacDill AFB. A large crowd was on hand to witness his last day as an Army Ranger. The event was officiated by Major General Sean Farrell, director for force structure, requirements, resources, and strategic assessments at SOCOM. In short, he is a J-8 in charge of the budget for Special Operations and its allocations.

The ceremony began with the MacDill AFB Silent Drill Team, the national anthem, then the invocation by Chaplain Lee Rutledge. General Farrell gave a full history of Colonel Getz's Army assignments from 1988 to the present. After attending the ROTC at Auburn University, he was assigned to 1st Battalion 505th PIR 82nd Airborne where he was stationed in European Command (EUROCOM) area of responsibility, which includes Morocco, Mali, and the Ivory Coast. Later he was assigned to Fort Leavenworth as a Global War on Terror planner and then on to Iraq. Then in 2009, he was assigned to Special Operations for Central Command (SOCCENT) on the Yemen Operational Planning Team. In 2013, he was reassigned to Special Operations for Southern Command (SOCSOUTH) in Homestead, Florida as the J33 chief of operations.

In 2016, Colonel Getz was deployed to Afghanistan, assisting the local police and responsible for the ministerial level advisory as the advanced logistics program director. In July of 2017, he came to Tampa to become the assessment director for J-8. In his last position, he was responsible for managing all aspects of resourcing required to organize, train, and equip SOCOM component forces. Colonel Getz has received many awards, among them the Purple Heart, Bronze Star, and Defense Meritorious Service Medal. He also earned a Ranger Tab and a Special Forces Tab.

Charles is married with two children and planned to stay in Tampa. Attending the event among all his friends, military leaders, and contemporaries were his four older sisters. In fact, one of them, Holly Grange, then a member of the North Carolina House of Representatives, ran for governor of North Carolina. Nick Zambito and I were fortunate to meet her after the ceremony and I presented her with our STAR challenge coin. The event was so emotional and memorable with the singing of "Old Glory." Everyone left the event with such a good feeling about the Getz family and the future they looked forward to in Tampa as he transitioned into the civilian world.

JUNE 30, 2022: RETIREMENT OF MAJOR GENERAL VINCENT K. BECKLUND

I was honored to be invited to attend General Vincent Becklund's retirement ceremony and appreciated that he had a reserved seat for me in the second row next to Major General Mark Clark (Ret.), former chief of staff for Admiral Olson at SOCOM and a close friend ever since. In the first row was the entire leadership of SOCOM with their wives. We had General Richard Clarke, commander, with his lovely wife, Suzanne; Admiral Colin Green, deputy commander, with his wife, Alyssa; General Marcus Evans, chief of staff, with his wife, Kelly; and Command Sergeant Major Greg Smith with his wife, Tina.

The ceremony commenced with an incredible rendition of the national anthem sung by Mr. Nathan West followed by the invocation by Father Eric Albertson. Lieutenant General James Slife gave remarks about the complete military career of General Becklund without the use of any notes, which was very impressive.

General Becklund began his military career at the US Air Force Academy in 1990. As a career helicopter pilot of the MH-53 (Sikorsky), he experienced assignments in rescue and special operations. He participated in Operations Joint Endeavor, Desert Thunder, Enduring Freedom, Iraqi Freedom, New Dawn, Inherent Resolve, and other worldwide operations.

General Slife emphasized that General Becklund was successful because of his courage, compassion, and commitment. With over 2,600 flying hours, he was considered the finest pilot of all fourteen Air Force wings and moved straight up to Special Operations. He was a flight instructor and then became a squadron, group, then wing leader.

On April 1, 2003, General Becklund planned and headed the team that recovered Jessica Lynch, who was a unit supply specialist captured and kidnapped in the Iraq War. He set up and flew the mission that recovered her. This was the first successful recovery of a kidnapped American soldier since WWII and the first woman ever recovered.

In addition, General Becklund was instrumental in the planning of the Osama Bin Ladin raid on May 1, 2011. General Becklund's last assignment was as a two-star general, head of operations for SOCOM (J-3). General Becklund received numerous merits and awards from the head of the Air Force, SOCOM, and the president of the United States.

General Slife closed by expressing what a great American leader and patriot we had before us. General Becklund took the podium and gave a very nice speech with great emphasis on his family and how important they were to him. He expressed his gratitude to his wife, Jennifer, and the important role she had in raising their three exceptional children. Then he thanked all his family members and friends who had helped and supported him during his thirty-two-year career in the military. As he closed his remarks, he mentioned the names of his fallen comrades, which choked him up and left tears in all our eyes.

I was honored to witness his retirement ceremony and was excited that he had decided to call Tampa his home as he retired into the civilian sector. He had joined our STAR program, participated in the dinners, met with local business leaders and was well on his way to determining his new future. Since he expressed an interest in the real estate field, I set up lunch at Palma Ceia Golf and Country Club and took him to my office. I shared the many experiences Deborah and I had enjoyed through real estate, and after mentioning other ideas like insurance and public adjusting, we walked through the office and talked about the many pictures hanging on the walls—Games and Trains Parties; military rides on an aircraft carrier, a nuclear submarine, and in an in-air refueler; generals in train conductor hats; military leaders and their wives; and a couple of awards.

General David Petraeus's retirement ceremony (photo courtesy of the US Department of Defense)

With Canadian General Dean Milner at his retirement ceremony in Ottawa, Canada

General John and Kathy Allen at John's retirement ceremony at Annapolis Naval Academy (photo courtesy of the Department of Defense)

With General James Mattis at General Allen's retirement ceremony

Me, General Boomer Smith, Brigadier General Mark Smethurst, and General Tim McOwen, all of the Australian Army, at General Allen's retirement

Celebrating General Allen's retirement with his family at Ruth Chris in Annapolis

Admiral Sean Pybus and family at his retirement ceremony at the SOCOM Memorial with Admiral Eric Olson and General Tony Thomas officiating

Lieutenant General James Slife officiating at General Vincent Becklund's retirement ceremony

In Conclusion . . . Gratitude

My fourteen-year experience (and counting!) with the military has been an incredible ride. I have learned about professional, dedicated, and truly humble American heroes and patriots who put their lives on the line each and every day so that we can enjoy freedom and safety in America. These American military families are strong and secure; their children are resilient and independent and exemplify all the best morals and structure to lead our nation. I hope that my experiences in this book will give each American the appreciation for the elite group of less than 1 percent of Americans who are at the tip of the spear protecting us. I am so grateful for the relationships I have developed with these patriots—foreign and domestic—and the insider view I have been given into the greatest military in the world. I am proud to be an American and I hope this book will inspire others to appreciate our military with its traditional values, devotion, loyalty, and commitment to the greatest country on earth!

Military Reference List

CEREMONIAL PRESENTATIONS

The core of the military is its traditions. These traditions connect decades of soldiers, sailors, airmen, and marines. They provide points of familiarity that are recognized by troops from all services, eras, jobs, and ranks and bind these men and women together through that recognition in a way that has no counterpart in other professions. Furthermore, these traditions have meanings that give them significance. Unlike many civilian practices, whose origins have been lost to obscurity, the military enshrines the roots of its rituals to ensure the purpose and point of it all is remembered, understood, and respected.

Among the most recognizable of military traditions are the many ceremonies that are conducted on a frequently recurring basis. Hardly a month goes by in any unit without some ceremonial event. In fact, the raising and lowering of the American flag on every military installation is performed with an exactly prescribed ritual that demonstrates the respect service members have for this symbol and the nation it represents.

As civilians, Deborah and I had never fathomed the place ceremonies hold in military life, nor the purpose they serve. In fact, we were a little surprised to discover that, at every military event that we attend, there are consistent ceremonial presentations we have been honored to witness and participate in. While these ceremonies are a normal part of the military world, as civilians who experience them for the first time, and for that matter, each and every time, these ceremonies have a profound impact.

The following are just a few of the revered rites we have been privileged to observe. I've selected the ones that are typical of the events we've attended.

PRESENTATION OF COLORS AND NATIONAL ANTHEM

The term *colors* refers to the flag of the United States of America. A color guard, or the small group of service members who conduct the presentation, may consist of two honor guards and two flag bearers who present the flag. A sergeant-at-arms calls the orders during the ceremony, so that all participants walk, turn, stop, and start again in complete unison. The national anthem is then sung by all. The audience stands for the entire ceremony, with hats removed. Military members in uniform stand and, when directed, salute.

INVOCATION

For many events, a chaplain or other appropriate person delivers a generally non-denominational prayer to request a blessing on the event, those present, and those being honored. The verbiage might be something like this.

> Dear Gracious Heavenly Father,
> I thank you for this day you have given us and for this occasion that we gather together to celebrate the alliance which exists between the United States and the democratic countries of this world, particularly tonight, in the Intelligence community.

We realize that it is our ability to work together that preserves the armistice and protects the freedom and independence of our friends.

I thank you for all of those involved in this task before us, from the newest private to the most experienced officer, and pray for each of them that they will be protected as they perform their duties but also that they will be blessed because of the significance of our mission.

I pray now that you will be with us tonight as we celebrate the successful, continued, execution of our mission and the alliance we enjoy with each other. Bless this time with your presence and bless each one here gathered.

God give us a joyous spirit of celebration of our nation's veterans and their families. Bless us now with your presence. In the name of our God who challenges us to care.

In your holy name I pray, Amen.

THE POW/MIA TABLE: A PLACE SETTING FOR ONE, A TABLE FOR ALL

This honor is generally observed at events that include meals. The example I described in a previous chapter was at a Navy event, but all the services observe very similar details. A small table is set at the entrance to the dining room or in another conspicuous location in the room. It is set for one person. A representative of the unit reminds the attendees out loud of the meaning behind the symbols displayed at the table. The script may differ from unit to unit, but the meaning and tone are consistent. In some readings, after each line, starting with the second, the audience replies with, "Remember!"

FLAG FOLDING: A TRIBUTE TO OUR NATION'S HONORED DEAD

If you've attended a funeral honoring a veteran who served our country, perhaps you witnessed the folding of the flag that once covered the casket of a loved one. Each of the thirteen folds of the flag holds great significance.

There are many sources where you can find information about flag-folding ceremonies. My favorite comes from Military.com. At the ceremony of retreat, a daily observance at bases during which all personnel pay respect to the flag, "the flag is lowered, folded in a triangle fold, and kept under watch throughout the night as a tribute to our nation's honored dead. The next morning, it is brought out and, at the ceremony of reveille, run aloft as a symbol of our belief in the resurrection of the body."

During the ceremony of retreat, the flag is folded thirteen times. Military.com describes the meaning behind each fold:

1. The first fold of our flag is a symbol of life.

2. The second fold signifies our belief in eternal life.

3. The third fold is made in honor and tribute of the veteran departing our ranks, and who gave a portion of his or her life for the defense of our country to attain peace.

4. The fourth fold exemplifies our weaker nature as citizens trusting in God; it is to Him we turn for His divine guidance.

5. The fifth fold is an acknowledgment to our country, for in the words of Stephen Decatur, "Our country, in dealing with other countries, may she always be right, but it is still our country, right or wrong."

6. The sixth fold is for where our hearts lie. It is with our heart

that we pledge allegiance to the flag of the United States of America, and to the republic for which it stands, one nation under God, indivisible, with liberty and justice for all.

7. The seventh fold is a tribute to our armed forces, for it is through the armed forces that we protect our country and our flag against all enemies.

8. The eighth fold is a tribute to the one who entered into the valley of the shadow of death, that we might see the light of day, and to honor our mother, for whom it flies on Mother's Day.

9. The ninth fold is an honor to womanhood, for it has been through their faith, love, loyalty, and devotion that the character of the men and women who have made this country great have been molded.

10. The tenth fold is a tribute to our father, for he, too, has given his sons and daughters for the defense of our country since he or she was first-born.

11. The eleventh fold, in the eyes of Hebrew citizens, represents the lower portion of the seal of King David and King Solomon and glorifies, in their eyes, the God of Abraham, Isaac, and Jacob.

12. The twelfth fold, in the eyes of a Christian citizen, represents an emblem of eternity and glorifies, in their eyes, God the Father, the Son, and Holy Ghost.

13. The last fold, when the flag is completely folded, the stars are uppermost, reminding us of our national motto, *In God We Trust*

Branch Creeds

THE US ARMY CREED
SOLDIER'S CREED

I am an American Soldier.
I am a warrior and a member of a team.
I serve the people of the United States of America
and live the Army Values.
I will always place the mission first.
I will never accept defeat.
I will never quit.
I will never leave a fallen comrade.
I am disciplined, physically and mentally
tough, trained and proficient in my
warrior tasks and drills.
I always maintain my arms,
my equipment and myself.
I am an expert and I am a professional.
I stand ready to deploy, engage, and destroy,
the enemies of the United States of America
in close combat.
I am a guardian of freedom and
the American way of life
I am an American Soldier.

US NAVY CREED
A SAILOR'S CREED

I am a United States Sailor.

I will support and defend the Constitution of the United States of America

and will obey the orders of those appointed over me.

I represent the fighting spirit of the Navy and those who have gone before me

to defend freedom and democracy around the world.

I proudly serve my country's Navy combat team with Honor, Courage, and Commitment.

I am committed to excellence and the fair treatment of all.

US AIR FORCE CREED
AIRMAN'S CREED

I am an American Airman.

I am a warrior.

I have answered my Nation's call.

I am an American Airman.

My mission is to fly, fight, and win.

I am faithful to a proud heritage,

a tradition of honor,

and a legacy of valor.

I am an American Airman.

Guardian of Freedom and Justice,

My Nation's sword and shield.

Its sentry and avenger.

I defend my Country with my life.

I am an American Airman.
Wingman, leader, Warrior.
I will never leave an Airman behind.
I will never falter,
and I will not fail.

US MARINE CREED
MARINES' RIFLE CREED

1. This is my rifle. There are many like it, but this one is mine.

2. My rifle is my best friend. It is my life. I must master it as I must master my life.

3. My rifle, without me, is useless. Without my rifle, I am useless. I must fire my rifle true. I must shoot straighter than my enemy who is trying to kill me. I must shoot him before he shoots me. I will . . .

4. My rifle and myself know that what counts in this war is not the rounds we fire, the noise of our burst, nor the smoke we make. We know that it is the hits that count. We will hit . . .

5. My rifle is human, even as I, because it is my life. Thus, I will learn it as a brother. I will learn its weaknesses, its strength, its parts, its accessories, its sights, and its barrel. I will ever guard it against the ravages of weather and damage. I will keep my rifle clean and ready. We will become part of each other. We will . . .

6. Before God, I swear this creed. My rifle and myself are the defenders of my country. We are the masters of our enemy. We are the saviors of my life.

7. So be it, until victory is America's and there is no enemy, but peace!

US COAST GUARD
CREED OF THE UNITED STATES COAST GUARDSMAN

I am proud to be a United States Coast Guardsman.
I revere that long line of expert seamen who by their devotion to duty and sacrifice of self have made it possible for me to be a member of a service honored and respected, in peace and in war, throughout the world.
I never, by work or deed, will bring reproach upon the fair name of my service, nor permit others to do so unchallenged.
I will cheerfully and willingly obey all lawful orders.
I will always be on time to relieve, and shall endeavor to do more, rather than less, than my share.
I will always be at my station, alert and attending to my duties.
I shall, so far as I am able, bring to my seniors solutions, not problems.
I shall live joyously, but always with due regard for the rights and privileges of others.
I shall endeavor to be a model citizen in the community in which I live.
I shall sell life dearly to an enemy of my country, but give it freely to Rescue those in peril.
With God's help, I shall endeavor to be one of His noblest Works—A United States Coast Guardsman.

Branch Songs

US ARMY
"THE ARMY GOES ROLLING ALONG"

March along, sing our song, with the Army of the free
Count the brave, count the true, who have fought to victory
We're the Army and proud of our name
We're the Army and proudly proclaim

First to fight for the right,
And to build the Nation's might,
And The Army Goes Rolling Along
Proud of all we have done,
Fighting till the battle's won,
And The Army Goes Rolling Along.

Then it's Hi! Hi! Hey!
The Army's on its way.
Count off the cadence loud and strong (TWO! THREE! FOUR!)
For where e'er we go,
You will always know
That The Army Goes Rolling Along.

US ARMY
"BALLAD OF THE GREEN BERETS"

Fighting soldiers from the sky
Fearless men who jump and die
Men who mean just what they say
The brave men of the Green Beret

Silver wings upon their chest
These are men, America's best
One hundred men will test today
But only three win the Green Beret

Trained to live off nature's land
Trained in combat, hand-to-hand
Men who fight by night and day
Courage take from the Green Berets

Silver wings upon their chest
These are men, America's best
One hundred men will test today
But only three win the Green Beret

Back at home, a young wife waits
Her Green Beret has met his fate
He has died for those oppressed
Leaving her his last request

Put silver wings on my son's chest
Make him one of America's best
He'll be a man they'll test one day
Have him win the Green Beret

US NAVY
"ANCHORS AWEIGH"

Anchors Aweigh, my boys, Anchors Aweigh.
Farewell to foreign shores,
We sail at break of day-ay-ay-ay.
Through our last night ashore,
Drink to the foam,
Until we meet once more.
Here's wishing you a happy voyage home.
Stand Navy out to sea,
Fight our battle cry
We'll never change our course,
So vicious foe steer shy-y-y-y.
Roll out the TNT,
Anchors Aweigh.
Sail on to victory
And sink their bones to Davy Jones, hooray!

US AIR FORCE SONG
"WILD BLUE YONDER"

Off we go into the wild blue yonder,
Climbing high, into the sun,
Here they come zooming to meet our thunder,
At 'em boys, Give 'er the gun!
Down we dive, spouting our flame from under,
Off with one helluva roar!
We live in fame, or go down in flame,
Hey! Nothing'll stop the US Air Force!

Minds of men fashioned a crate of thunder,
Sent it high into the blue,
Hands of men blasted the world asunder,
How they lived God only knew!
Souls of men dreaming of skies to conquer,
Gave us wings ever so soar,
With scouts before and bombers galore, Hey!
Nothing'll stop the US Air Force!

Off we go into the wild sky yonder,
Keep the wings level and true,
If you'd live to be a gray-haired wonder,
Keep your nose out of the blue! (Out of the blue, boy!)
Flying men, guarding the nation's border,
We'll be there, followed by more,
In echelon we carry on, Hey!
Nothing'll stop the US Air Force!

US MARINE CORPS HYMN
"FROM THE HALLS OF MONTEZUMA"

From the Halls of Montezuma
To the shores of Tripoli;
We will fight our country's battles
In the air, on land, and sea;
First to fight for right and freedom
And to keep our honor clean;
We are proud to claim the title
Of the United States Marine.

Our flag's unfurled to every breeze
From dawn to setting sun;

We have fought in every clime and place
Where we could take a gun;
In the snow of far-off Northern lands
And in sunny tropic scenes;
You will find us always on the job
The United States Marines.

Here's to health to you and to our Corps
Which we are proud to serve
In many a strife we've fought for life
And never lost our nerve;
If the Army and the Navy
Ever look on Heaven's scenes;
They will find the streets are guarded by
The United States Marines.

US COAST GUARD
"SEMPER PARATUS"

From Aztec shore to Arctic zone, to Europe and Far East.
The Flag is carried by our ships in time of war and peace;
And never have we struck it yet in spite of foe-men's might,
Who cheered our crews and cheered again for showing how to fight.

So here's the Coast Guard marching song.
We sing on land or sea.
Through surf and storm and howling gale,
High shall our purpose be.
"Semper Paratus" is our guide, our fame, our glory too,
To fight to save or fight and die! Aye!
Coast Guard we fight for you!

Branch Rankings and Positions

ARMY RANKINGS

E-1 Private
E-2 Private Second Class
E-3 Private First Class
E-4 Specialist
E-5 Sergeant
E-6 Staff Sergeant
E-7 Sergeant First Class
E-8 Master Sergeant
E-9 Command Sergeant Major
W-1 Warrant Officer 1
W-2 to 5 Chief Warrant Officer
O-1 Second Lieutenant
O-2 First Lieutenant
O-3 Captain
O-4 Major
O-5 Lieutenant Colonel
O-6 Colonel
O-7 Brigadier General (one-star)
O-8 Major General (two-star)
O-9 Lieutenant General (three-star)
O-10 General (four-star)

NAVY RANKINGS

E-1 Seaman Recruit
E-2 Seaman Apprentice
E-3 Seaman
E-4 Petty Officer 3rd Class
E-5 Petty Officer 2nd Class
E-6 Petty Officer 1st Class
E-7 Chief Petty Officer
E-8 Senior Petty Officer
E-9 Master Chief Petty Officer
W-2 Warrant Officer 2
W-3 Warrant Officer 3
W-4 Warrant Officer 4
W-5 Warrant Officer 5
O-1 Ensign
O-2 Lieutenant Junior Grade
O-3 Lieutenant
O-4 Lieutenant Commander
O-5 Commander
O-6 Captain
O-7 Rear Admiral Lower Half (one-star)
O-8 Rear Admiral Upper Half (two-star)
O-9 Vice-Admiral (three-star)
O-10 Admiral (four-star)
O-11 Fleet Admiral (five-star)

AIR FORCE RANKINGS

E-1 Airman Basic
E-2 Airman

E-3 Airman First Class
E-4 Senior Airman
E-5 Staff Sergeant
E-6 Technical Sergeant
E-7 Master Sergeant
E-8 Senior Master Sergeant
E-9 Chief Master Sergeant
O-1 Second Lieutenant
O-2 First Lieutenant
O-3 Captain
O-4 Major
O-5 Lieutenant Colonel
O-6 Colonel
O-7 Brigadier General (one-star)
O-8 Major General (two-star)
O-9 Lieutenant General (three-star)
O-10 General (four-star)

MARINE CORPS RANKINGS

E-1 Private
E-2 Private First Class
E-3 Lance Corporal
E-4 Corporal
E-5 Sergeant
E-6 Staff Sergeant
E-7 Gunnery Sergeant
E-8 Master Sergeant
E-8 First Sergeant
E-9 Mastery Gunnery Sergeant
E-9 Sergeant Major

E-9 Sergeant Major of the Marine Corps
O-1 Second Lieutenant
O-2 First Lieutenant
O-3 Captain
O-4 Major
O-5 Lieutenant Colonel
O-6 Colonel
O-7 Brigadier General (one-star)
O-8 Major General (two-star)
O-9 Lieutenant General (three-star)
O-10 General (four-star)

Military Management Positions: All Branches

J-1 Manpower and Personnel—provides the manpower and personnel support for planning and operations for the command.

J-2 Intelligence—provides accurate, detailed, and relevant information and knowledge for the command.

J-3 Operations—conducts operational and cyber planning, organizes forces for assigned missions, coordinates movement and employment of the forces, and monitors and directs operations.

J-4 Logistics—optimizes logistics in order to achieve command objectives and enterprise logistical goals.

J-5 Strategy, Engagement, and Programs—develops strategic guidance, plans military campaigns and operations, and conducts security cooperation activities.

J-6 Command, Control, Communications, and Computer/Cyber—provides the best military advice while advancing cyber defense, joint and coalition interoperability, and provides leadership with up-to-date operational information and the ability to convey coordinating instructions to operational element capabilities required by the Joint Force to preserve the nation's security.

J-7 Joint Force Development—supports the chairman of the Joint Chief of Staff (CJCS) and the joint warfighter through joint force development (JFD) in order to advance the operational effectiveness of the current and future joint force.

J-8 Resources and Assessment—plans, programs, budgets, and

executes fiscal resources to deliver the best capability and value from the resources provided.

J-9 Soldier/Airmen and Family Readiness—provides guidance and directs actions that will produce healthy life choices and promote resiliency with the Guard family.

www.ingramcontent.com/pod-product-compliance
Lightning Source LLC
LaVergne TN
LVHW091706070526
838199LV00050B/2295